The Unmasking of

Oscar Wilde

JOSEPH PEARCE

HarperCollins*Publishers*

HarperCollins*Publishers*
77–85 Fulham Palace Road, London w6 8jb
www.fireandwater.com

First published in Great Britain in 2000
by HarperCollins*Publishers*
This edition 2001

1 3 5 7 9 10 8 6 4 2

Copyright © 2000 Joseph Pearce

Joseph Pearce asserts the moral right to
be identified as the author of this work.

A catalogue record for this book is
available from the British Library.

ISBN 0 00 274051 6

Printed and bound in Great Britain by
Omnia Books Ltd, Glasgow

For Derek and Jo Barrel

You knew what my Art was to me, the great primal note by which I had revealed, first myself to myself, and then myself to the world; the real passion of my life; the love to which all other loves were as marsh-water to red wine ...

Contents

Acknowledgements

Such has been the depth of research into all aspects of Oscar Wilde's life and legacy that the search for new primary source material is akin to prospecting for gold. The precious few nuggets which adorn this volume were collected during sorties to Oxford and London, most particularly to the Bodleian Library, to the Archives of Magdalen College and to the British Library Department of Manuscripts. Gratitude is due to Greg Glazov and Stratford Caldecott at Plater College for furnishing me with hospitality during my trips to Oxford. I am indebted to Father Charles Dilke of the London Oratory and to the Archivist at the Jesuit church in Farm Street for their valuable time and assistance in providing background material. Staff at the Department of Manuscripts and Records of the National Library of Wales in Aberystwyth were most helpful in providing me with copies of several unpublished letters.

I am grateful to Merlin Holland, Wilde's grandson, for his help and advice. As always, I am indebted to Sarah Hollingsworth for her reading of the original manuscript and for her comments and suggestions. Alfred Simmonds continues to offer support whenever needed. Dr Michael Nicholson, Rupert Hart-Davis and Katrina White have also provided valuable assistance.

Finally, I must thank James Catford, Elspeth Taylor, Kathy Dyke, Gina Sussens and everyone at HarperCollins for their continued faith in my work and for all their efforts to bring this and my other volumes to satisfactory fruition.

Preface

Oscar Wilde died a pariah. He was scorned by the world and was ostracized by all except a loyal handful of friends. Today, a hundred years after his poverty-stricken death, he is the adored and idolized icon of a growing cult. In the past few years any item of memorabilia connected with him has been sold for large sums at auction. A questionnaire filled in by Wilde when he was at Oxford sold for £23,000; an inscribed cigarette case apparently given to Wilde by Lord Alfred Douglas sold for £14,000 despite its doubtful authenticity; and two letters from Wilde to Philip Griffiths, described as one of his lovers, reached £16,000 at Christie's. The letters were themselves innocuous and there is no evidence that Wilde ever had a sexual relationship with Griffiths but the letters sold nonetheless. Wilde's grandson, Merlin Holland, expressed a sense of exasperation at the cult surrounding his grandfather, but added philosophically that he could 'appreciate the humour of questionable pieces of memorabilia from Saint Oscar the Sinner being offered to a credulous public at absurd prices and be proud of my ancestor's ability to take his revenge a century later'.[1]

The irony of the present situation is that Wilde is remembered far more for his private life than for his art. It is not a state of affairs which would have pleased him. In fact, it would have horrified him. He would have seen it as the last and worst insult to his battered reputation. For Wilde, art was always Art and it was by this alone that he desired to be judged, both by his peers and by posterity. Furthermore, he believed that life followed art and, consequently, that life was best understood through the prism of art. Whether this is a universal law, as Wilde claimed, it is certainly a law which applies to Wilde himself.

There is no way of understanding the true Wilde without first understanding the truth of his art. This was Wilde's view and this is also the view which underpins the approach of this study.

'Every great man nowadays has his disciples,' Wilde wrote, 'and it is always Judas who writes the biography.' These should be cautionary words for any prospective biographer, yet, in Wilde's case, they have been all too tragically ignored. Over the years he has been served by a string of biographers who have betrayed him with either a kiss or a curse. Robert Sherard and Frank Harris, both journalists by profession and inclination, wrote with vivid sensationalism but questionable accuracy about their friendship with Wilde. Alfred Douglas spent most of his life trying to explain, or explain away, his relationship with Wilde, so that his views on the subject must be regarded as exercises in self-justification with little effort at objectivity. Later biographies of Wilde have sought to sensationalize his life, sacrificing truth on the altar of scandal if necessary. Perhaps the most obvious example was the illustration in Richard Ellmann's biography, published in 1987, purporting to show 'Wilde in costume as Salomé'. This was duly reproduced in many reviews of Ellmann's book as a previously unpublished photograph of Wilde, depicting previously unsuspected transvestism. The 'exclusive' was no doubt greatly beneficial to sales and the photograph was subsequently included in half a dozen works wholly or partially concerned with Wilde. Such was Ellmann's reputation as a scholar that no one questioned the photograph's authenticity. Then, in 1994, an article in the *Times Literary Supplement* proved beyond doubt that the 'Salomé' in the photograph was in fact a Hungarian opera singer, Alice Guszalewicz, photographed in Cologne in 1906.

The worst example of this sensationalist approach was the allegation that Wilde contracted syphilis as an undergraduate at Oxford and that, twenty-five years later, he died of the disease. According to Ellmann, and also to Melissa Knox in a more recent study, the 'fact' that Wilde had syphilis is crucial to any understanding of his life or his work. Yet Wilde almost certainly never had the disease and certainly never died of it (see chapter 5). Thus Ellmann's and Knox's crucial understanding becomes a crucial misunderstanding at the very heart of their respective studies.

It was a growing uneasiness at the misconceptions of these previous studies which was the principal motivation behind the writing of the present work. In particular, the enshrining of Ellmann's study as the 'definitive biography' was in need of serious reappraisal. As a life of Wilde it is fairly comprehensive in facts while remaining largely uncomprehending of truth. In this context it must be remembered that the distinction between fact and truth was one which Wilde reiterated often. A collage of facts, carefully constructed, can either present a kaleidoscopic truth or a colossal lie. Ellmann's study may not be a colossal lie but what emerges from its pages is not a true picture of its subject. Certainly, it cannot be considered either final or definitive in its presentation of the man who was Oscar Wilde.

For a purely factual knowledge of Wilde there is no better source than his letters. These were edited with great objectivity and meticulousness by Rupert Hart-Davis whose footnotes are invaluable. Yet for an understanding of the enigmatically elusive truth it is necessary to read between the lines of his letters and beyond the facts of his everyday life. In this respect, no adequate study exists. The transcendent reality at the heart of the man remains an untold mystery.

The problem stems from an inability to see Wilde except through the lens of either puritan or prurient motives. The prurient see Wilde as a subversive hero who undermines traditional values. For this school of thought his value is not primarily in his art but in his licentious life, encapsulated in the lurid title of Melissa Knox's study as Wilde's 'long and lovely suicide'. Against the prurient is counterposed the puritan who believes that Wilde's work lacks value because of his immoral life. The most extreme example of the puritan school of thought was St John Ervine whose conclusion to his 'appraisal' of Wilde, published in 1952, is particularly scathing:

Wilde came into the world with a small talent and made little of it. He did worse than that. He denied his principles by his practice. He cast such pearls as he had before swine, and then wallowed with the swine at the troughs in the sty. He was a flippant man who turned high matters to bibbers' jests, and would not forgo a witticism to spare a friend's wound. A brawler in the temple may be sincerely affirming a faith, but a man who titters in the temple and is flippant about his faith is a recusant who denies without any affirmation in the denial. The steward who hid his talent in a napkin was cursed and condemned, but what punishment is fitting for the man who takes his gift from God and drops it in the mire? That was the sin committed by Oscar Wilde. It was the sin against the Holy Ghost.[2]

The prurient and the puritan are both blinded by their bias. To one Wilde is a war-cry, to the other he is a warning. One betrays him with a kiss, the other with a curse. It is a choice between Judas and the Pharisee. George Bernard Shaw, in his preface to the 1938 edition of Frank Harris's biography of Wilde, admitted that he had 'somewhat Pharisaically' summed up Wilde's last days in Paris as those of 'an unprofitable drunkard and swindler'. Yet, he argued, those of Wilde's admirers who had objected to this description of their hero had forgotten 'that Wilde's permanent celebrity belongs to literature, and only his transient notoriety to the police news'. It is a fact which is forgotten by Wilde's detractors as much as by his admirers. In both cases he is condoned or condemned in accordance with the personal prejudices of those sitting in judgement. He is presumed innocent or guilty before the evidence is heard. Both sides pontificate before pondering Wilde's own words, and come to conclusions before hearing and comprehending the arguments of the case. They are too busy casting stones at Wilde or each other to remember that the subject of their passion was first and foremost an artist who expressed the deepest secrets about himself in his art.

'We are all in the gutter,' says Lord Darlington in *Lady Windermere's Fan*, 'but some of us are looking at the stars.' To look for Wilde in the gutter, whether to wallow with him in the mire or to point the finger of self-righteous scorn, is to miss the point. Those wishing a deeper understanding of this most enigmatic of men should not look *at* him in the gutter but *with* him at the stars.

1 *Daily Telegraph*, 23 February 1998.
2 St John Ervine, *Oscar Wilde: A Present Time Appraisal*, New York: William Morrow & Co, 1952, p. 336.

ONE

Mother of Masks

Even as above her nest goes circling round
   The stork when she has fed her little ones,
   And he who has been fed looks up at her,

So lifted I my brows, and even such
   Became the blessed image, which its wings
   Was moving, by so many counsels urged.
Dante, Paradiso, Canto XIX

In 1885 Oscar Wilde wrote 'The Truth of Masks' in which he claimed that there was no such thing in art as a universal truth. Attitude, he wrote, was everything.

The truth, or otherwise, of masks is crucial to any understanding of Wilde's complex character. His public persona, cultivated carefully from his youth onwards, was a calculated pose. He became the poseur *par excellence*, creating masks for himself which amused his friends, beguiled his disciples and infuriated his critics. Yet do the masks conceal the truth or do they reveal it? This question lies (in both senses of the word) at the very centre of any quest for a fuller understanding of this most elusive of characters.

Since the facts of his life are an elaborate masquerade one must seek the truth beyond the facts, for, as Wilde stated in the essay on masks, 'Truth is independent of facts always.' Truth, in Wilde's case, is the transcendent reality at the heart of the actor.

Oscar Wilde inherited the truth of masks from his mother.

Lady Wilde wore masks as others wore clothes and her attire was anything but modest. Beginning with the assumption that a rose by any other name would smell sweeter, she set about reinventing herself. She had always disliked her first name, which was Jane, and was not quite satisfied with her second, almost certainly Frances. The latter was improved to Francesca which she felt was more befitting the dignity of her alleged Italian ancestry. Lady Wilde's maiden name was Elgee and, according to family tradition, or so Lady Wilde maintained, the Elgee family were originally called Algiati. It was easy to imply that Algiati was itself a corruption of Alighieri and *ipso facto* that Dante himself was one of her ancestors. In later years her son would take this ingenious genealogy one fanciful step further, claiming a visual resemblance to, and a spiritual kinship with, both Shakespeare and Nero.

Lady Wilde wore her various names as fashion statements. To tradesmen or others of no consequence she signed herself Jane Wilde. To her friends or those of higher station she was Francesca or J. Francesca Wilde. Yet even these were insufficient. She felt the need for an altogether more elaborate and grandiose title. This was Speranza, her *nom de guerre*, which was plucked from the motto with which her notepaper was embossed: *Fidanza, Speranza, Costanza*. In her correspondence with Henry Wadsworth Longfellow, translator of Dante, she adopted the most impressive combination of all these names, signing herself Francesca Speranza Wilde.

The flight of fancy into the Tuscan mists to claim Dante's inheritance may have been wishful thinking but Lady Wilde's verifiable ancestors are themselves of considerable interest. On her mother's side she could boast the Reverend Charles Maturin who died in 1824, two years before her own birth. Maturin was a famous novelist and playwright. His tragedy *Bertram* had a successful run at Drury Lane in 1816, although its successors, *Manuel* and *Fredolpho*, failed to emulate its popularity. He is most remembered for a series of extravagantly macabre novels including *The Fatal Revenge*, *The Albigenses* and, most notably, *Melmoth the Wanderer* which was published in 1820 to immediate critical acclaim. Its mysterious, some would say satanic, hero held a morbid fascination for Sir Walter Scott, and for Honoré de Balzac who wrote a sequel. The poet Charles Baudelaire claimed to have found in Melmoth an alter ego; Baudelaire's own considerable influence on the young Oscar Wilde ensured that Maturin's hero held Wilde even more in his thrall than he might otherwise have done.

Wilde was beguiled both by Melmoth himself and by Melmoth's French alter ego. Perhaps it was not so surprising, therefore, that Wilde would one day take Melmoth as his own name, emulating for more practical and tragic reasons his mother's predilection for nominal masks.

Maturin's son, William, was a controversial High Churchman whose Anglo-Catholic views kept him from preferment. William's son, Basil William Maturin, took his father's stance to its logical conclusion, becoming a Roman Catholic in 1897. Following his ordination, Father Maturin gained a reputation as a well-known pulpit orator, becoming chaplain to the undergraduates at Oxford where he exerted an important influence on the conversion of Ronald Knox. Father Maturin became one of the earliest victims of the First World War when he perished as a passenger on the torpedoed *Lusitania*. Paying tribute, Knox wrote of the horror of the circumstances surrounding the priest's death, stating that 'it was easy to conjure up the picture of him, as he moved fearlessly to and fro in those last moments on the *Lusitania*'.[1]

Lady Wilde's maternal great-grandfather, Dr Kingsbury, was a well-known physician and friend of Jonathan Swift, while her great-grandfather on her father's side, Charles Elgee (1709–87), was a rich farmer in County Down. His son, John Elgee (1753–1823), was a rector and archdeacon in the Church of Ireland, and his grandson, also named Charles, Lady Wilde's father, became a lawyer. Lady Wilde's mother, Sarah, was the daughter of another Protestant cleric, Thomas Kingsbury, who divided his time between his duties as vicar of Kildare and his secular responsibilities as Commissioner of Bankruptcy. The token tradesman among Lady Wilde's ancestors was an English immigrant from County Durham – a bricklayer who came to Ireland in the 1770s and died in 1805.

Wilde's ancestry on his father's side was a cause of some embarrassment both to Lady Wilde and to Oscar himself. They both considered themselves Irish nationalists, which made any mention in public of Sir William Wilde's ancestral links with the invading army of William of Orange a serious *faux pas*. Oscar's paternal grandfather, Thomas Wills Wilde, was a country doctor from Castlerea in County Roscommon; his great-grandfather, Ralph Wilde, farmed the land near Castlerea and also managed the property of the local landowner,

Lord Mount Sandford. Ralph Wilde prospered in his dual role as land agent and farmer, no doubt fuelling the resentment of his master's tenants in the process, and he passed on the benefits of his wealth to his three sons. His eldest son, Ralph, went to Trinity College, Dublin, so that he could pursue a career in the Anglican Church; his second son, Thomas, Oscar's grandfather, was sent to England to complete his medical studies; and the third son, William, was shipped off to Jamaica to seek his fortune in the sugar plantations. Yet it was Ralph Wilde's ancestor, Colonel de Wilde, a Dutch army officer, who was the principal cause of uneasiness to Lady Wilde and her son. Colonel de Wilde accompanied King William of Orange to Ireland where he helped the Protestant monarch, who had previously usurped power in England, to defeat the Catholic King James II at the Battle of the Boyne. This defeat, along with the earlier atrocities believed to have been carried out by Oliver Cromwell against the Irish Catholics, had bred the hatred and resentment which has afflicted Ireland ever since, in the days of Wilde's childhood no less than today.

Colonel de Wilde was granted lands in Connaught for his services to King William during the military campaign in Ireland and this formed the basis of the Wilde family's wealth and social position. In a further example of Lady Wilde's ability to embellish the truth, she sought to conceal this aspect of her husband's past by suggesting that the Wildes were in fact descended from a northern English family. Although Oscar didn't go this far, he did seem a little uneasy about the orange skeleton in his family's cupboard. According to the American writer Vincent O'Sullivan, who befriended Wilde during his last years in Paris, Wilde 'did not seem particularly proud' of his Dutch descent; 'at least he liked to say that he took after his mother's family which, it seems, was pure Irish, more than his father's'.[2]

It is intriguing to compare Wilde's ancestry and social position within Irish society with that of his great contemporary, George Bernard Shaw. In 1689 Captain William Shaw had sailed from Hampshire to Ireland to fight at the Battle of the Boyne. His reward was a grant of land in Kilkenny. There, as landed gentry, the Shaws lived in considerable comfort, marrying into the families of those who had come to Ireland in similar circumstances. As a class apart, these descendants of earlier invaders shunned the indigenous population and took their politics and religion from Dublin Castle, the bastion of the Protestant ascendancy in Ireland. 'The Shaws made no secret of being aristocrats,' wrote Michael Holroyd, Shaw's biographer. 'Their aristocracy was a fact of natural history and the ... social order of Ireland. No Shaw could form a social acquaintance with a Roman Catholic or tradesman. They lifted up their powerful Wellingtonian noses and spoke of themselves ... in a collective spirit ... using the third person: "the Shaws".'[3]

G.K. Chesterton, in his earlier study of Shaw, discussed the implications and ramifications, and the psychological consequences, of such an upbringing. Shaw's ancestry precluded the possibility of his ever being a typical Irishman, in the sense of being part of the common culture of Catholic Ireland. He was doomed to being a 'separated and peculiar kind of Irishman'.

'This fairly educated and fairly wealthy Protestant wedge which is driven into the country at Dublin and elsewhere,' Chesterton wrote, 'is a thing not easy superficially to summarize in any terms.'

> There is only one word for the minority in Ireland, and that is the word that public phraseology has found; I mean the word 'Garrison'. The Irish are essentially right when they talk as if all Protestant Unionists lived inside 'The Castle'. They have all the virtues and limitations of a literal garrison in a fort ... their curse is that they can only tread the flag-stones of the courtyard or the cold rock of the ramparts; they have never so much as set their foot upon their native soil.

In reading about Shaw's youth, Chesterton observed, it was easy to forget that it was passed on the island which is 'still one flame before the altar of St Peter and St Patrick', adding wryly that Shaw's formative years, to all intents and purposes, might have been happening in Wimbledon. Typically, Chesterton overstates and caricatures his case in order to make his point and ends plaintively by stating that Shaw had rejected all forms of Christianity without ever understanding the Catholicism of the vast majority of his fellow countrymen: 'It could never cross the mind of a man of the garrison that before becoming an atheist he might stroll into one of the churches of his own country, and learn something of the philosophy that had satisfied Dante and Bossuet, Pascal and Descartes.'[4]

Chesterton went still further, drawing psychological conclusions that push his argument to the limit, and perhaps beyond. His comments, though caricatured to hammer home his case, raise questions which are as applicable to Wilde as they are to Shaw:

> He who has no real country can have no real home. The average autochthonous Irishman is close to patriotism because he is close to the earth; he is close to domesticity because he is close to the earth; he is close to doctrinal theology and elaborate ritual because he is close to the earth. In short, he is close to the heavens because he is close to the earth. But we must not expect any of these elemental and collective virtues in the man of the Garrison. He cannot be expected to exhibit the virtues of a people, but only (as Ibsen would say) of an enemy of the people.[5]

In stating his case so forcefully, Chesterton is in danger of overstating it farcically. It would certainly be unfair to suggest that Wilde or Shaw were enemies of the Irish people; still less, as Chesterton implied on another occasion, that they were, in the words of a nationalist song, 'anti-Irish Irishmen'. Yet his general point, however stridently stated, is valid. The Protestants of the plantation were a privileged class apart, distinct from the Catholic majority and unwilling and unable to be a part of the wider cultural and religious life of Ireland. They were a 'separated and peculiar kind of Irishman'. In this context it is at least pertinent to conjecture that Wilde's upbringing imbued him with the psychology of the privileged outsider and that this, in turn, contributed to the emotional rootlessness and restlessness which was a major factor in the unfolding of his life.

For all the similarities, real and superficial, in the circumstances surrounding the early years of Wilde and Shaw, significant differences remain. Whereas Shaw shrugged off the Protestantism of his upbringing without ever seriously considering the Catholic alternative, Wilde rebelled against Protestantism and courted conversion to Rome. Furthermore, whereas Shaw remained a puritan even when he had ceased to be a Protestant, Wilde's whole life was a war against puritanism. In this, as in so much else, Wilde was merely following a trail which his mother had blazed before him.

Lady Wilde was a rebel who relished the opportunity to cause controversy. Counting among her relatives and ancestors several

Protestant clerics, she flirted with the 'Scarlet Woman' of Rome; belonging to a class which upheld the Union, she proclaimed her Irish nationalism.

Her flirtation with Catholicism was to have practical consequences for the young Oscar and his brother Willie. When the brothers were quite young, probably under five years of age, Lady Wilde took them to stay at a farmhouse in the vale of Glencree about fifteen miles from Dublin. During their stay she met a young convert Catholic priest, Father Lawrence Fox, and asked him whether she could bring the two children to Mass. Soon afterwards she requested that Oscar and Willie be baptized as Catholics. Father Fox duly obliged. 'After a few weeks I baptized these two children,' Father Fox wrote, 'Lady Wilde herself being present on the occasion.' Mentioning that one of the two infants was 'that future erratic genius Oscar Wilde', Father Fox added that Lady Wilde then requested that he call on her husband to inform him of what had been done. Such was the anti-Catholic prejudice at the time that the young priest must have been expecting a tyrannical tirade when he broke the news and would have been considerably relieved when Sir William merely informed him that 'he did not care what they were so long as they became as good as their mother'.[6] Father Fox's recollections of these events were recalled more than fifty years afterwards, only months before his death at the age of eighty-five. By that time, Lady Wilde and her two sons had predeceased him so that corroboration of his story was not possible. There is, however, no reason to doubt the elderly priest's story, especially as Oscar declared more than once to intimate friends in later years that he had a distinct recollection as a child of being baptized in a Catholic church.[7]

The clandestine baptism of her two children was the only practical result of Lady Wilde's fling with Catholicism, other than the lingering ghost of her son's memory. Whether her attraction was ever more than a mask, a skin-deep shallowness designed to shock or provoke reaction, is difficult to discern. Certainly it appeared that at least one of her correspondents, Sir William Hamilton, was sufficiently concerned about the possibility of her own conversion to express fears that the Catholic poet Aubrey De Vere could 'succeed in converting, or perverting you'.[8] He need not have worried. Lady Wilde's brief affair with the Church appeared to be little more than a fleeting passion, aroused perhaps by nothing other than a desire for a little naughtiness and illicit excitement. If her motives were more noble than this, or her attraction deeper, her resolve must have faltered soon after the initial urge took hold. She showed little inclination to pursue the matter further in future years, and never felt it necessary to take the step which she had desired for her sons.

Lady Wilde's attraction to Irish nationalism seemed more serious and was expressed in the dedication to her sons in the first edition of her poems, published in 1864:

> Dedicated to my sons Willie and Oscar Wilde
> 'I made them indeed
> Speak plain the word country. I taught them, no doubt,
> That country's a thing one should die for at need'

Lady Wilde's nationalism predated the births of her sons and had its roots in a pamphlet by Richard D'Alton Williams, who was tried for treason, though acquitted, in 1848. D'Alton Williams was the author of 'The Nation's Valentine, To the Ladies of Ireland', a poem which called upon women to 'sing us no songs but of FATHERLAND now'. Lady Wilde was bowled over by the naked romance of Williams' words though she seemed to be moved more by his poetry than his patriotism. 'Then it was I discovered I was a poet,' she proclaimed.[9] As the entirely different account given to W.B. Yeats testifies, her words should not be taken at face value. She told Yeats that she was walking through a street in Dublin when she came across a crowd so vast that she could go no further. Asking one of the spectators the reason for such a crowd she was told that it had assembled for the funeral of Thomas Davis. Who was Thomas Davis, she enquired. On being told that he was a poet she was astounded to think that a poet could be responsible for bringing so many people on to the streets. It was then, she told Yeats, that she decided to be a poet.[10] Again, it was Davis's position as a poet rather than his role as an Irish nationalist which was efficacious.

There was also more than a little poetic licence employed in Lady Wilde's weaving of the tale. It is extremely unlikely, for instance, that she could have been ignorant of Thomas Davis's identity. She was probably twenty-three at the time of his funeral in 1845 and it seems

inconceivable that she had not heard of the famous nationalis
who was the talk of Ireland in the 1840s. It is likely, however, that s.
made her story more plausible by implying or explicitly stating that
she was several years younger at the time. She allowed it to be known
that she was born in 1826, a fact still recorded as her date of birth in
most biographies and in respected works of reference such as the
Chambers Biographical Dictionary. Yet when pressed on the matter of
her age she invariably replied evasively, stating that her birth had
never been recorded. The parish register that might have refuted her
has not been discovered so that biographers have been forced to
accept Lady Wilde's word, never the most reliable of sources. It is
interesting, however, that she recorded her date of birth as 27 December 1821 on her application for a grant from the Royal Literary Fund
in November 1888, by which time age rather than youth was to her
advantage.

Lady Wilde's son appeared to approve of his mother's evasiveness. 'No woman should ever be quite accurate about her age,' says
Lady Bracknell in *The Importance of Being Earnest*. 'It sounds so calculating.' Indeed, Oscar was more than a match for his mother. He regularly claimed to be two years younger than he was, even on his
marriage certificate, and his mother seemed delighted at her son's
deception. In 1878 she wrote to congratulate him on winning the
Newdigate Prize 'at the age of only 22' when she knew he was nearer
twenty-four. Years later this apparently harmless lying was to prove
disastrous. During his trial in 1895, Oscar endeavoured to keep up
the pretence about his age even in the dock and had the mask
stripped away by examining counsel. It was a serious blow to his
credibility. If he could lie so brazenly under oath about something as
superficial as his age, how could the judge or jury be expected to
believe anything else he said?

Perhaps Lady Wilde's disingenuousness throws the very nature of
her nationalism into question. Whereas Thomas Davis wrote poetry
as an expression of deeply rooted beliefs, it seemed that Lady Wilde,
or Speranza as she preferred to be known in her poetic guise, used a
set of beliefs as an expression of her poetry. Nonetheless, whether her
nationalism was a means or an end, it constituted a powerful compound of emotions with which to inflame her muse. She wrote verse
on the coming revolution, on the famine, and on the exodus from

Ireland of the famished, all of which were published in the *Nation*, a nationalist journal which had been founded in 1842.

The suspicion that Speranza's nationalism was not as deep-rooted as her verse suggested was heightened by her growing disillusionment. She and her husband dissociated themselves from the republican Fenianism of the 1860s, relapsing into a blurred and vague vision of Irish nationhood which was out of step with the increasingly vociferous Catholic majority. It is tempting to conclude, even though it may be taking the case a step further than the evidence will carry it, that Speranza's nationalism was, like her hankering after Catholicism, little more than a provocative posture. A pose. A mask.

What then of her son's reputed Irish nationalism? Was it any deeper and less ambivalent, or was it merely a reflection of his mother's mask? 'It must not be forgotten,' wrote Shaw, 'that though by culture Wilde was a citizen of all civilized capitals, he was at root a very Irish Irishman, and as such, a foreigner everywhere but in Ireland.'[11] Yet, if this is so, it seems odd that Wilde only returned to Ireland twice after he settled in London, and then only when he was paid to do so as a lecturer. He did not consider himself an Irish expatriate and seldom referred to either his own Irishness or the thorny question of Irish politics. The only exception to this conspicuous silence was on his lecture tour of the United States when he spoke to Irish-American audiences. The fact that he broke his silence on these occasions with a bravado and bravura in defence of Irish nationalism notably absent elsewhere in any of his speeches or writings, signifies an element of artificiality. Was his playing up to the audience on these occasions merely a further elaborate pose? If there was any truth in Wilde's nationalism, was it only the truth of masks? Returning to Shaw's assertion, it is tempting to suggest that Wilde was a foreigner everywhere, *even* in Ireland.

If Wilde's lifelong sense of alienation was rooted in his being a 'separated and peculiar kind of Irishman' of the 'garrison' class, exacerbated by his mother's masks and her ambivalence towards truth, it was probably reinforced by his father's premarital promiscuity. When Wilde was born on 16 October 1854, he already had one illegitimate half-brother and two illegitimate half-sisters to go with his legitimate older brother, William, who had been born on 26 September 1852.

His sister, Isola, would be born on 2 April 1857.

Sir William Wilde was twenty-three when the first of his illegitimate children, a boy named Henry Wilson (as in William's or Wilde's son?), was born in Dublin in 1838. He looked after his son, educated him, and took him into his surgery as a fellow practitioner. There is no mention of the mother, nor have the mother or mothers of his two other illegitimate offspring been identified. Emily and Mary, born in 1847 and 1849 respectively, were adopted by Sir William's eldest brother, the Reverend Ralph Wilde, thereby retaining the family name.

It is likely that Oscar's knowledge of these unorthodox family relations influenced his art, much of which is permeated with an interest in foundlings, orphans and the murkier mysteries of birth. Thus, for example, Dorian Gray falls in love with a young woman of illegitimate birth, whose brother reproaches her mother for her fall; Lady Windermere has been abandoned by her errant mother; a cloud hangs over Jack Worthing's birth in *The Importance of Being Earnest*; and young Arbuthnot's mother in *A Woman of No Importance* is unmarried.

When Sir William Wilde married Jane Elgee on 14 November 1851 there was little doubt that his new wife was fully conversant with her husband's past. She didn't appear to resent it and John Butler Yeats, the distinguished artist and father of W.B. Yeats, privately attributed her indulgence to the fact that she had herself, before her marriage, been discovered with the politician Isaac Butt in circumstances 'that were not doubtful' by Mrs Butt.[12] She was certainly an admirer of Butt, who preceded Charles Stewart Parnell as leader of the Irish party in Parliament, describing him in print as 'the Mirabeau of the Young Ireland movement, with his tossed masses of black hair, his flashing eyes, and splendid rush of cadenced oratory'.[13]

Passion, it seems, was an integral part of Lady Wilde's character which she retained, in theory at least if not in practice, until her last days. 'Give me passion!' she exclaimed in full hearing of all those present during a lull in proceedings at a dinner party in London in the 1880s, and her rejoinder to a young man when she was in her sixties reads like a line from one of her son's plays: 'When you are as old as I, young man, you will know there is only one thing in the world worth living for, and that is sin.'[14] Yet even Lady Wilde's liberal attitude to sin was sorely tried by a sordid episode involving her husband which ended in the law courts at the end of 1864. A woman named Mary

Travers, who had become a patient of William Wilde in 1854, the year of Oscar's birth, claimed that he had given her chloroform and then raped her. The alleged rape occurred in October 1862 when she was twenty-six years old. Curiously, she remained his patient and, even more curiously, accepted money from him to cover her fare to Australia. She failed to embark and kept silent throughout the following year. It was, she claimed, the conferring of a knighthood on Sir William on 28 January 1864 which had incensed her sufficiently to spur her into action. Realizing that an allegation of rape after such an interval would have had little chance of a favourable verdict, Mary Travers wrote letters containing dark hints to newspapers. She also composed a scurrilous pamphlet about the Wildes, who were characterized as Dr and Mrs Quilp, which she cheekily signed as 'Speranza'. Lady Wilde responded on 6 May 1864 by protesting to Mary Travers' father, a professor of medical jurisprudence at Trinity College, that his daughter was making 'unfounded' allegations. When Mary Travers discovered the letter among her father's papers she sued Lady Wilde for libel.

The case was heard over five days from 12 to 17 December 1864. There was much speculation as to whether Sir William would take the stand to clear his name, but since it was not he who was being sued there was no compulsion that he do so. His failure to make an appearance was seen as a telling point in Mary Travers' favour. In a bizarre twist of events, counsel for Miss Travers emerged as the ubiquitous Isaac Butt, with whom Lady Wilde had herself been discovered *in flagrante delicto* some years earlier. He had no intention of allowing any earlier liaison to inhibit him in the pursuit of his quarry and, like a praying mantis, employed his erstwhile charms to deadly effect. It is easy to imagine Butt's polished performance as he exhibited all his legal and political experience, his 'splendid rush of cadenced oratory' accentuated by 'tossed masses of black hair' and flashing eyes. Lady Wilde was, however, no mean adversary and when asked by Butt why she had ignored Mary Travers' charges that she had been raped by Sir William, she replied with majestic indifference: 'I really took no interest in the matter. I looked upon the whole thing as a fabrication.'[15] The jury did not agree and upheld the charge of libel against her. They had been swayed in their judgement by letters from her husband to Mary Travers which, produced in evidence, illustrated a good deal of fluster on Sir William's part. Although the jury found in Mary Travers' favour, the court placed little value on her outraged innocence, awarding her a farthing in damages. This was cold comfort for either Lady Wilde or Sir William who had to pay £2,000 in legal costs.

The publicity surrounding the trial brought the Wildes notoriety, so much so that they became one of the most talked-about couples in Irish society. 'I inherited a famous name,' Oscar would write in *De Profundis* and he wasn't referring solely to the scandal of the libel trial. His father, recently knighted, was a pioneering eye surgeon as well as the author of several books on Irish history and topography; his mother was a flamboyantly famous poet and a high-profile champion of the nationalist cause. Of the two, Lady Wilde was the more colourful character and her perceived dominance in their relationship was exacerbated by their difference in height. Sir William was of average height whereas Lady Wilde was nearly six feet tall. The result was that they were often caricatured as a giantess and a dwarf.

In later years Lady Wilde became so large in the lumbar region that Shaw attributed her condition to giantism, concluding, with a singular lack of medical evidence, that this was an hereditary cause of Oscar's homosexuality. Whether or not Shaw's theory was justified, there is little doubt that Lady Wilde was a larger-than-life character in far more than the physical sense and that she exerted a giant's influence on the development of her son's personality.

William Wordsworth wrote that the child is father of the man. In Wilde's case a matriarchal element must be added. It could be claimed, in Wildean fashion, that the mother was father of the man; or, more perversely and paradoxically, that the mask was mother of the man. It was certainly true that Wilde's life contradicted one of his most celebrated epigrams: 'All women become like their mothers. That is their tragedy. No man does. That's his.' In many respects Wilde *was* made in the image of his mother and in many ways that was his tragedy.

1 Ronald Knox, *A Spiritual Aeneid*, London: Burns & Oates, 1958 edn., p. 162.
2 H. Montgomery Hyde, *Oscar Wilde: A Biography*, London: Eyre Methuen, 1976, p. 4.
3 Michael Holroyd, *Bernard Shaw, Volume I: The Search for Love*, London: Chatto, 1988, p. 5.
4 G.K. Chesterton, *George Bernard Shaw*, London: John Lane, 1909, pp. 34–6 and 57–8.

5 Ibid., pp. 37–8.
6 Rev. L.C. Prideaux Fox, 'People I Have Met', *Donahoe's Magazine* (Boston, Mass.), LIII, no. 4 (April 1905), p. 397.
7 Stuart Mason, *Bibliography of Oscar Wilde*, London, 1914, p. 118; quoted in Hyde, *Oscar Wilde*, p. 8.
8 Horace Wyndham, *Speranza: A Biography of Lady Wilde*, New York, 1951, p. 56; quoted in Richard Ellmann, *Oscar Wilde*, London: Penguin edn., 1988, p. 18.
9 Ibid., p. 23; quoted in Ellmann, *Oscar Wilde*, p. 7.
10 Quoted in Ellmann, *Oscar Wilde*, p. 7.
11 Quoted in H. Montgomery Hyde (ed.), *The Annotated Oscar Wilde*, London: Orbis, 1982, p. 11.
12 J.B. Yeats, *Letters to His Son*, ed. Joseph Hone, New York, 1946, p. 277; quoted in Ellmann, *Oscar Wilde*, p. 13.
13 Ellmann, *Oscar Wilde*, p. 13.
14 Ibid.
15 Ibid., p. 14.

TWO

Star in the Ascendancy

LADY CHILTERN: We were at school together, Mrs Cheveley.
MRS CHEVELEY (superciliously): Indeed? I have forgotten all about
my schooldays. I have a vague impression that they were detestable.

In February 1864 Willie and Oscar Wilde were sent to the Portora
Royal School in Enniskillen, County Fermanagh, a small public
boarding school of between eighty and a hundred pupils. Willie was
eleven but Oscar was still barely nine years old at the time, much
younger than most entrants. This must add to the suspicion that he
and his brother had been shipped out of Dublin to escape the coming
scandal surrounding Mary Travers' allegations about their father.
Although the libel case did not go to trial until the following December, Mary Travers was commencing her campaign against Sir William
and Lady Wilde in the printed media during the early months of 1864.
Storm clouds were gathering and it looks as though the boys may
have been sent to the remote north to escape the deluge. It is not clear
to what extent their remoteness shielded them from the scandal but
there is no question that it would return to haunt them in later years.
When Willie and Oscar proceeded from Portora to Trinity College,
Dublin, in 1869 and 1871 respectively, they could not have helped
hearing an irreverent ballad about their father which was commonly
sung by the students, the Travers case having become a lewd legend:

An eminent oculist lives in the Square.
His skill is unrivalled, his talent is rare,
And if you will listen I'll certainly try
To tell how he opened Miss Travers's eye.[1]

Little is known of Wilde's schooldays, principally due to Wilde's own reluctance to discuss them. When pressed on the subject he invariably lied, as, for example, when he informed D.J. O'Donoghue, the tireless compiler of an Irish biographical dictionary, that he had spent 'about a year there'. He was in fact at Portora for seven years, from the age of nine to sixteen. Interviewed for the *Biograph*, an English annual which published a six-page life of Wilde when he was only twenty-six, he said that he had been privately tutored at home.

It is not clear why Wilde should have been so unwilling to discuss his time at school. Perhaps it was nothing more sinister than the simple fear that hard facts about his formative years would weaken the myth with which he was seeking to surround himself. There was certainly no reason why he should have been ashamed of the reputation of the school itself. Portora may not have been 'the Eton of Ireland', as Lady Wilde claimed pretentiously, but it was a respectable public school preparing the future pillars of the Protestant ascendancy for their role in public life. Wilde's earliest surviving letter, written in September 1868 to his mother, throws valuable light on life at the school and on that of its thirteen-year-old pupil. 'Darling Mama, The hamper came today, and I never got such a jolly surprise, many thanks for it, it was more than kind of you to think of it.'[2] In the same letter the young Wilde showed especial interest in the publication of his mother's poetry and demonstrated an early dandyism when describing his flannel shirts as being lilac and 'quite scarlet'. His humour is evident in a sketch which accompanied the letter depicting 'ye delight of ye boys at ye hamper and the sorrow of ye hamperless boy'.[3] The remainder of the letter referred to a cricket win over a regimental side, and to 'that horrid regatta'. At this stage, Wilde still expressed a mild interest in cricket but his disdain for rowing shows the early signs of the aesthete's distaste for the athlete. Later, he would deride cricket in the same breath as the horrid regattas, dismissing them jointly as 'bats and boats'.

The seemingly untroubled innocence of this early letter disguised a deep emotional scar which had been inflicted the previous year. On 23 February 1867 his sister Isola had died. She was only nine years old. 'Such sorrows are hard to bear,' wrote Lady Wilde. 'My heart seems broken. Still I feel I have to live for my sons and thank God they are as fine a pair of boys as one could desire.' Even three years after the tragedy, Lady Wilde would write to a friend that since Isola's death she had gone to no dinner, soiree, theatre or concert, 'and never will again'. Her husband was equally distressed, declaring that 'it has left me a mourner for life'.[4] Oscar was utterly devastated. The doctor who attended Isola during her final illness thought him 'an affectionate, gentle, retiring, dreamy boy', deeper than his brother Willie.[5] He paid regular visits to his sister's grave and later wrote a poem, 'Requiescat', about her. The potency of the loss and the poignancy of the memory are vividly evident in this verse, which serves as a graphic illustration of the way that Wilde's mask is lifted in the greatest of his art. Here is to be seen the soul stripped of its disguises, the broken heart laid bare:

Tread lightly, she is near
 Under the snow,
Speak gently, she can hear
 The daisies grow.

All her bright golden hair
 Tarnished with rust,
She that was young and fair
 Fallen to dust.

Lily-like, white as snow,
 She hardly knew
She was a woman, so
 Sweetly she grew.

Coffin-board, heavy stone,
 Lie on her breast,
I vex my heart alone,
 She is at rest.

Peace, peace, she cannot hear
 Lyre or sonnet,
All my life's buried here,
 Heap earth upon it.

On reading this verse it is easy to believe that his sister's death had awakened the melancholy which Wilde in later years insisted was hidden behind the jocular pose. Thereafter, as Wilde heaped layers of earth upon it, his heart was carefully hidden from public view, protected by a mask of mirth brandished with deflective wit. It was only through his art that the heart would emerge, broken.

Shortly after Wilde left Portora for Trinity College, the family suffered another tragic loss when both his illegitimate half-sisters died in horrific circumstances. In November 1871, Emily and Mary, now both in their early twenties, were showing off their ball gowns before a party when one went too close to an open fire. The crinoline of her dress caught in the flames and she was terribly burned. Her sister, who tried frantically to rescue her, suffered the same fate and both died from their injuries. Their gravestone records them as dying on the same day, 10 November, but the *Northern Standard* reported on 25 November that Emily had in fact died on the 8th and Mary on the 21st. Sir William's grief was intense and his groans could be heard outside the house. He had now lost all three of his daughters. Lady Wilde's reaction is not known but the sexton at the local church in Monaghan, where the girls are buried, recalled that a woman in black made an annual pilgrimage by train from Dublin, hiring a car to drive her from the station to the graveyard. This went on for twenty years, but the only admission she made to the sexton was that the two dead girls 'were very dear to me'. The sexton was never able to discover whether the anonymous visitor was Lady Wilde or the girls' mother.[6] Oscar's reaction is also shrouded in mystery but his sisters' deaths in such horrific circumstances must have cast a further shadow on his psyche.

These personal tragedies and traumas did not appear to affect Wilde's academic progress. In 1869 Lady Wilde had reported that her two sons were 'fine clever fellows'. By this time, however, the younger son was beginning to outshine his brother. Oscar, for example, was fourth in classics when Willie was thirteenth. The difference did not escape the notice of their mother who remarked to George Henry Moore, father of the novelist George Moore, that 'Willie is all right, but as for Oscar, he will turn out something wonderful'.[7]

The extent to which Oscar was beginning to show himself as something of a child prodigy during his last years at Portora is illustrated by the speed with which he could digest information. 'When I was a boy at school,' he informed the American humorist Eugene Field, 'I was looked upon as a prodigy by my associates because, quite frequently, I would, for a wager, read a three-volume novel in half an hour so closely as to be able to give an accurate résumé of the plot of the story; by one hour's reading I was enabled to give a fair narrative of the incidental scenes and the most pertinent dialogue.'[8] In similar vein, he told the novelist W.B. Maxwell that he read facing pages of a book simultaneously, demonstrating the fact by showing that he had mastered the intricacies of a novel in three minutes.

It was also during his last year at Portora that Wilde displayed an early interest in theology. He and his schoolfriends became captivated by an ecclesiastical prosecution then making the news in England. Presumably this was the case of the Reverend W.J.E. Bennett, vicar of Frome Selwood, who had been accused of heresy by the Anglican authorities for insisting that Christ was physically present in Holy Communion. The case was heard three times at the Court of Arches, the provincial court of appeal of the Archbishop of Canterbury, on 30 April and 18 November 1869 and on 20 July 1870. Eventually Bennett was found guilty. Wilde was fascinated by the case and announced to his friends that he would like to emulate the Reverend Bennett's 'heresy'. He wanted, he said, 'to go down to posterity as the defendant in such a case as "Regina versus Wilde"'.[9] Even at such an early age, Wilde was playing up to his audience with remarks that were deliberately designed to shock. As his mother's son, he was determined to make a sensation, whatever the cost.

Perhaps a similar desire to shock was behind Wilde's response to the death of Dickens in 1870. While everyone else was eulogizing, Wilde pointedly expressed his dislike for the dead man's novels, preferring, he said, those of Disraeli. Many years later, his disdain for Dickens and his desire for effect were once more combined in one of his most amusing and memorable aphorisms. 'One must have a heart of stone to read the death of Little Nell without laughing,' he quipped to Ada Leverson.[10] Wilde's own taste in contemporary literature at this time included William Morris and the Pre-Raphaelites. He read Dante Gabriel Rossetti's first volume of poems, published in 1870, and would have been aware of Robert Buchanan's strident attack on Rossetti's sensuality in his article 'The Fleshly School of Poetry' in 1871. By this time, the sixteen-year-old Wilde was a thoroughgoing convert to the 'Fleshly School', discovering Swinburne and, through him, Baudelaire and Whitman. The seed of Wilde's future flowering was being sown.

Wilde's extra-curricular reading had no noticeable effect on his academic achievement at Portora. He emerged triumphant in his last two years at the school, the highest accolade being his winning of the Carpenter prize for Greek Testament in 1870. When the Reverend William Steele, the school's headmaster, summoned him to the platform to collect the prize he read out his name in full, calling out 'Oscar Fingal O'Flahertie Wills Wilde'. His friends were highly amused at this, having no previous idea that Wilde could boast so many flamboyantly extravagant appendages. In the following year, Wilde was one of only three pupils awarded a Royal School scholarship to Trinity College, Dublin, and in recognition of his achievement his name was duly inscribed in gilt letters on Portora's black noticeboard. This would be painted out in 1895, the year of Wilde's disgrace, and the initials O.W. which he had carved by the window of a classroom were scraped away by the headmaster. His name has since been regilded.

When Wilde arrived at Trinity College it was a bastion of Unionism, holding out against the rising nationalist tide. The college was still largely the preserve of the Protestant ascendancy, even though Roman Catholics had been permitted to enter and take degrees from as early as 1793. Furthermore, in 1873, two years after Wilde's arrival, all religious tests except for the Divinity School were abolished. Yet the underlying bias remained. As a member of Ireland's ruling class, Wilde was typical of most of his Trinity contemporaries. When he was a child, the Wilde household at 1 Merrion Square boasted a German governess and a French maid, together with six servants. Oscar was both conscious and proud of his elevated class, as was his brother Willie, whose nickname at Portora had been 'Blue Blood' because he had protested, when accused of having failed to wash his neck, that its colour came not from the dirt but from the blue blood of the Wilde family. Nonetheless, politically if not socially, the family's nationalist background put the brothers in the minority when they arrived at Trinity.

Far more typical of the sort of undergraduate in the 1870s was Edward Carson, destined to play a crucial role in Wilde's downfall more than twenty years later.

Carson was an exact contemporary of Wilde, born in the same city and in the same year. It is even said that the two boys became friends, playing on the beach together. It seems that they shared the same fifteen-year-old nanny for a time in 1859, when Wilde and Carson would have been four or five years old. It was she who remembered the two boys playing together on the seashore.[11] Commenting wryly that this episode may have explained Carson's role as prosecuting counsel against Wilde in 1895, Michael MacLiammoir observed that 'Oscar probably upset Edward's sandcastle'.[12] Their paths would cross again at Trinity and at the Old Bailey but otherwise the two childhood friends retained little in common. Carson would become a Conservative MP, representing Dublin University from 1892 until 1918, and the Duncairn division of Belfast from 1918 to 1921. It was, however, as a rabble-rousing orator against Home Rule that he gained fame and notoriety. Prior to the outbreak of the First World War he organized the Ulster Volunteer Force, a paramilitary private army which effectively ensured the partition of Ireland by threatening civil war if the British government attempted to force Home Rule on the Protestants of the north. In the event, civil war was still not avoided in the south, and in the north a civil war in slow motion has been simmering for three quarters of a century. Carson's career in the law was as successful as his career in politics. He was called to the Irish Bar in 1880 and the English Bar in 1894. In 1892 he became Solicitor-General for Ireland and eight years later for England. He was appointed Attorney-General in 1915 and two years later became First Lord of the Admiralty and a member of the War Cabinet.

Wilde would later claim that when he and Carson arrived at Trinity they became good friends, walking about arm in arm, or with arms draped round each other's shoulders. Carson, on the other hand, denied such intimacy, claiming that he had disapproved of Wilde's 'flippant approach to life'.[13] Whichever version is true, there was no denying that the two erstwhile friends were growing apart during their time at Trinity. Carson was developing politically into the stern upholder of law and order. Wilde was evolving apolitically, towards an iconoclastic and 'flippant' aestheticism.

An intriguing picture of Wilde during his days at Trinity was given by a contemporary, Horace Wilkins. Wilde, Wilkins recalled, was 'a queer, awkward lad ... big, ungainly and clumsy to such a degree that it made him a laughing stock'. He was a 'big-hearted, liberal fellow, who never did a mean, underhanded thing, and his last shilling was at anybody's disposal'. Outwardly Wilde appeared distant, 'ever moping and dreaming', but a very different side of his character was displayed at one of the class symposiums when he read one of his poems to the assembled students. As he finished reading, one of the students, described by Wilkins as the bully of the class, laughed sneeringly. Wilde responded angrily, his face a 'savagery of hate'. He strode across the room, confronted his detractor and demanded what right he had to sneer at his poetry. The man responded by laughing again and Wilde struck him across the face. The class intervened to keep the protagonists apart but within an hour a crowd had gathered behind the college to witness a fight. Everyone expected the bully to make short work of the dreamy aesthete but Wilde led with a right which, according to Wilkins, was like a pile-driver. He followed up with half a dozen 'crushers' after which the surprised bully cowered submissively.

Wilkins claimed that he always thought of Wilde's pugilistic prowess whenever he read descriptions in the press of him as a 'pallid young man'. Less credibly, Wilkins alleged that this one incident was a major turning point in Wilde's fortunes at the college. 'It seemed to put new ambition into him and the next term found him at the head of all his classes. He seemed to be able to master everything he tackled.'[14]

Although it is unlikely that this particular incident had much to do with it, Wilde certainly succeeded in mastering everything he tackled at Trinity. At the end of his first year he was named first of those in the first class, finishing ahead of Louis Purser, who was a contemporary of Wilde's at Portora and destined to become an eminent Professor of Latin at Trinity. Purser eventually overtook his competitor but Wilde remained one of the brightest lights at the college. In a competitive examination in 1873 he received a much sought after Foundation Scholarship. He had come sixth out of the ten successful candidates, one place ahead of William Ridgeway, later Professor of Archaeology at Cambridge. The crowning achievement of Wilde's classical career at Trinity came with his winning the Berkeley Gold Medal for Greek, achieving the highest mark in a difficult examination on Meineke's *Fragments of the Greek Comic Poets*. In later years he would repeatedly pawn and redeem this medal to stave off penury.

Wilde's accumulation of new interests at Trinity led to a further weakening, or diluting, of his Irish nationalism. By this time the nationalism of his parents had lost some of its passion, becoming more lukewarm as they felt increasingly alienated from the direction in which the Fenians were taking the nationalist cause. Added to this was Wilde's growing indifference to politics and his impassioned adherence to aestheticism. His cultural enthusiasms, his Hellenism, his dandyism, his love for the Pre-Raphaelites, for Whitman, for Swinburne and for Baudelaire, made Ireland seem too parochial, too claustrophobic and inhibiting. What had the earthy demands of the Irish peasants in common with the aesthetic demands of the universal critic? The Pre-Raphaelites were singularly and peculiarly English; Whitman exuded the passionate optimism of America; Baudelaire the seductive fruits of French decadence. These literary passions were, Wilde believed, beyond the narrow minds and narrower hearts of the provincial Irish. The Catholic peasants were too uneducated to understand such things and his Protestant peers too puritanical and parochial to care.

Wilde, savouring academic success at Trinity and spreading his wings with new-found confidence, was ready to fly the provincial nest. His star, he felt, was in the ascendant, and had already risen beyond the reach of the Protestant ascendancy from which it had sprung. That ascendancy, historically, culturally and politically, had already waxed and waned; it was a spent force, exhausted and bankrupt. Wilde was now ready to cast it off like an unwanted garment that he had outgrown and which, in any case, was embarrassingly out of fashion. The only ascendancy to which Wilde now owed any allegiance was his own.

1 Ellmann, *Oscar Wilde*, p. 15.
2 Rupert Hart-Davis (ed.), *The Letters of Oscar Wilde*, London: Hart-Davis, 1962, p. 3.
3 Ellmann, *Oscar Wilde*, p. 4.
4 Ibid., p. 24.
5 Ibid.
6 Hyde, *Oscar Wilde*, p. 8.
7 Ellmann, *Oscar Wilde*, p. 21.
8 Ibid.
9 Frank Harris, *Oscar Wilde*, London: Constable & Co., 1938, pp. 17–18.
10 Ellmann, *Oscar Wilde*, p. 441.
11 Ibid., p. 18 and footnote 62, p. 557.

12 Ibid., p. 18.
13 Ibid., p. 25.
14 E.H. Mikhail (ed.), *Oscar Wilde: Interviews and Recollections*, London: Macmillan, 1979, vol. 1, p. 2.

THREE

Oxford Donned

LADY BRACKNELL: Untruthful! My nephew Algernon? Impossible!
He is an Oxonian.

Neither Wilde's dabbling in French decadence, nor his fetish for Rossetti's fleshly school of poetry, caused his liberal-minded parents any concern. His father, however, was very much perturbed by another interest which his intellectually adventurous son had picked up at Trinity College. On discovering that Oscar had befriended a number of Catholic priests, Sir William made no secret of his displeasure at the disreputable company his son was keeping.

Wilde's interest in Catholicism had little to do with any sense of solidarity with Ireland's indigenous population. The faith of the peasants was not for him. Rather, he had become attracted to the fashionable Catholicism surrounding the charismatic figure of John Henry Newman. Under Newman's patronage, which had itself been inspired by the example of St Philip Neri, Oratory churches had been founded twenty years earlier in Birmingham and London and these had quickly become centres of fashion as well as of faith, attracting many converts from the higher echelons of Victorian society. In the 1850s Newman's proselytizing influence spread across the Irish Sea when he became involved in the founding of the Dublin Catholic University which prospered under his rectorship between 1854 and 1858. When Newman returned to England, the seeds of his influence remained, growing and ripening into a garden of well-bred converts whose success in winning others to Rome was causing considerable alarm among the hierarchy of the (Protestant) Church of Ireland. It was Wilde's wanderings in this garden which had so alarmed his father who feared that his son could be seduced into the arms of the Scarlet Woman of Rome. For Wilde himself the garden was one of delights, offering a paradoxical mixture of aesthetic experiences: the odour of sanctity and the scent of scandal. His conversion, if he took the decisive step, would certainly alienate his family but it would also add a certain *savoir vivre*. The temptation was alluring, presenting the precociously ambitious young dilettante with the prospect of an upwardly mobile scandal.

It would, however, be unfair to suggest that Wilde's dabbling was only dalliance and nothing more. He was a great admirer of Newman's prose style, the beauty of which was once more evident in his *Grammar of Assent*, published in 1870, the year before Wilde's arrival at Trinity. In this book, Newman elucidated the philosophy of faith and it is difficult to conceive that Wilde could appreciate the style with which Newman made his case without also appreciating the substance which had inspired it. The stylistic surface was, after all, merely the masterly expression of its spiritual source, so that Wilde could hardly assent to the grammar without assenting also to the grain of truth from which it sprang and to which it was put in service.

The year in which Newman published his *Grammar of Assent* was also the year in which the Church pronounced the doctrine of papal infallibility at the Vatican Council. The doctrine caused much controversy among Catholics, with lines being drawn in England between the Inopportunists led by Newman and the Ultramontanes led by Manning. Both sides of the dispute would eventually be reconciled and, in 1875 and 1879 respectively, Manning and Newman would be named cardinal. Not surprisingly, the declaration of the doctrine heightened tensions between the Catholic Church and other denominations. For many Protestants the promulgation of such a dogma merely reinforced their protest against Rome, confirming their suspicions that there was something inherently pernicious about Catholicism. It is interesting, therefore, that Wilde should find himself attracted to Rome at such a volatile time. Evidently he did not find the doctrine of papal infallibility unpalatable. Perhaps, on the contrary, it was one of the causes of his attraction. If so, it is possible that Wilde's principal motivation was little more than a desire to shock his Protestant contemporaries, but it may also have been part of a genuine quest for a concrete reality – an unambiguous creed, permitting no ambivalence – which would act as a stabilizing influence, counterbalancing the flux and fluctuation of the masks he was beginning to adopt.

Whatever lay at the root of his attraction, the greatest obstacle to Wilde's conversion was the obstinacy of his father. Eventually, Sir William would employ the ultimate deterrent, the threat of disinheritance, to deter his son from taking the decisive step. In the meantime, he sought to employ more subtle methods. Encouraged by Wilde's tutor at Trinity, the Reverend Dr John Pentland Mahaffy, Sir William hatched the idea of saving his son from the clutches of Dublin priests by sending him to Oxford. It was an ill-conceived idea, not least because Oxford's dreaming spires had already been the breeding ground for many converts, including Newman himself. Only a few years earlier, Newman had received the young Gerard Manley Hopkins into the Church while the latter was still an Oxford undergraduate. Hopkins, arguably the greatest poet to emerge from the Victorian era, became a Catholic in spite of the opposition of his family and the great grief it caused his mother. Within two years, having graduated from Oxford with first class honours, Hopkins was training for the Jesuit priesthood. Clearly, in spite of Sir William's best laid schemes, Wilde would not be safe from the clutches of papist priests in Oxford. In fact, even though Wilde was not to emulate Hopkins' achievement in the spiritual sphere, or for that matter his achievement as a poet, he very nearly did emulate his predecessor's undergraduate conversion, following Hopkins to the very threshold of the Church.

With his father's encouragement, Wilde responded to an announcement in the *Oxford University Gazette* on St Patrick's Day 1874, that Magdalen College would award two Demyships (scholarships) in classics by examination on 23 June. Each paid £95 a year and could be held for five years. Wilde felt so confident of success that he did not even bother to sit for the third year examinations at Trinity. He strolled through the Magdalen examination, easily beating the other four applicants. G.T. Atkinson, who came second to Wilde, thereby receiving the other Demyship, recalled how Wilde was older than the others and much more self-assured. During the examination he kept coming up to the invigilator for more paper because, as Atkinson remembered, his writing was 'huge and sprawling, somewhat like himself'.[1]

From Oxford, Wilde travelled to London where his brother was pursuing a career in the law at the Middle Temple. Lady Wilde had travelled from Ireland to meet up with her two sons and orchestrated the celebration of her younger son's success by conducting the family on a tour of London's literati. Most memorable was a visit to the home of Thomas Carlyle, by this time a grand old man approaching his eightieth year. Lady Wilde had become acquainted with Carlyle when he had visited Ireland some years earlier. On that occasion he had sent her a volume of Tennyson's poems and he later presented her with another book, inscribed with his own translation of four lines from Goethe:

Who never ate his bread in sorrow,
Who never spent the midnight hours
Weeping and wailing for the morrow,
He knows you not, ye heavenly powers.[2]

Lady Wilde was greatly taken by these lines and would often quote them to her son. Years later, in Reading gaol, they returned to haunt him, their spirit inspiring the Ballad for which they could easily serve as an epigraph.

Oscar's impressions of London during this visit are not recorded but it is likely that his mother spoke for both of them when she wrote in a letter to a friend that London was 'truly a great and mighty city – the capital of the world'.[3] For once her grandiloquent phraseology was not given to exaggeration. In economic and political terms, London was indeed a great and mighty city, the hub of an Empire which was larger than any the world had ever seen. Its effect on Lady Wilde's brilliant and precocious son, impatient for new experiences away from the perceived sterility of Dublin, can only be imagined.

More new experiences followed. In July, Lady Wilde took her two sons to Geneva and then to Paris. It was while they were staying at the Hôtel Voltaire in Paris that Wilde began work on early drafts of his poem 'The Sphinx'. Undoubtedly inspired by the excitement of his new surroundings, 'The Sphinx' also exhibited the exotica and erotica of the decadent literature which had influenced him since his days at Portora. Wilde's sphinx sang with the seductive licentiousness of Swinburne, the darkness of Poe and the acid boredom of Baudelaire.

The young poet, liberated from Dublin's dreary limitations into the fresher air of a freer world, was finding his voice.

Returning to Ireland briefly before re-embarking once more for his new life in England, Wilde received the congratulations of his Trinity College tutors. Mahaffy, delighted by his pupil's success, quipped mischievously that 'you're not quite clever enough for us here, Oscar. Better run up to Oxford.' Robert Yelverton Tyrrell, the young Professor of Latin at Trinity, remarked, with equal mischievousness but greater profundity, that Oxford was the place where German philosophies go when they die.[4]

Wilde's life as an Oxford undergraduate commenced on 17 October 1874, the day after his twentieth birthday. The next four years would see a major metamorphosis in many aspects of his personality which would, in turn, affect, and effect, the way in which he perceived art, society and religion. The most important element in this metamorphosis involved the way in which Wilde perceived himself; or, more important still, the way in which he failed to perceive himself. The first stage of this fundamental transformation was the consciously ruthless shedding of the last vestiges of his Irishness. During his years at Oxford Wilde customized and acclimatized himself to the culture of his peers, to the old Etonians, Harrovians and Wykehamites who dominated the city's hallowed halls. Meticulously he cultivated an English public school accent. Soon he had exorcized any remnants of an Irish twang so that the actor Seymour Hicks, among others, could vouch that no trace of it was audible. 'My Irish accent was one of the many things I forgot at Oxford,' Wilde said, yet the forgetfulness was deliberate. He had become oblivious to it only because he had consciously consigned it to oblivion. In calculated fashion, and in cold blood, he had murdered any outward sign of his Irish identity.

Wilde's auto-anglicization found expression in an affected Englishness which reached almost obsessive and absurd proportions in his poem 'Ave Imperatrix'. This verse retains a subtle sense of his smothered Irishness in the implicit condemnation of Cromwell and in the lament over those who had died in foreign lands, though tellingly it is the English dead he laments:

O Cromwell's England! must thou yield
   For every inch of ground a son?

Yet even though 'Ave Imperatrix' is not, as its title would suggest, a hymn of praise to the Empire or a genuflection to the glories of the Pax Britannica, Wilde's eulogizing of 'our English chivalry' and 'quiet English fields' is indicative of a change of heart, or at any rate of an altered pose. It was certainly not the language of the Fenian uprising which had ripped his native land apart only a few years earlier or that of his mother's Irish nationalism. Perhaps, as with his mother's verse, his poetic posturing was little more than a mask. It is tempting to search for a sense of irony in 'Ave Imperatrix' which would convey layers of meaning beyond the almost jingoistic surface. There is a subversive subtlety in the republicanism of the final stanza but it is an English republicanism, distinct from its Irish equivalent, and rooted in a feigned English patriotism:

> Peace, peace! we wrong the noble dead
> > To vex their solemn slumber so;
> Though childless, and with thorn-crowned head,
> > Up the steep road must England go.
>
> Yet when this fiery web is spun,
> > Her watchmen shall descry from far
> The young Republic like a sun
> > Rise from these crimson seas of war.

It seems that Wilde was being earnest in 'Ave Imperatrix', even if only on a shallow and superficial level. The whole verse resonates with the uncomplicated earnestness of youth and there are none of the deft and devious *distinguo*s which characterize his later criticism. The irony was that there was no irony.

Wilde's determination to conform to the conventions of Victorian Oxford extended to his choice of dress. Initially, conformity meant formality and Wilde developed an exaggerated taste for formal wear. 'If I were all alone marooned on a desert island and had my things with me, I should dress for dinner every evening,' he told a friend.[5] His biographer, Richard Ellmann, wondered mirthfully who would actually cook for him in such circumstances. The exaggerated taste was not restricted to evening wear. By day, he discarded his Dublin clothes and bought new outfits designed to be sportier than those of his friends. His tweed jackets boasted larger checks than theirs and he wore bright blue neckties, tall collars and curly brimmed hats balanced on one ear. This, of course, was the early flourishing of the dandyism which would make Wilde something of a legend at Oxford. Beginning with a desire to conform, his playing the role of an English gentleman developed, in a personality such as his, into an element of exaggeration, of hamming it up for his audience. Thus the adopted character became an adept caricature. In this way the transmogrification from a singular and peculiar sort of Irishman into a very un-English Englishman would be achieved. The chrysalis of conformity would crystallize itself into a singular non-conformity with Wilde emerging from the process as a rare and outwardly beautiful butterfly, a dandy dilettante in disguise. Henceforth Wilde's disguise would be a statement, and his statements a disguise. The truth and the mask would be one. Wilde, as the world would know him, was born.

Not surprisingly, Wilde's emergence as a self-conscious dandy met with a mixed response from his fellow students in classics, many of whom considered him a freak. The more robustly athletic of his contemporaries scorned both his aestheticism and his affected mannerisms, and he in turn treated his detractors with contempt. Conflict was inevitable. It was said that on one occasion Wilde was dragged to the top of a high hill by a group of students who only released him once they had reached the summit. Wilde was said to have got to his feet, dusted himself off and remarked casually that the view from the top of the hill was really very charming. Atkinson expressed doubts that the incident ever took place but it was the sort of story around which the Wilde legend would be constructed. In fact, much of the legend would be constructed on the misconstrued, something which Wilde actively encouraged. 'What is true in a man's life is not what he does,' he later remarked, 'but the legend which grows up around him ... You must never destroy legends. Through them we are given an inkling of the true physiognomy of a man.'[6]

Wilde was anything but effete beneath the aesthetic surface. In his memoirs, Sir Frank Benson recalls an incident which parallels Wilde's robust defence of his poetry at Trinity. According to Benson, Wilde was 'far from being a flabby aesthete'. On the contrary, the only man in Magdalen College who, in Benson's view, 'had a ghost of a chance in a tussle with Wilde' was J.T. Wharton, who rowed seven in the

Varsity Eight. Wharton held Wilde in considerable respect, commenting on the latter's deceptive muscularity. Benson confirmed Wharton's judgement, remembering Wilde's response to a group of students who arrived at his rooms intent on giving him a beating. Four undergraduates were deputed to burst into Wilde's rooms while the rest watched from the stairs. The assailants received more than they expected. According to Benson, Wilde booted out the first, doubled up the second with a punch, threw out the third through the air, and taking hold of the fourth – a man as big as himself – carried him down to his rooms and buried him beneath his own furniture. As a final *coup de théâtre* Wilde helped himself to his assailant's wines and spirits and invited the astounded spectators to join him.

Wilde's solid grounding in the classics, the fruit of his labours at Portora and Trinity, gave him an advantage over most of his contemporaries. Handling his studies with ease, he was left with plenty of time for extra-curricular reading. He retained his admiration for Swinburne, whose *Essays and Studies*, published in 1875, gave him the idea of uniting 'personality' with 'perfection'. This potent union would result in the conception of much of Wilde's own art in later years. Wilde's other reading spanned the spectrum of philosophy from Plato and Aristotle through to Kant, Hegel, Locke, Hume, Berkeley, Mill and Spencer. Such a combination of ancient and modern was illustrative of Wilde's desire to make sense of, and to embrace, both the eternal verities of classical thought and the newer agnostic speculations of the evolutionary philosophers and 'progressive' thinkers.

The desire to unite the classical with the modern was as true of his approach to art as it was to his approach to philosophy. He would write in the Commonplace Book which he kept while at Oxford that Dante and Dürer, Keats and Blake were the best representatives of the Greek spirit in modern times. Wilde also considered himself a representative of this spirit, distilling his views into an aesthetic fundamentalism which espoused the doctrine of Beauty for Beauty's Sake: 'Beauty is perfect. Beauty is capable of all things. Beauty is the only thing in the world which does not excite desire.'[7] At this stage, Wilde's enshrining of beauty was reconciled with, and dependent on, his belief in God. It would lead, however, to further metaphysical speculation, culminating for a time in a belief that beauty was self-sufficient, an end in itself. Art as deity. Yet beauty was blasphemed by ugliness which, at its deepest, was exhibited in man's conception of sin. Thus Wilde scribbled in his Commonplace Book the words of Baudelaire: 'O Lord! Give me the strength and the courage to contemplate my heart without disgust!' In this short phrase Baudelaire had summed up the tension in his own heart and the paradox at the heart of the decadent movement. It was certainly applicable to Wilde whose whole life would be a war between his consciousness and his conscience, between the masks of beauty and the mark of the beast.

These paradoxes of life and art became Wilde's principal preoccupation during his first year at Oxford. This can be readily gauged by the main headings which he chose for the Commonplace Book: Culture, Progress, Metaphysics, Poetry ... In 1875 he was – as he would always remain, in spite of his inner contradictions and rebellions – a conscientious seeker after truth in all its guises. It was inevitable, therefore, that Wilde should become fascinated with the two ultimately opposing schools of thought at Oxford represented by John Ruskin and Walter Pater. The extraordinary influence of these two men on Wilde's subsequent development was so ubiquitous that only the French decadents could rival them in importance.

At the time of Wilde's arrival at Oxford, Ruskin, at fifty-five, was probably the most celebrated art critic in England. He had been the most vociferous champion of J.M.W. Turner, helping to restore and secure the great painter's reputation, and had been an early champion of the Pre-Raphaelites. In 1870 Oxford had paid him the honour of making him its first Slade Professor of Fine Art, a position he held during Wilde's days as an undergraduate. During his first term at Oxford, Wilde attended a series of eight lectures given by Ruskin between 10 November and 4 December 1874. The theme of the lectures was 'The Aesthetic and Mathematic Schools of Art in Florence'. By 'Mathematic' Ruskin meant the science of perspective, but it was his discussion of the 'Aesthetic' which would most have interested Wilde. For Ruskin aestheticism in art was inseparable from morality which, in the case of Florentine art, had its roots in the moral foundations of medieval Christendom. Consequently, the aesthetic inevitably suffered when the humanism of the Renaissance weakened the link with these Christian roots. As such, Ruskin argued, the more the Renaissance bloomed, the more it decayed.

Wilde seems to have attended all eight lectures. Atkinson recalled that 'Wilde was always there', and another contemporary, W.H. Nevinson, remembered him in constant attendance, 'leaning his large and flabby form against the door upon our right, conspicuous for something unusual in his dress, still more in his splendid head, his mass of black hair, his vivacious eyes, his poet's forehead, and a mouth like a shark's in formlessness and appetite'.[8]

Ruskin's influence on Wilde was both lasting and ingrained. Wilde became a disciple of Ruskin's social teaching which echoed that of William Blake in its disdain for industrialism's 'dark satanic mills'. 'At Paddington station I felt as if in hell,' Ruskin remarked, and in similar vein, Wilde, as a loyal disciple of both Blake and Ruskin, told his friends that all the factory chimneys and vulgar work-shops should be transported to some far-off island. 'I would give Manchester back to the shepherds and Leeds to the stockfarmers,' he declared.[9] Echoing Ruskin, Wilde believed that art could play a part in the social regeneration of England and much of his talk at Magdalen was devoted to social issues. Perhaps it was this romantic spirit which inspired the anglophile republicanism of 'Ave Imperatrix'. So enthused was he by these utopian visions of a rustic England that he joined a team of student volunteers on one of Ruskin's schemes to improve the neighbouring countryside. Intent on practising what he preached, Ruskin joined his undergraduate recruits and helped with the labour. It was on one of these work excursions that Wilde met his mentor, bragging humorously in later years that he had been privi-leged to fill 'Mr Ruskin's especial wheelbarrow' and that he had been solemnly instructed by the master himself in the mysteries of wheel-ing such a vehicle from place to place. Ruskin and Wilde became friends, seeing each other regularly, and Wilde gained a great deal from the master–disciple relationship. Writing to Ruskin many years later, Wilde paid homage:

the dearest memories of my Oxford days are my walks and talks with you, and from you I learned nothing but what was good. How else could it be? There is in you something of prophet, of priest, and of poet, and to you the gods gave eloquence such as they have given to none other, so that your message may come to us with the fire of passion, and the marvel of music, making the deaf to hear, and the blind to see.[10]

Within a few years Wilde was to lose his enthusiasm for Ruskin's social vision. His apolitical nature and his restless, rootless, nomadic soul could not find their fulfilment or their true home in England's green and pleasant land, any more than in Ireland's forty shades of green. Yet Ruskin's vision of art and aestheticism would be more enduring. Wilde accepted Ruskin's view of late Renaissance decadence and was struck by his conception of Venice as a medieval Virgin who became a Renaissance Venus, specific works of art and architecture marking the change. In *De Profundis* Wilde would echo his master's voice:

> To me one of the things in history the most to be regretted is that the Christ's own renaissance which had produced the Cathedral of Chartres, the Arthurian cycle of legends, the life of St Francis of Assisi, the art of Giotto, and Dante's *Divine Comedy*, was not allowed to develop on its own lines but was interrupted and spoiled by the dreary classical Renaissance that gave us Petrarch, and Raphael's frescoes, and Palladian architecture, and formal French tragedy, and St Paul's Cathedral, and Pope's poetry, and everything that is made from without and by dead rules, and does not spring from within through some spirit informing it.[11]

Like Wilde, Walter Pater had once been Ruskin's disciple. Yet by the time Wilde arrived at Oxford the disciple was in rebellion. Twenty years Ruskin's junior, Pater saw himself as the older man's natural successor. He was still only in his mid-thirties when, in 1873, as a fellow of Brasenose College, he had published his *Studies in the History of the Renaissance*. A year later, during his first term at Magdalen, Wilde fell under its spell. Henceforth, in Wilde's imagination, Pater's seductively amoral approach to the Renaissance would serve as a counterpoise to Ruskin's morality. According to Pater's 'progressive' view, the Renaissance was neither defined by, nor confined to, medieval Christendom. In many respects, the medieval period was only of value insofar as it laid the basis for the early Renaissance, while the late Renaissance represented a liberation from the strictures of medievalism. As for Ruskin's assertion that the late Renaissance had declined into decadence, Pater's riposte in his preface to *Studies in the History of the Renaissance* was to heartily welcome what he called 'a refined and comely decadence'. Yet it was Pater's controversial 'Conclusion' to his *Studies* which affected Wilde most deeply. Pater declared that life was merely a drift of momentary acts and that, in consequence, each act must be experienced to the full and each moment magnified. Life should be lived for the instant, seeking 'not the fruit of experience, but experience itself'. Since life was to be judged from this perspective, Pater asserted, success in life was to 'burn always with this hard gemlike flame'. This was a vision that fired Wilde's imagination. He absorbed Pater's 'Conclusion' and would refer to *Studies in the History of the Renaissance* as 'my golden book'. Yet from prison, looking back wistfully at the price he had paid for living for the moment, he referred to Pater's *Renaissance* only as 'that book which has had such a strange influence over my life'.[12]

Pater's influence, both strange and important, should not be understated. It is, however, often overstated. It is suggested, for instance, that Pater liberated Wilde from the inhibitions of Victorian morality, enabling him to experience sensual pleasures which would otherwise have been beyond his reach. This may be so, but Wilde always believed that such pleasures were, at best, a distraction from higher and more satisfying pleasures. At worst, they erected an insurmountable obstacle to the realization of the higher pleasures. This is readily illustrated by Wilde himself in two of the poems often cited as evidence of Pater's influence. In 'The Burden of Itys' the following lines are quoted as proof of Wilde's debt to Pater:

> I would be drunk with life,
> Drunk with the trampled vintage of my youth.

Wilde, however, had no illusions about the effects of drunkenness, or that the 'highs' to be attained from drink, drugs or other addictive pleasures were an illusory diversion from higher realities or truth. The very next lines of the stanza from which these lines are plucked suggest as much:

> I would forget the wearying wasted strife,
> The riven veil, the Gorgon eyes of Truth,
> The prayerless vigil and the cry for prayer,
> The barren gifts, the lifted arms, the dull insensate air!

These lines, and the two which preceded them, were written while Wilde was at Magdalen. The influence of Pater is all too evident, but only as an escape from, and not as an access to, his quest for the higher goal for which he was groping, 'the Gorgon eyes of Truth'.

The other verse often quoted to illustrate Pater's influence is 'Humanitad'. Wilde's desire 'to burn with one clear flame' is compared with Pater's maxim that a successful life is to 'burn always with this hard gemlike flame'. Wilde, however, does not offer the image as part of a Conclusion, as does Pater, but sets his gemlike flame within a deeper question:

> To burn with one clear flame, to stand erect
>   In natural honour, not to bend the knee
> In profitless prostrations whose effect
>   Is by itself condemned, what alchemy
> Can teach me this?

Wilde's question asks more than Pater's conclusion ever answers. The flame cannot burn in the stale air of transient pleasures and the quest for natural honour is inhibited by momentary acts condemned by their own effects. This is expressed later in the same poem with succinct, flamelike brilliance:

>   Anarchy
>   Freedom's own Judas, the vile prodigal
> Licence who steals the gold of Liberty
>   And yet has nothing ...

In many respects these eighteen words could serve as a key to understanding the truth behind Wilde's many masks. They could serve as both epigraph and moral to many of his works, and indeed to his life. They also serve as a definitive refutation of Pater's position.

Wilde's most elaborate and memorable refutation of Pater came through the unravelling of the plot of *The Picture of Dorian Gray*. At the outset of Wilde's novel, Dorian Gray is corrupted by the Pateresque sermons of Lord Henry Wotton. Gray accepts Lord Henry's position, stating in a direct and unacknowledged quotation from Pater's 'Conclusion' that he was seeking 'not the fruit of experience, but experience itself'. Ultimately, Gray's practising what Pater preached has disastrous and murderous consequences.

Faced with such evidence of Pater's direct influence on what is arguably Wilde's greatest literary achievement, the extent of his importance can scarcely be denied. His influence, however, was primarily that of a catalyst, sparking luridly imaginative reactions. Pater prompted the loins of Wilde's creativity, arousing the urge to probe into the lowest depths of human existence, life's lusts and not its loves. Yet Pater was too shallow to reach the heart and mind of Wilde's creativity and intellect. Even at Magdalen Wilde had perceived as much, which is why he became Ruskin's disciple not Pater's. Wilde knew, though sometimes he chose to forget, that the highest common factors of life were its loves and not its lusts. It was these that transfused and transformed his art, imbuing the Pater-inspired *facts* with the Ruskin-inspired *truth*.

The aesthetic battle between Ruskin and Pater was, in Wilde's judgement, resolved very soon after his arrival at Oxford, the former being declared victor. The other metaphysical battle which raged across the frontiers of Wilde's heart and mind during his years at Magdalen would not be resolved as easily. This was the struggle with religious truth, the battle of belief and unbelief. For Wilde this was a battle which would be fought with varying degrees of intensity throughout the whole of his life. For long periods the struggle was subdued but it was always rejoined with renewed vigour, depriving Wilde of the peace he desired.

1 Ellmann, *Oscar Wilde*, p. 33.
2 Ibid., p. 34.
3 Ibid.
4 Ibid., p. 35.
5 Ibid., p. 37.
6 Ibid., p. 42.
7 Ibid., p. 41.
8 Ibid., p. 47.
9 Ibid., p. 48.
10 Hart-Davis, *Letters of Oscar Wilde*, p. 218.
11 Ibid., p. 482.
12 Ibid., p. 471.

FOUR

Courting Conversion

The truths of metaphysics are the truths of masks.

A t Oxford the flirtation with Catholicism which Wilde had initiated in Dublin was roused to new levels of intensity. Ruskin and Pater, through their enticing evocations of the Renaissance spirit, were at least partially responsible for this. Whether the Renaissance was an expression of Catholicism, as Ruskin maintained, or a liberation from it, as Pater countered, it remained at the centre of the discussion. If one loved the Renaissance it was essential to feel something about the faith which had spawned it.

A year before he and Wilde first met, Ruskin had spent the summer in a monastic cell in Assisi, basking in the Franciscan spirit. In the end he refused to be converted, claiming to be more Catholic than the Roman Catholics. Pater, on the other hand, was a great admirer of the rituals and decorations in Catholic churches. Ten years later, in *Marius the Epicurean*, he was to praise the 'aesthetic charm' of Catholic art and ritual while treating the doctrines of the Church with reserve.

Following Ruskin's example, Wilde travelled to Italy in the summer of 1875, visiting Florence, Bologna, Venice and Milan. Journeying by train from Florence to Bologna, Wilde wrote to his mother of the beautiful mountain scenery, 'above us pine-forests and crags, below us the valley, villages and swollen rivers'. Arriving in Venice, Wilde let his Renaissance imagination run wild. The Church of San Marco was 'most gorgeous': 'a splendid *Byzantine* church, covered with gilding and mosaics, inside and out. The floor of inlaid marbles, of colour and design indescribable.'[1]

His impressions of Italy found poetic expression in several religious verses. On 15 June, after a visit to San Miniato in Florence, he was inspired to unite his love for Fra Angelico with the artist's angelic visions of the Virgin:

> See, I have climbed the mountain side
> Up to this holy house of God,
> Where the Angelic Monk has trod
> Who saw the heavens opened wide,
>
> And throned upon the crescent moon
> The Virginal white Queen of Grace, –
> Mary! Could I but see thy face
> Death could not come at all too soon.

Similarly, studying a fresco of the Annunciation in Florence, possibly with the parallel image of Dante Gabriel Rossetti's *Ecce Ancilla Domini* in mind, he wrote:

> With such glad dreams I sought this holy place,
> And now with wondering eyes and heart I stand
> Before this supreme mystery of Love:
> A kneeling girl with passionless pale face,
> An angel with a lily in his hand,
> And over both with outstretched wings the Dove.

On 25 June, having spent all his money, Wilde was forced to cut short his holiday, abandoning the planned visit to Rome. His disappointment found voice in 'Rome Unvisited', possibly the best known and most accomplished of his religious verse. At the heart of this poem, which apparently elicited the praise of Newman when Wilde sent it him, was the desire for conversion.

As a poet Wilde reveals himself as his mother's son. 'Rome Unvisited' is shrouded in the imagery of masks. There is, however, a crucial and fundamental difference. Whereas physical masks can be lies or distortions which conceal the *facts*, metaphysical masks can be signs or sacraments which reveal the *truth*. As Wilde would state many years later, 'the truths of metaphysics are the truths of masks'.[2] Thus, in 'Rome Unvisited', the Pope, in elevating the consecrated host, 'shows his God to human eyes / Beneath the veil of bread and wine'. The Blessed Sacrament is a mask which shows God to the people. It is a veil that reveals. The poem reaches its climax with Wilde calling upon the name 'Of Him who now doth hide His face'. Thus the *coup de grâce* and the *coup de théâtre* are one: even God wears a mask.

Returning to Oxford, Wilde found himself discussing the teachings of the Church with fellow undergraduates. In the rooms of his friend W.W. Ward, he argued through the night with Ward and another friend, David Hunter Blair. The latter was described by Ward as 'a new and eager convert to Roman Catholicism' and 'a man of singular enthusiasm and vivacity'. Ward recalled that, as the sound of the dawn chorus in the trees that fringe the river Cherwell accompanied the theological debate, Wilde was seemingly convinced by Hunter Blair's apologetics, and was suspended, 'poised in a paradox, between doubt and dogma'. Hunter Blair, sensing that Wilde's poise was not so much a pause as an impasse, suddenly exclaimed in exasperation: 'You will be damned, you will be damned, for you see the light and will not follow it!'[3]

Hunter Blair was received into the Church in 1875 and he recalled that Wilde was greatly interested in the step he had taken. 'Oscar ... asked me many questions, and showed me what I had not known before; how deep, and I am sure genuine, was his own sympathy with Catholicism, and how much moved he was by my having taken the step which I did.'[4] Wilde then told of his own attendance at Catholic services when he was at Trinity College and his father's wrath when he had discovered his friendship with several Catholic priests: 'I am sure that if I had become a Catholic at that time he would have cast me off altogether, and that he would do the same today. That is why he rejoiced at my winning a scholarship at Oxford, where I should not be exposed to these pernicious influences. And now my best friend turns out to be a Papist – perhaps, for anything I know, a "Jesuit in disguise", a real wolf in sheep's clothing!'[5] Wilde concluded by reminding Hunter Blair, who belonged to a family of landowning gentry in Galloway, that he was fortunate to be financially independent of his father and so free to do what he liked. '*My* case is very different.'

In the months following his conversion, Hunter Blair took an increasing interest in the Catholic life of the university and city, and

Wilde often accompanied him to Catholic gatherings and functions. They were present at the laying of the foundation stone of the new church of St Aloysius, and Wilde was much impressed by Bishop Ullathorne's address to mark the occasion. 'That little old gentleman with the big silver spectacles certainly spoke like one having authority,' he remarked as he and Hunter Blair walked away after the ceremony. A few months later, on 23 November 1875, the two friends returned to St Aloysius' to hear Cardinal Manning preach at the dedication service on the university motto, *Dominus Illuminatio Mea*, the Lord is my enlightenment. The Cardinal was in fighting mood, employing his abrasive oratory to denounce the secular tone of much of the university's teaching.

By the beginning of 1876 Wilde was making no secret of his Catholic sympathies, to such an extent that, according to Hunter Blair, he considerably bored those of his acquaintances who were not in the slightest degree interested in such matters.[6] Others were openly hostile, such as Lord Ronald Gower, younger son of the second Duke of Sutherland, who was related to Hunter Blair through marriage. Lord Ronald had first met Wilde on 4 June 1876, describing him as 'a pleasant cheerful fellow but with his long-haired head full of nonsense regarding the Church of Rome'.[7] With evident distaste, he added that Wilde's rooms were filled with photographs of the Pope and Cardinal Manning.

Wilde's choice of Pope Pius IX and Cardinal Manning as objects of adoration is itself interesting. The Pope and Manning were pillars of the uncompromising Ultramontane school within the Church, distinct from the more moderate elements represented most notably in England by Newman. The ageing Pope, a voluntary prisoner within the Vatican since the soldiers of Victor Emmanuel had entered Rome in 1870, had become something of an icon of resistance to secular incursions into the life of the Church. In 1875 Wilde had written plaintively in verse how 'far away at Rome / In evil bonds a second Peter lay' and in another verse had called him 'the prisoned shepherd of the Church of God'.[8] (It was no coincidence that Evelyn Waugh should invoke Pius IX nearly a century later to justify his own bitter opposition to what he believed were secular incursions into the Church's liturgy following the reforms of the Second Vatican Council.)

In 1854, by the bull *Ineffabilis Deus*, Pope Pius had decreed the Immaculate Conception which was attacked by Protestants as further evidence of the Church's mariolatry. Yet it was the decision of the Vatican Council in 1870 to proclaim the infallibility of the Pope which had most outraged hostile observers. It had also unsettled many Catholics, including Newman. Manning, however, was as uncompromising as the Pope himself and it is interesting, when seen in this light, that Wilde should have switched his allegiance from the moderate Newman, the object of his admiration when he was at Trinity, to the 'hard-line' Manning. It would certainly appear to illustrate that he was thoroughly *au fait* with the doctrinal disputes within the Church at the time. This is borne out by a letter which Wilde wrote to W.W. Ward in July 1876. He recommends that his friend read a new 'really wonderfully dramatic book' on the Vatican Council: 'How strange that on the day of the Pope publicly declaring that his Infallibility and that of the Church were identical a fearful storm broke over Rome *and two thunderbolts fell from heaven*.' He also responds to Anglican opposition to the Pope's earlier Promulgation of the Immaculate Conception with the cuttingly orthodox wit more often associated in later years with G.K. Chesterton or Ronald Knox. It was, he wrote, 'very strange that they should be so anxious to believe the Blessed Virgin conceived in sin'.[9]

In marked contrast to his lauding of the Church Militant to anyone who would listen in Oxford, Wilde was careful to keep his Papist sympathies a carefully concealed secret from his father in Dublin. Wilde's duplicity was not due merely to a fear of incurring his father's wrath but arose from a genuine concern for Sir William's ailing health. The news of a further deterioration in his father's condition reached Wilde during the spring vacation in 1876. Conscientiously, he was spending the vacation in Oxford studying for the examination in Honour Moderations which he would have to take in June. On hearing that his father was bedridden and that the worst was feared he abandoned his studies and travelled to Ireland. He was saddened by his father's condition but marvelled at his mother, for during what were obviously her husband's last weeks, she permitted an unidentified veiled woman – presumably the mother of one or more of Sir William's illegitimate children – to come and sit by the bedside, silent and grief-stricken. The mysterious woman's appearance would suggest that Sir William had maintained some degree of intimacy with her and that Lady Wilde had, to some degree, knowingly acquiesced. Whatever her other faults may have been, Lady Wilde could not be accused of jealousy.

Sir William died on 19 April, with his family at his bedside. His wife's grief would later find an expressive outpouring in verse. 'In the Midnight', published in an issue of the *Dublin University Magazine* later in the year, palpitates with pathos:

Read till the warm tears fall my love,
With thy voice so soft and low,
And the Saviour's merits will plead above
For the soul that prayeth below.

This was probably the poem which Wilde enclosed in a letter to W.W. Ward on 3 January 1877. 'I know your mother is fond of reading Sacred Poetry,' Wilde wrote, 'so I have taken the liberty of sending her a Magazine with a poem of Mamma's in it ...'[10] In the same letter, Wilde criticized Ward for being 'an awful cynic about women' and expressed the hope 'some day to hear you raving about pretty lips and blue eyes'. Wilde's own enthusiasm for pretty lips and blue eyes had been aroused a few months earlier, in August 1876, when he first met Florence Balcombe, third of five daughters of a retired lieutenant-colonel who had served in India and the Crimea. It is quite possible that her father's service in the Crimean War was responsible for her being named after Florence Nightingale. She and Wilde met at her home in Dublin when she was seventeen and he was twenty-one. In a letter to another college friend, Reginald Harding, Wilde enthused that he had just met an 'exquisitely pretty girl' who had 'the most perfectly beautiful face I ever saw', promising to show him a photograph of her when they next met.[11] Wilde's appraisal of Florence's beauty was shared by the artist and author George du Maurier, who considered her one of the three most beautiful women he had ever seen.[12]

Wilde informed Harding that he was taking Florence to the afternoon service at Dublin's Protestant cathedral, St Patrick's. A lively friendship developed and by Christmas Wilde and Florence Balcombe were in love. The idea of marriage was aired and Wilde presented her with a small gold cross which united their names. It was, therefore, with an air of superciliousness that Wilde was able to admonish Ward on 3 January for his failure to appreciate feminine charms.

Florence Balcombe's charms excited Wilde's muse in a way that only the Church had done previously and for a while caritas gave way to eros, not only in his affections but in the affectations of his poetry. In the first flush of first love Venus had vanquished the Virgin:

> She is too fair for any man
>   To see or hold his heart's delight,
> Fairer than Queen or courtesan
>   Or moonlit water in the night.
>
> Her hair is bound with myrtle leaves,
>   (Green leaves upon her golden hair!)
> Green grasses through the yellow sheaves
>   Of autumn corn are not more fair.
>
> Her little lips, more made to kiss
>   Than to cry bitterly for pain,
> Are tremulous as brook-water is,
>   Or roses after evening rain.
>
> Her neck is like white melilote
>   Flushing for pleasure of the sun,
> The throbbing of the linnet's throat
>   Is not so sweet to look upon.
>
> As a pomegranate, cut in twain,
>   White-seeded is her crimson mouth,
> Her cheeks are as the fading stain
>   Where the peach reddens to the south.
>
> O twining hands! O delicate
>   White body made for love and pain!
> O house of love! O desolate
>   Pale flower beaten by the rain.[13]

Throughout 1876 and 1877, Wilde's poems were published in various journals. The above verse was published in 1876, as were 'Rome Unvisited' and 'San Miniato' among others. In the following year, his published verse included 'Sonnet on Approaching Italy', 'Urbs Sacra Aeterna', 'Sonnet, Written during Holy Week', 'The Grave of Keats', 'Madonna Mia' and 'Vita Nuova'. His literary achievement was paralleled by a similar success in his studies when he gained a first in Classical Moderations in 1876. All the while, as the subject matter of his verse testified, he was preoccupied with the issue of religion. Roman Catholicism threaded its way omnipresently through his years as an undergraduate without ever gaining, on Wilde's part, the omnipotence of final acceptance. He courted it romantically, sought it intellectually, but it seemed to flit elusively just out of his grasp.

In 1876 he took Newman's books with him to Ireland for the summer vacation, presumably anxious to understand the reasoning and motivation behind Newman's conversion thirty years earlier. In the autobiographical *Apologia pro Vita Sua*, and the semi-autobiographical novel *Loss and Gain*, Newman had delivered masterful accounts of the spiritual and psychological processes, and the intellectual stimuli, that had led to his own acceptance of the Church's creed and authority. Wilde must have hoped that Newman's style and brilliance would settle his own difficulties. Yet if he believed that Newman would sweep him off his feet and into the comforting arms of Rome he was to be disappointed. Newman's calm and arid path to Rome, rooted in reason, was not for the tempestuous and sensation-seeking Wilde. In a letter to Ward in July 1876, Wilde stated that he thought Newman's 'higher emotions' had revolted against Rome 'but that he was swept on by Logic to accept it as the only rational form of Christianity'.[14] This was the opposite of Wilde's approach. Wilde's 'higher emotions', his aesthetic sensibilities, were attracted to Rome but he was troubled by a pessimistic rationalism which led him towards scepticism. The warring paradox at the centre of his psyche was that he was emotionally attracted to faith but temperamentally tempted to doubt. Logic, as perceived by the pessimistic side of his character, led him away from the Church and not towards it. He accepted, with Newman, that Catholicism was the only rational form of Christianity, but he was beginning to fear that Christianity was itself irrational. He was, at least in his most sceptical moments, at one with Maurice Baring who, twenty-three years later, would state that he understood the logic of the Catholic position without accepting the ultimate logic of Christianity itself: 'My trouble is I cannot believe in the first proposition, the source of all dogma. If I could do that, if I could tell the first lie, I quite see that all the rest would follow.'[15] In his darker moments Wilde began to fear that behind the beautiful mask which was Rome there was Nothing.

More stimulating and constructive for a man of Wilde's disposition was Thomas à Kempis's *Imitation of Christ*, which he purchased on 6 July, about the time that he had bought most of Newman's books. Thomas à Kempis's Christocentric Catholicism struck an aesthetic chord, accentuating and inflaming Wilde's love for the person of Christ, a love which would always remain with him, even in – especially in – his darkest hours. 'I am now off to bed after reading a chapter of S. Thomas à Kempis,' he wrote to Ward on 26 July. 'I think half-an-hour's warping of the inner man daily is greatly conducive to holiness.'[16]

Wilde spent the summer with his mother who seems to have shared her late husband's distaste for their son's continuing love affair with Catholicism. Taking it upon herself to open her son's mail she was 'greatly troubled' to learn that Wilde had been attending Catholic services at St Aloysius' in Oxford. Religion was certainly a topic of conversation between them and Lady Wilde revealed that she, too, was battling with the twin giants of faith and doubt. She told her son that dogma was necessary for the 'people', who presumably could not be expected to know any better, but that she rejected all forms of superstition and dogma, particularly any notion of priest and sacrament standing between her and God. The aspect of God which she found most attractive was the concept of the divine intelligence of which humanity could partake. Against this divine intelligence, Lady Wilde took an interest in what could be termed the counter-intelligence offered by pessimistic philosophers. According to her son, the philosopher with whom she was most enamoured in the summer of 1876 was Artur Schopenhauer.

It is implicit in Wilde's correspondence that he and his mother discussed Schopenhauer at some length during July 1876. The importance of these discussions has been overlooked by Wilde's biographers even though it is likely that their impact on Wilde's future development was considerable. In Wilde's approach to metaphysics Schopenhauer would come to rival Christ, each struggling with the other for supremacy. For the greater part of his life neither would be victorious so that Wilde often espoused an incongruous and indigestible mixture of both. Schopenhauer's pessimism would only partially eclipse Wilde's latent Christianity, creating a hybrid whose contradictions and confusions masked his true meaning, even from himself.

There are, in fact, some remarkable, and perhaps not entirely superficial, similarities between the lives of Schopenhauer and Wilde. Schopenhauer's father was a banker and his mother was a novelist who in later life kept a literary salon at Weimar. Lady Wilde was of course a poet and would, upon her arrival in London three years later in 1879, keep a literary salon of her own at which she played a *grande dame*, dressed flamboyantly in the style of the 1860s and wearing a black wig which was often topped with an imposing headdress. Her weekly salons became almost legendary in London literary circles with guests coming to marvel at Lady Wilde's presence and her son's wit. As for Schopenhauer, he considered himself a genius, the natural heir of Socrates, and was resentful that the world paid more attention to what he considered the fatuous ravings of Hegel, Schelling and Fichte than to his own thought. He retired to Frankfurt-am-Main where he became a lonely, violent and unbefriended man, who shared his bachelor's existence with a poodle named 'Atma', or 'world soul'. Wilde was certainly not violent, and he was only unbefriended and lonely during his final years of enforced exile, but it was in their philosophy that the two men had much in common. In Schopenhauer, as in Wilde, feeling and reason were in perpetual conflict and this appears to have shaped Schopenhauer's philosophy. His *weltanschauung* was preconditioned by his *weltanschmerz*, his world-view the child of his angst. In essence, Schopenhauer's creed was based on the concept of Subjective Idealism, the belief that the world is my idea, a mere phantasmagoria of my brain, and therefore in itself nothing. He also elevated Art, the ideas of which were accessible to the intuition of genius, and, as such, the only knowledge which was not subservient to the Will and to the needs of practical life.

Schopenhauer was an atheist and it is easy to imagine the mental contortions of Lady Wilde's mind, no doubt exacerbated by grief at the recent loss of her husband, as she struggled to accommodate this atheistic pessimism into the remnants of her own esoteric Protestantism. Wilde, always open to his mother's influence, must have found their discussions discomforting and sought to shrug them off, even to laugh them off, in a letter to Ward. Schopenhauer was, he wrote, his mother's 'last', i.e. her latest, pessimist, implying that she collected pessimists as others collected postage stamps. Wilde summed up Schopenhauer's pessimism with a caustic mix of wit and whimsy, declaring that the German philosopher believed that the whole human race ought to walk into the sea and leave the world tenantless. The problem was, Wilde added, that 'some skulking wretches would hide and be left behind to people the world again I am afraid'.[17] At this stage, Wilde's interest in Catholicism served as an antidote to Schopenhauer and it was only after the former faltered in his affections that the latter emerged as a formative influence.

Immediately after his whimsical appraisal of pessimism, Wilde's letter to Ward turned to the 'beauty and necessity' of the Incarnation, stating that it helped humanity 'grasp at the skirts of the Infinite': 'since Christ the dead world has woke up from sleep. Since him we have lived. I think the greatest proof of the Incarnation aspect of Christianity is its whole career of noble men and thoughts and not the mere narration of unauthenticated histories.' He cites St Bernard, St Augustine, St Philip Neri, and contemporaries such as Newman and Henry Parry Liddon, as being 'good philosophers and good Christians'.[18]

When he wasn't receiving the comfort of Thomas à Kempis or the discomfort of Schopenhauer, Wilde sought physical release from his metaphysical speculations in a variety of recreations. In the evenings he sometimes went riding and during the day he bathed in the sea. Yet even on the beach he couldn't entirely escape the persistent longing for conversion. In a letter to Ward he confessed to feeling 'slightly heretical when good Roman Catholic boys enter the water with little amulets and crosses round their necks and arms that the good S. Christopher may hold them up'.[19] Such sentiments had been echoed a couple of weeks earlier, just before Wilde returned to Ireland. On Sunday, 9 July he had gone to the church of Our Lady of Victories in Kensington High Street, which was used as the Pro-Cathedral until the consecration of Westminster Cathedral in 1903. There he had heard Cardinal Manning preach, declaring him 'more fascinating than ever'. After the service he met a couple of Oxford acquaintances, most notably Archibald MacCall who had converted the previous year and who was about to become a member of the London Oratory.

Wilde found MacCall's sense of vocation and evident peace of mind disconcerting. By comparison, he was all confusion and indecision. 'I feel an impostor and traitor to myself on these occasions,' he wrote, 'and must do something decided.'[20]

Wilde's attendance at the Catholic Mass was sandwiched on either side by visits to, and arguments with, Anglican clergymen. He had stayed the week before with his uncle, the Rev. John Maxwell Wilde, his father's elder brother, who was vicar of West Ashby in Lincolnshire. John Wilde was sufficiently scandalized by his nephew's Catholic sympathies that he preached two sermons on Sunday aimed indirectly at his incorrigible guest. In the morning he preached in opposition to Rome and in the evening held forth on the need for humility. A week later, Wilde stayed at Bingham Rectory in Nottinghamshire, home of his friend Frank Miles whose father was an Anglican clergyman. 'Have had some good arguments with Dean Miles,' Wilde wrote, 'who was a great friend of Newman, Pusey and Manning at Oxford and a very advanced Anglican.'[21]

Wilde appeared less impressed by Dean Miles's arguments than with the more obvious charms of his four daughters, describing them as 'all very pretty indeed, one of them who is writing at the other side of the table quite lovely', adding that his heart was 'torn in sunder with admiration for them all'.[22] A week later he returned to Ireland where, as well as the company of his mother and her latest pessimist, he would have the company of Florence Balcombe, whose charms were more accessible than those of his friend's sisters. These distractions kept the spiritual charms of the Scarlet Woman largely at bay during the summer months, apart from any latent temptations aroused by his nightly reading of Thomas à Kempis. Throughout the summer he corresponded with Aubrey De Vere, his mother's friend, describing him as 'a cultured poet (though sexless) and a convert to Catholicity'.[23] He had taken an interest in Wilde's religious verse and was responsible for getting 'Rome Unvisited' published in the *Month* in September 1876. The *Month* was edited by Father Henry James Coleridge, SJ, a great-nephew of the poet, whom Wilde had heard preach at St Aloysius' during the previous Lent.

The religious question was largely neglected until Wilde's return to Oxford when it re-emerged with renewed vigour. David Hunter Blair recalled that he and Wilde walked over Magdalen Bridge each

Sunday morning to the old Catholic chapel in St Clement's. Wilde became friendly with one of the priests and Hunter Blair hoped that this would finally prompt his friend to take the decision to be received into the Church. The priest, however, was more perceptive. 'Your friend interests me much,' he remarked.

> He has brains, many good qualities, and an undoubted charm of manner and address. But at present he is in earnest about nothing except his quite laudable ambition to succeed in the schools, and even that he keeps in the background. Behind his superficial veneer of vanity and foolish talk there is, I am convinced, something deeper and more sincere, including a genuine attraction towards Catholic belief and practice. But the time has not come. The finger of God has not yet touched him. There will come some day, I am convinced, a crisis in his life when he will turn to the Ark of Peter as his only refuge. Till then we can only pray. And you, his friend, for whom he has a true affection, can help him in that way, and in many others.[24]

The conflicts and contradictions in Wilde's approach to Catholicism were highlighted most conspicuously by the other interest in his life – freemasonry. The freemasons were much in fashion in Oxford during the 1870s, partly because Prince Leopold, Queen Victoria's youngest son, then a commoner at Christ Church, was Grand Master of the Order. Wilde had become a mason on 23 February 1875, partly no doubt because of his determination to be accepted into the old school network and partly because of a curiosity to know freemasonry's secrets and 'mysteries'. He was also attracted to the elaborate flamboyance of the costume. The Apollo Lodge into which he was initiated required its members to wear knee breeches, tail coat, white tie, silk stockings and pumps, as well as the usual masonic paraphernalia of apron, gloves and sash. Wilde took to the costume as much as to the ritual and plunged himself into debt to ensure that he had all the accessories a well turned-out member of the Lodge required. The supplier was still requesting payment for many of these items months after Wilde had obtained them on credit.[25]

After the meeting at which he was initiated, there was a dinner at which he rose, or sank, to the occasion by making irreverent references to St John the Baptist. He had heard that John the Baptist was the founder of the Order, he told his audience, who responded with yells of laughter. 'I hope we shall emulate his life but not his death,' he quipped, 'I mean we ought to keep our heads.'[26] It was a perfect example of Wilde's developing table manner, the wit of which ensured that he soon became a popular and successful member of his Lodge. On 24 April 1875 he was raised to the second degree, and on 25 May to the third, that of Master Mason. As well as ensuring his further integration into fashionable English society, Wilde was following in the footsteps of his father who in 1841 had become the Worshipful Master of the Shakespeare Lodge (no. 143) in Dublin.

Wilde took to the pomp and quasi-religious ritual of freemasonry with real enthusiasm. At times it rivalled his interest in Catholicism and in the autumn of 1876 he was fired with a new burst of interest in the masonic life. On 27 November he elected to proceed not into the Apollo Royal Arch Chapter but into the Apollo Rose-Croix Chapter, which had been 'consecrated' only four years earlier, because, unlike the other, it was High Church. Whereas the lower degrees of masonic ritual had been based on the allegorizing of the building of Solomon's Temple, the higher degrees, which Wilde now took, allegorized the death and resurrection of Christ. The quasi-religious ceremony presented a ritualized progress towards illumination and a communion rite.

Wilde was well aware that the Catholic Church condemned freemasonry, and aware too that Catholics were not permitted to become or, in the case of converts, remain masons. Hunter Blair had relinquished his membership of the freemasons upon his own conversion and Wilde knew that the same would be expected of him should he become a Catholic. In the meantime he was as avid a proselytizer for freemasonry as Hunter Blair was for the Church, ushering in as many undergraduates to the Apollo Lodge as his charm could beguile. It all served to add to his dilemma. In March 1877 he wrote to Ward, himself a mason, of the problematic nature of his position. 'I have got rather keen on Masonry lately and believe in it awfully – in fact would be awfully sorry to have to give it up in case I secede from the Protestant Heresy.'[27]

Wilde was increasingly perplexed at the anomalous nature of his own position. During the spring of 1877 he was a regular Mass attender at St Aloysius' and breakfasted with Father Thomas Parkinson, SJ, who had become the Superior at St Aloysius' in 1875. It is even possible, though no record of a meeting exists, that he may later have met Gerard Manley Hopkins, who returned to Oxford in November of the following year to become a curate at St Aloysius'.

Throughout 1877 Wilde continued to discuss the possibility of conversion with Hunter Blair and with Archibald Dunlop, another friend who had been received into the Church as a Magdalen undergraduate. The inner peace of these two friends must have struck him as being in stark contrast to his own inner turmoil. (Hunter Blair entered the Benedictine Order in the following year, was ordained priest in 1886, and became the Abbot of Fort Augustus in 1913. In 1896 he succeeded his father as fifth baronet. Archibald Dunlop remained a layman and was responsible for the building, largely at his own expense, of St Boniface's Catholic church in Southampton.) Wilde longed for such peace but already sensed that it was tantalizingly beyond his reach. He still claimed, in a letter to Ward, that he was 'caught in the fowler's snare, in the wiles of the Scarlet Woman', adding that he 'may go over' during the next vacation. 'I have dreams of a visit to Newman, of the holy sacrament in a new Church, and of a quiet and peace afterwards in my soul.' Yet the desire was overshadowed by doubt. 'I need not say, though, that I shift with every breath of thought and am weaker and more self-deceiving than ever.'

> If I *could hope* that the Church would wake in me some earnestness and purity I would go over *as a luxury*, if for no better reasons. But I can hardly hope it would, and to go over to Rome would be to sacrifice and give up my two great gods 'Money and Ambition'.[28]

Wilde's flirtation with faith, his courting conversion, had been the overriding passion of the previous three years. Now, however, his great love affair with the Church was at the crossroads. He must either surrender himself to the God of the Church or abandon himself to the two great gods of the world.

1 Hart-Davis, *Letters of Oscar Wilde*, p. 7.

2 Oscar Wilde, *The Complete Works of Oscar Wilde*, London: Collins, 1966 edn., p. 1078.

3 Vyvyan Holland, *Son of Oscar Wilde*, London: Rupert Hart-Davis, 1954; quoted in Mikhail, *Interviews and Recollections*, vol. 1, pp. 13–14.

4 Sir David Hunter-Blair, *In Victorian Days and Other Papers*, New York: Longmans, 1939, pp. 115–43; quoted in Mikhail, *Interviews and Recollections*, vol. 1, p. 6.

5 Ibid.
6 Ibid., p. 7.
7 Hyde, *Oscar Wilde*, p. 19.
8 *Complete Works of Oscar Wilde*, pp. 725 and 730.
9 Hart-Davis, *Letters of Oscar Wilde*, pp. 17–18.
10 Letter from Wilde to W.W. Ward, 3 January 1877, Magdalen College Archives.
11 Hart-Davis, *Letters of Oscar Wilde*, p. 24.
12 E.V. Lucas in *The Times*, 6 March 1934; quoted in Hart-Davis, *Letters of Oscar Wilde*, p. 36.
13 From 'La Bella Donna Della Mia Mente', *Complete Works of Oscar Wilde*, pp. 751–2.
14 Hart-Davis, *Letters of Oscar Wilde*, p. 20.
15 Maurice Baring, *The Puppet Show of Memory*, London: Heinemann, 1930, p. 259; quoted in Joseph Pearce, *Literary Converts*, London: HarperCollins, 1999, p. 13.
16 Hart-Davis, *Letters of Oscar Wilde*, p. 21.
17 Ibid., p. 20.
18 Ibid.
19 Ibid., p. 21.
20 Ibid., p. 16.
21 Ibid., p. 17.
22 Ibid.
23 Ibid., p. 26.
24 Mikhail, *Interviews and Recollections*, vol. 1, p. 7.
25 Unpublished letter, Bodleian Library, Oxford.
26 Ellmann, *Oscar Wilde*, p. 39.
27 Hart-Davis, *Letters of Oscar Wilde*, p. 30.
28 Ibid., p. 31.

FIVE

Roman Fever

I have suffered very much for my Roman fever in mind and pocket and happiness.

The myriad confusions and contradictions besetting Wilde's psyche in March 1877 were heightened by the prospect of a trip to Rome. His friends Ward and Hunter Blair had already arrived in Italy and were urging him to join them. Writing to Ward, Wilde expressed his hope that his friend's arrival in 'the Sacred City' would waken him from the 'Egyptian darkness' that had blinded him. Unable to commit himself to Catholicism, Wilde nonetheless urged it upon his reluctant friend: '*Do* be touched by it, *feel* the awful fascination of the Church, its extreme beauty and sentiment, and let every part of your nature have play and room.' Wilde had now retreated from Newman's logical path to Rome and argued for the Church purely from an aesthetic perspective. He implored his friend not to approach Rome 'with the bugbear of formal logic'. On the contrary, he should reject the aridity of the intellect in favour of the delights of the senses. 'I know you are keenly alive to beauty ... do try and see in the Church not man's hand only but also a little of God's.'

There was an element of desperation in Wilde's almost shrill exhortations to his friend. 'I only say that for *you* to feel the fascination of Rome would to me be the greatest of pleasures: I think it would *settle me*.' Unable to act decisively on his own, he hoped to enter the Church by clinging to his friend's coat-tails.

The pathetic state of Wilde's mind is evident elsewhere in the same letter when he seems to view the Church as little more than a panacea for life's problems. 'I get so wretched and low and troubled that in some desperate mood I will seek the shelter of a Church which simply enthralls me by its fascination.' Wilde had ceased to seek the Church for its truth but merely for the comfort it could offer a desperate soul. 'God! How I have wasted my life up here! I look back on weeks and months of extravagance, trivial talk, utter vacancy of employment, *with feelings so bitter that I have lost faith in myself.* I am too ridiculously easily led astray.'[1]

Two weeks later, Wilde was again writing to Ward, this time informing him that he would not be able to join him and Hunter Blair in Rome. He explained that he had recently been elected to his first London club and the membership fee of £42 had made any further expenditure beyond his means. Instead, he announced that he intended to visit Newman in Birmingham 'to burn my fingers a little more'. The idea had come to him following conversations with another Magdalen undergraduate, Henry Wise, who was 'awfully caught with the wiles of the Scarlet Woman' and had written to Newman. Wise received the 'most charming' replies which apparently he had shown to Wilde, one of which was an invitation to come and see Newman in Birmingham. This had given Wilde the idea of doing the same. 'I am awfully keen for an interview, not of course to argue, but merely to be in the presence of that divine man.' Wilde promised to give Ward a long account of the interview, but added that 'perhaps my courage will fail, as I could hardly resist Newman I am afraid'.[2]

There is no evidence that the interview ever took place, though this may not necessarily have been due to a lack of courage on Wilde's part. Rather, it seems that other events intervened. Hunter Blair, hearing that Wilde's inability to travel to Rome was the result of straitened financial circumstances, provided him with £60, allegedly the return on a £2 stake placed at Monte Carlo where he had stopped off en route to Italy. There being now no obstacle to his joining them, Wilde made plans to meet up with Ward and Hunter Blair in Rome. Clearly excited at the prospect of finally setting eyes on 'the golden dome of St Peter's and the Eternal City', he wrote to another friend, Reginald Harding:

> This is an era in my life, a crisis. I wish I could look into the seeds of time and see what is coming.
>
> I shall not forget you in Rome, and will burn a candle for you at the Shrine of Our Lady.[3]

Wilde arranged to travel as far as Genoa with his old Trinity College tutor, Professor Mahaffy, who was taking two young men to Greece. They met at Charing Cross station where Mahaffy introduced Wilde to his two companions: William Goulding, with whom Wilde was already acquainted, the son of a wealthy Dublin businessman, and George Macmillan, son of Alexander Macmillan, one of the two founding brothers of the publishing firm. George Macmillan, who had joined the family firm on leaving Eton in 1874 and would be made a partner in 1879, wrote to his father on 28 March, shortly after their arrival in Genoa, to which they had travelled by way of Paris and Turin. His letter is of interest, not merely as a lucid description of Wilde but as an insight into the lengths to which Professor Mahaffy went in order to deter Wilde from proceeding to Rome. Macmillan described Wilde as 'aesthetic to the last degree, passionately fond of secondary colours, low tones, Morris papers, and capable of talking a good deal of nonsense thereupon, but for all that a very sensible, well-informed and charming man'.

> Being very impressionable he is just now rather fascinated by Roman Catholicism, and is indeed on his way to Rome, in order to see all the glories of the religion which seems to him the highest and most senti- mental. Mahaffy is quite determined to prevent this if possible, and is using every argument he can to check him. At first he tried hard to persuade him to come to Greece with us, pointing out to him by the way all the worst faults of Popery. Finding this not altogether effective, though it had some weight, he changed his tack, and when Wilde began to say that perhaps he would come, Mahaffy said 'I won't take you. I wouldn't have such a fellow with me,' which of course, as Wilde is somewhat of a wilful disposition, has raised in him a firm determina- tion to come, and I quite expect he will, and hope so.[4]

The temptation to forsake Rome for the pagan pleasures of Greece was playing on Wilde's mind as he watched the Genoese enjoying the celebrations of Holy Week. His 'Sonnet, Written in Holy Week at Genoa' climaxes with a cry of conscience, culminating in an apology for the culpable decision he is about to take:

Ah, God! Ah, God! Those dear Hellenic hours
Had drowned all memory of Thy bitter pain,
The Cross, the Crown, the Soldiers and the Spear.

'No, Oscar, we cannot let you become a Catholic,' Mahaffy was reported to have said, 'but we will make you a good pagan instead.'[5] Mahaffy's success was evident in a triumphant letter home to his wife. Written from Corfu on 2 April, Mahaffy boasted that Wilde had been clutched from Rome's grip at the last moment and had accompanied them to Greece. Wilde had 'come round under the influence of the moment from Popery to Paganism', he wrote, adding that 'the Jesuits had promised him a scholarship in Rome, but, thank God, I was able to cheat the Devil of his due'.[6]

On the same day that Mahaffy was informing his wife of his triumph, Wilde was scribbling a note of explanation to Reginald Harding: 'I never went to Rome at all! What a changeable fellow you must think me, but Mahaffy my old tutor carried me off to Greece with him to see Mykenae and Athens. I am awfully ashamed of myself but I could not help it and will take Rome on my way back.'[7]

Considering that Wilde was travelling with money given him by Hunter Blair with the express purpose that he use it to join his friends in Rome, his behaviour in aborting his plans at the last moment was reminiscent of his words in the recent letter to Ward: *I am too ridiculously easily led astray.*

On their way to Greece, Wilde and his adoptive companions stopped at Ravenna, the ancient churches of which impressed Wilde immensely. He was particularly struck by some mosaics of the fourth century which depicted two figures of the Virgin enthroned and receiving adoration. In a letter to one of his Oxford tutors, Wilde wrote that these presentations of the Madonna 'completely upset the ordinary Protestant idea that the worship of the Virgin did not come in till late in the history of the Church'. In the same letter Wilde appeared to have moderated the ultramontane position he had held previously, shrinking back from the 'hard-line' Catholicism of the Pope and Cardinal Manning. Referring to a book which the tutor, the Rev. H.R. Bramley, had lent him Wilde agreed that 'the Roman Catholics certainly do seem to confuse together Catholic doctrines which we may all hold and the supremacy of the Pope which we need not hold'.[8]

As promised, Wilde visited Rome before returning to England, meeting up belatedly with Ward and Hunter Blair. Hunter Blair was well connected in Rome and Wilde was immediately welcomed in cultivated Roman society. In the evenings the three friends dined with Hartwell de la Garde Grissell and Ogilvie Fairlie, both of whom were Chamberlains of Honour to the Pope. The climax of the visit was an audience with the Pope himself, secured by Hunter Blair through his friendship with Monsignor Edmund Stonor. Hunter Blair recalled that Wilde was awestruck as he knelt to receive the Papal blessing. Afterwards he remained speechless all the way back to the hotel where he locked himself in his room. When he emerged he presented Hunter Blair with a sonnet inspired by the Papal audience, possibly 'Urbs Sacra Aeterna'. That evening, as the three friends were on their way to the basilica of St Paul's Without the Walls, Wilde had insisted on stopping at the Protestant cemetery where he prostrated himself on the grass before the grave of John Keats. Wilde's audience with the departed soul of Keats inspired another sonnet in which the poet was compared with the martyred St Sebastian. Hunter Blair was not pleased with Wilde's act of reverence to Keats, sensing perhaps that Wilde's piety before the Poet rivalled his earlier piety before the Pope.

While Wilde enjoyed the last few days in Rome problems were brewing back in Oxford. He had not sought permission to absent himself from college at the start of term and the unscheduled trip to Greece had made him even later than he had originally envisaged. The Easter term had begun on 4 April 1877 but, three weeks later, Wilde had still not returned. On 26 April the officers of Magdalen College resolved that

> Mr Wilde having absented himself during this term up to the present time without permission, be not allowed to reside for the Easter and Trinity Terms, and that he be deprived of the emoluments of his Demyship for the half-year ending Michaelmas 1877; and that he be informed that unless he return punctually on the appointed day of October Term, 1877, with an amount of work prescribed by his Tutor satisfactorily prepared, the officers will consider whether he shall retain his Demyship.[9]

The dryness of the official language barely disguised the evident fury with which the Magdalen officers regarded Wilde's effrontery in

absenting himself without leave. Apart from an official admonish-
ment by the College President in January 1875 when he had failed in
Responsions,[10] Wilde had never fallen foul of the college authorities.
With this in mind, he appealed for leniency. The officers were
unmoved, resolving on 4 May to maintain their earlier order, 'with
the proviso that half the fine shall be remitted, if in October the work
prescribed by his Tutor be satisfactorily prepared'.[11] Wilde was left
with no option but to return to Dublin with his tail between his legs
and was reduced to writing sulking letters to friends about the
'wretched stupidity of our college dons'.[12]

He found a degree of consolation in the continuing love affair with
Florence Balcombe who was 'more lovely than ever'. Otherwise he
was utterly disconsolate. His Christian faith was faltering. In a sonnet
he sent to William Ewart Gladstone, who was then Leader of the
Opposition, on recent massacres of Christians by Moslems in Bul-
garia, he appeared to be demanding of God a sign:

> If thou in very truth didst burst the tomb,
>   Come down, O Son of Man, and show thy might,
>   Lest Mahomet be crowned instead of Thee.

The emergence of further doubts didn't prevent Wilde from fraterniz-
ing with Catholic priests. In June he wrote to Father Matthew Russell,
the Jesuit editor of the *Irish Monthly*, who had published several of
Wilde's poems in previous issues. Father Russell had objected to the
words *'our* English Land' in Wilde's sonnet 'The Grave of Keats', and
Wilde's reply illustrates his own ambivalence towards Irish nationalism
by this time. 'It is a noble privilege to count oneself of the same race as
Keats or Shakespeare,' he declared, wishing away his Irish blood in
favour of an imagined Englishness. In the same letter, Wilde expressed
his pleasure that one of his sonnets had been admired by Wilfrid
Meynell, the Catholic journalist who had married the poet Alice
Thompson two months earlier. The sonnet in question was presumably
the 'Sonnet on Approaching Italy' which had been published in the
June issue of the *Irish Monthly*. Wilde remarked how he had been surprised at the way this particular sonnet had 'touched the hearts of the
Catholic priests I have met'.[13] He had been told that it was recited nine
times at the Glencree Reformatory on the day it arrived there.

Unfortunately, the very sonnets that had warmed the hearts of Catholic priests had hardened the heart of Wilde's half-brother, Henry Wilson, who was alarmed at the publication of Wilde's poems in Catholic magazines. After his early death from pneumonia on 13 June 1877 it emerged that he had left £8,000 to St Mark's Hospital, £2,000 to Wilde's brother Willie, and only £100 to Oscar, and that only if he remained a Protestant. Worse was to follow. Wilson's will also stipulated that his half-share of Illaunroe, the fishing lodge in Connemara which he owned jointly with Oscar, would only be made over to Wilde conditionally upon his not becoming a Catholic for five years. Failure to comply would mean that Wilson's half-share would revert to Willie's ownership. According to Richard Ellmann, Oscar persuaded Willie to give up his reversionary interest for £10, which would seem to indicate that Wilde still considered conversion to Catholicism within the next five years a distinct possibility.

Wilde had paid heavily for his flirtation with the Church. He had expected, along with Willie, to be the joint heir to his half-brother's considerable fortune so the revelation that he had been virtually excluded from the will was a bitter blow. Wilde struggled to avoid becoming embittered, describing his half-brother as 'bigotedly intolerant of the Catholics' and wondering how he could go before God 'with his wretched Protestant prejudices and bigotry clinging still to him'. Counting the personal cost to himself Wilde wrote wistfully to a friend: 'you see I suffer a good deal from my Romish leanings, in pocket and mind'.[14] These sentiments were repeated, almost word for word, a month later, when Wilde wrote to Ward that he had 'suffered very much for my Roman fever in mind and *pocket* and happiness'.[15]

Wilde spent the remainder of the summer in enforced idleness, sending copies of his poems to various luminaries in the hope of getting them published. In between he bathed and fished, lazing away several weeks at the Connemara fishing lodge. He seems, however, to have paid little attention to his studies throughout the term of rustication and failed to complete the work prescribed by his tutor as stipulated by the college officers the previous May. As such, he risked losing his Demyship and being sent down without a degree but on his return to Oxford in October he managed to come up with a plausible excuse. At a meeting on 15 October it was resolved that the officers, 'having considered the reasons given by Mr Wilde for not having prepared the work assigned to him by his Tutor ... are so satisfied that they will inflict no further penalty than that already imposed, of the loss of the emoluments of his Demyship for the half-year ending Michaelmas 1877'.[16]

Apart from his studies, Wilde's abiding interest in his last year at Magdalen remained poetic composition. Two of his longest and most important poems were written during these months: 'The Sphinx', which he had begun writing in 1874 and would not finish for several years to come, was probably largely written in the final year at Oxford; and 'Ravenna', the poem inspired by his visit to the Italian city, would be completed by the end of March 1878. Both poems represent significant shifts in Wilde's artistic vision, as well as signifying shifts in his self-perception and his perception of life itself.

'The Sphinx' exudes decadent sensuality, to which Wilde is obviously attracted, but its climax is not sexual but anti-sexual:

> Get hence, you loathsome mystery! Hideous animal, get hence!
> You wake in me each bestial sense, you make me what I would not be.
> You make my creed a barren sham, you wake foul dreams of sensual
>   life,
> And Atys with his blood-stained knife were better than the thing I am.
> False Sphinx! False Sphinx! By reedy Styx old Charon, leaning on his
>   oar,
> Waits for my coin. Go thou before, and leave me to my crucifix,
> Whose pallid burden, sick with pain, watches the world with wearied
>   eyes,
> And weeps for every soul that dies, and weeps for every soul in vain.

The overpowering presence of self-loathing is paralleled by the presence of omnipotent paganism. Wilde is attracted to, and disgusted by, a power he feels unable to resist. The Sphinx will not be denied. She is seductress turned rapist. Against this pagan omnipotence, Christ, shrivelled to christ, is impotent. He is nothing but a pallid burden weeping hopelessly for a world he is powerless to save. 'The Sphinx' is lust triumphant and love betrayed. It is easy to see the climactic lines of this poem as a parable on Wilde's own position at the end of 1877. Losing his faith in Christianity, he senses that the spiritual vacuum is being filled by less noble impulses. Sickened by his own weakness, he is filled with anxiety and remorse. Desolation turning to despair.

Richard Ellmann, in his biography of Wilde, follows the example of others by suggesting that Wilde's self-loathing at this time was due to his having contracted syphilis from a prostitute. Ellmann's evidence is highly circumstantial, a fact he readily admits, adding that it 'might not stand up in a court of law'. In spite of the tenuous nature of the assertion, Ellmann insists that his conviction that Wilde had the disease 'is central to my conception of Wilde's character and my interpretation of many things in his later life'.[17] The whole issue deserves greater scrutiny.

It is of course possible that Wilde used the services of prostitutes at Oxford. There is, however, no evidence that he did so. Ellmann offers none. Still less is there any evidence that *if* he used prostitutes he had contracted syphilis by doing so. The only evidence offered to back up the assertion are the words of Wilde's friend, Reginald Turner, in a letter written in 1934: 'The ear trouble, which I believe began in prison, was only shortly before his death diagnosed as a tertiary symptom of an infection he had contracted when he was twenty.'[18] The letter's recipient, Robert Sherard, another of Wilde's friends, drew the conclusion that Wilde may have been infected by an Oxford prostitute. Ellmann transforms Sherard's conjecture into an established fact, employing the imaginary prostitute as evidence that Wilde had died of syphilis, itself a *non sequitur* considering that the 'fact' only rested on the alleged diagnosis at the time of death. Furthermore, Ellmann offers Turner's letter to Sherard as evidence of the death-by-syphilis theory without quoting the next sentence: 'The doctor told him that he would live many years if he took care of himself ...' which is totally inconsistent with a diagnosis of tertiary, i.e. terminal, syphilis. Ellmann also ignores a later letter in which Turner states: 'Nor was there ever any question at the real mode and cause of his death. He died of meningitis ...'[19]

Ellmann does cite the diagnosis of the two doctors who attended Wilde on his deathbed, neither of whom detected any evidence of syphilis:

The undersigned doctors, having examined Mr Oscar Wilde ... established that there were significant cerebral disturbances stemming from

an old suppuration of the right ear, under treatment for several years ...
The diagnosis of encephalitic meningitis must be made without doubt.[20]

Merlin Holland, Wilde's grandson, points out that one of the two doctors who made this diagnosis, Dr Paul Claisse, had specialized in venereal diseases during his medical training at the Sorbonne. This fact was unearthed by Dr Macdonald Critchley in a scientific paper entitled 'Oscar Wilde's Fatal Illness: The Mystery Unshrouded' in which Dr Critchley refers to a paper written by Dr Claisse on tertiary syphilis.[21] Holland discovered, too, that the doctors who treated Wilde for his 'ear trouble' when he was in prison were also specialists in venereal diseases.[22] It is, therefore, unfeasible that these experts would not have diagnosed tertiary syphilis if Wilde had been suffering from it. Their failure to do so must surely be taken as evidence that he did not have the disease.

Such evidence has done little to deter the sensationalist school. Melissa Knox, in a recent 'psychoanalytic biography',[23] is forced to bow to the weight of medical evidence and accepts, begrudgingly, that Wilde probably did not die from the disease. Yet she insists that he probably had it anyway. No fresh evidence is offered beyond some superficial leaps of logic, themselves little more than attempts to fit the square pegs of fact into the round hole of supposition. 'The Knox strain is nothing if not contagious,' Merlin Holland complains, 'by the end of the book "possibly, even probably" Wilde's two sons have it, his wife has died of it, and the Canterville Ghost has it by implication.'[24]

At the outset of her study Knox, mindful of the recent medical evidence, states that 'it is not so important that Wilde had contracted this dread disease as that he appears to have believed he had: he behaves as though he were living under the shadow of the horror, the uncertainty, the guilt of the feeling that he had committed a crime against himself by contracting the disease and of having bestowed it again and again with a kiss'.[25] Yet, as Holland remarks, Knox is at pains elsewhere to show that Wilde's wife had actually died of it.[26] Is imaginary syphilis contagious? Only, it seems, to Wilde's biographers who have gone to great pains to pass it on to one another.

The error originated with Arthur Ransome who, in his 1912 biography of Wilde, claimed, without offering any evidence, that the cause of death 'was directly due to meningitis, the legacy of an attack of tertiary syphilis'.[27] Having made the error, Ransome repented and removed all reference to syphilis in the second edition. The damage had been done, however, and most later biographers have picked up Ransome's statement and repeated it. Ellmann, however, went one step further, repeating Ransome's statement as a direct quotation from Wilde's friend, Robert Ross.[28] Presumably, Ellmann felt justified in doing this because Ransome had acknowledged Ross's help in verifying certain details and had dedicated his book to him. Yet this is surely no justification for putting words in Ross's mouth in order to provide added authority to a precariously argued theory, especially as the words in question were removed from the second edition.

'The impact of Wilde's syphilis on his development as a writer is hard to overestimate,' writes Knox. 'His dread of the disease permeated every aspect of his life and work.'[29] In reality, the impact of the *invention* of Wilde's syphilis by his biographers is hard to overestimate. As Ellmann claims, his conviction that Wilde had the disease 'is central to my conception of Wilde's character and my interpretation of many things in his later life'. But if Wilde did not have the disease where does that leave Ellmann's book?

After the evidence, or its lack, is considered, all that remains to substantiate the insubstantial is the adage that there is no smoke without fire, the last refuge of the scandal-monger. In this case, it is safe to assume that any smoke is merely another screen, or mask, that must be removed if the real Wilde is to emerge.

It can be fairly safely assumed that the self-loathing and guilt-laden recriminations in 'The Sphinx', which are a recurring motif in much of Wilde's art, have their origin elsewhere than in the syphilitic. It is likely, in fact, that they are rooted in nothing more, or less, than a healthy conscience, accompanied by a consciousness of the objective nature of sin. In April 1878 this led Wilde to make one last desperate effort to reconcile himself to the Church of Rome. He approached Father Sebastian Bowden at the Brompton Oratory, whose acquaintance he may have made through the auspices of Archibald MacCall, a former Magdalen undergraduate. MacCall had graduated in 1876 having become a Catholic the previous year. It was in July 1876 that Wilde had met MacCall, remarking on that occasion how meeting MacCall had made him feel an 'impostor and traitor' to himself, adding that he 'must do something decided'. Almost two years later he appears to have reached the same conclusion and MacCall, who had joined the Oratory about eighteen months before Wilde's visit, would have been well placed to make the necessary arrangements for Wilde's meeting with Father Bowden on 14 April.

Father Henry Sebastian Bowden was one of the fashionable priests of the day with a reputation for facilitating the conversions of many dignitaries from the higher echelons of Victorian society. Born in 1836 he was part of what could be termed a priestly dynasty. His aunt, Elizabeth Bowden, had two sons who also became priests of the Oratory. The Bowdens were related to Algernon Swinburne, one of Wilde's artistic mentors. Swinburne wrote to Father Charles Bowden on the occasion of Elizabeth Bowden's death, mourning 'my dear aunt' and assuring the priest of his 'deep sympathy and sincere sorrow'.[30]

The fact that Wilde was teetering on the brink, either of conversion or rejection, at the time of his meeting with Father Bowden can be divined from the contents of the letter which the priest wrote to him afterwards. It needs quoting *in extenso* for the deep insight into Wilde's psyche that it provides.

My dear Mr Wilde,

Whatever your first purpose may have been in your visit yesterday there is no doubt that as a fact you did freely and entirely lay open to me your life's history and your soul's state. And it was God's grace which made you do so.

You would not have spoken of your aimlessness and misery or of your temporal misfortune to a priest in a first interview unless you hoped that I should have some remedy to suggest, and that not of man's making. Be true to yourself then, it was no power or influence of mine (which is nonsense to speak of) but the voice of your own conscience urging you to make a new start, and escape from your present unhappy self, which provoked your confession. Let me then repeat to you as solemnly as I can what I said yesterday, you have like everyone else an evil nature and this in your case has become more corrupt by bad influences mental and moral, and by positive sin; hence you speak as a dreamer and sceptic with no faith in anything and no purpose in life. On the other hand God in His mercy has not let you remain contented in this state. He has proved to you the hollowness of this world in the unexpected loss of your fortune and has removed thereby a great obstacle to your conversion; He allows you to feel the sting of conscience and the yearnings for a holy pure and earnest life. It depends therefore on your own free will which life you lead. As God calls you, He is bound, remember, to give you the means to obey the call.

Do so promptly and cheerfully and difficulties disappear and with your conversion your true happiness would begin. As a Catholic you would find yourself a new man in the order of nature as of grace. I mean that you would put from you all that is affected and unreal and a thing unworthy of your better self and live a life full of the deepest interests as a man who feels he has a soul to save and but a few fleeting hours in which to save it. I trust then you will come on Thursday and have another talk; you may be quite sure I shall urge you to do nothing but what your conscience dictates. In the meantime pray hard and talk little.[31]

It appears that Wilde never arrived for the next meeting. Father Bowden told Wilde's erstwhile friend, André Raffalovich, that Wilde sent him a bunch of lilies on the morning they were due to meet, presumably as an apology for his non-attendance. In fact the two men never met again.

The reason for Wilde's non-attendance at the second meeting is a matter of conjecture. Possibly it had as much to do with a loss of courage as a loss of faith. His fear of Father Bowden, Newman's disciple at the Oratory in London, may have been the same as the fear he had expressed a year earlier about meeting Newman himself at the Oratory in Birmingham: *perhaps my courage will fail, as I could hardly resist Newman I am afraid.* Wilde's sending flowers in lieu of himself would certainly suggest that he felt unable to make his apology in person.

It is clear from Father Bowden's letter that he was capable of penetrating to the very heart of Wilde's psyche, his doubts and fears as much as his hopes and aspirations. The priest was providing a mirror for Wilde's soul, stripping away the masks to reveal the spiritual reality beneath. It required courage to look oneself in the eye and Wilde evidently felt it easier to look the other way. If he couldn't face the truth about himself, the only option was to hide from it. From now on, masks would become more important than ever.

1 Hart-Davis, *Letters of Oscar Wilde*, pp. 31–2.
2 Ibid., p. 33.
3 Ibid., p. 34.
4 Rupert Hart-Davis (ed.), *More Letters of Oscar Wilde*, London: John Murray, 1985, pp. 24–5.
5 Ellmann, *Oscar Wilde*, p. 67.
6 Ibid.
7 Hart-Davis, *Letters of Oscar Wilde*, pp. 34–5.
8 Ibid., p. 35.
9 President's Notebook entry for 26 April 1877, Magdalen College Archives.
10 President's Notebook entry for 18 January 1875, Magdalen College Archives.
11 President's Notebook entry for 4 May 1877, Magdalen College Archives.
12 Hart-Davis, *Letters of Oscar Wilde*, p. 36.
13 Ibid., p. 40.
14 Ibid., p. 43.
15 Ibid., p. 45.
16 President's Notebook entry for 15 October 1877, Magdalen College Archives.
17 Ellmann, *Oscar Wilde*, p. 88.
18 Reginald Turner, letter to Robert Sherard, 3 January 1934; quoted in Peter Rabey (ed.), *The Cambridge Companion to Oscar Wilde*, Cambridge University Press, 1997, p. 12; and in Ellmann, *Oscar Wilde*, p. 546.
19 Rabey, *Cambridge Companion to Wilde*, p. 13.
20 Ellmann, *Oscar Wilde*, p. 547.
21 Macdonald Critchley, 'Oscar Wilde's Fatal Illness: The Mystery Unshrouded', in *Encyclopaedia Britannica Medical and Health Annual 1990*, pp. 190–207; referred to in Rabey, *Cambridge Companion to Wilde*, p. 13.
22 Merlin Holland, in conversation with the author, 20 April 1999.
23 Melissa Knox, *Oscar Wilde: A Long and Lovely Suicide*, London: Yale University Press, 1994.
24 Rabey, *Cambridge Companion to Wilde*, p. 14.
25 Knox, *Long and Lovely Suicide*, p. xx.
26 Ibid., pp. 42–3.
27 Arthur Ransome, *Oscar Wilde*, London: Martin Secker, 1912, p. 199.
28 Ellmann, *Oscar Wilde*, p. 546.
29 Knox, *Long and Lovely Suicide*, p. 45.
30 Algernon Swinburne, letter to Father Charles Bowden, 7 October 1896, Brompton Oratory Archives.
31 Quoted in Ellmann, *Oscar Wilde*, p. 90.

SIX

Love's Web

> It shall be, I said, for eternity
>   'Twixt you and me!
> Dear friend, those times are over and done;
>   Love's web is spun.

Two weeks before his visit to Father Bowden, Wilde entered the finished version of his long poem 'Ravenna' as a contender for the Newdigate Prize, the university prize for English verse. A little over two months later, on 10 June 1878, it was declared the winner. Wilde's triumph turned him into an overnight hero in the eyes of the college authorities who were overjoyed that the prize had been won by a Magdalen undergraduate for the first time in more than half a century. On the next day the President of Magdalen noted Wilde's success in his Minute Book, adding that 'the last time the College gained the Newdigate was in 1825 by R. Sewell':

> By obtaining this Prize Mr Wilde becomes entitled to the following bequest of Dr Daubeny, who died December 13, 1867: 'I desire my Executor to retain my Marble Bust of the young Augustus, and give it as a Prize to the first member of Magdalen College after my decease who shall gain the Newdigate Prize Poem.'[1]

Ten days later, in the college hall at the terminal examination, the marble bust was duly presented to Wilde by the President.[2] The sweet taste of success continued on 26 June when Wilde gave the traditional public reading of his prizewinning poem. 'The Newdigate was listened to with rapt attention and frequently applauded,' reported

The Oxford and Cambridge Undergraduate's Journal on the following day. Not surprisingly, Lady Wilde rejoiced at her son's success, revelling in the reflected glory: 'Oh, Gloria, Gloria! ... It is the first pleasant throb of joy I have had this year. How I long to read the poem. Well, after all, we have *Genius* ...'[3]

Elsewhere in her congratulatory letter, Lady Wilde laid emphasis on the words 'honour' and 'recognition', indicating her own assessment of the two most important results of her son's success. Honour, however, is of two sorts. There is the honour possessed through integrity and the honour bestowed through celebrity. Wilde appears to have sacrificed the former in order to receive the latter, as a later conversation with Hunter Blair makes manifest. Hunter Blair had objected to the lines in the prizewinning poem praising the triumphant entry of King Victor Emmanuel II into Rome in 1870 which had led to the subsequent imprisonment of the Pope in the Vatican:

> ... for at last
> Italia's royal warrior hath passed
> Rome's lordliest entrance, and hath worn his crown
> In the high temples of the Eternal Town!
> The Palatine hath welcomed back her king,
> And with his name the seven mountains ring!

Recalling Wilde's earlier references to the same subject, when he had invariably supported the imprisoned Pope, Hunter Blair accused his friend of hypocrisy: 'You know that all your sympathies were with the dethroned Pope, not with the invading and usurping King. You know they were.' Wilde could only reply apologetically, urging Hunter Blair not to be angry: 'You must know that I should never, never have won the Newdigate if I had taken the Pope's side against the King's.'[4]

When Hunter Blair had first accused him of writing 'humbug', Wilde had protested that he had written the poem '*ex imo corde*, from the bottom of my heart, red-hot from Ravenna itself'. Now, however, the mask had slipped and, for a fleeting moment, the real Oscar emerged. As Hunter Blair rose to leave, Wilde suddenly knelt and kissed his hand. 'Pray for me,' he muttered, tears in his eyes.[5] The two friends were destined never to see each other again.

Any pangs of conscience Wilde may have been experiencing in private were eased to a great degree by further accolades in public. Hard on the heels of his Newdigate success came a further superlative achievement. The examiners in Final Schools summoned him for his *viva voce* on his written papers and, to Wilde's surprise, were full of compliments for his work. His tutor told Hunter Blair that, as with his Honour Moderations examination two years earlier, Wilde's examination as a whole was the best of his year. He was awarded a rare double first, a fact which made almost as much impact as the Newdigate when it was announced on 19 July, especially in Magdalen. 'The dons are "astonied" beyond words – the Bad Boy doing so well in the end!' Wilde wrote to William Ward. 'It is too delightful altogether this display of fireworks at the end of my career.'6

The fact that the Magdalen authorities had forgiven the 'Bad Boy' for his earlier misdemeanour was confirmed at a meeting of the college officers on 20 October. Following an application by Wilde for the remission of the fine imposed the previous year for his absence without permission, the officers recommended that 'the sum ... withheld from Mr Wilde's Demyship, be placed with the consent of the College (after deducting £7 for Tuition) to the account of Mr Wilde'.7 The decision was ratified by a full college meeting on 7 November.

The note of triumph which accompanied Wilde's departure from Oxford in the summer of 1878 was marred by the devastating news that awaited him upon his return to Dublin. He discovered, though not from her, that Florence Balcombe was engaged to be married to another man. Her future husband, to whom she would be married on 4 December 1878, was Bram Stoker, later to achieve fame as the author of *Dracula*. Stoker, an Irish civil servant with literary and dramatic ambitions, was seven years Wilde's senior. Two years earlier he had done much to promote Henry Irving's successful visit to Dublin, and Irving repaid the debt by appointing Stoker business manager of the Lyceum Theatre in October 1878. It has been suggested that this may have been a determining factor in Florence Balcombe's decision to transfer her affections to the older man, not least because she made no secret of her aspirations to become an actress. Yet it seems likely, considering that their wedding was less than two months later, that Stoker had proposed marriage some time before his appointment to the Lyceum. The most likely explanation, apart from considerations of physical attraction and sexual chemistry, is that Stoker merely filled the vacuum left by Wilde's prolonged absence from Dublin.

During the previous April, Wilde had chosen not to return to Dublin to see Florence at Easter but went for a short holiday to Bournemouth instead. He reminded her in a letter sent from Bournemouth that a year earlier she had sent an Easter card to him in Greece 'over so many miles of land and sea – to show me you had not forgotten me'.[8] It is implicit in Wilde's letter that this year she had forgotten him, or at least that no Easter card was sent, because it is he who is sending Easter greetings and it is clear from his wording that he is not replying to any letter of hers. Perhaps, as early as April 1878, Florence Balcombe's ardour was cooling. Perhaps she was already seeing Stoker.

Such facts appear to have escaped the notice of Richard Ellmann, or at least were not considered worthy of mention. Instead, evidence of the growing estrangement is put to one side to make way for the recurring fantasy at the centre of Ellmann's biography: 'In any case,' he writes dismissively, 'Wilde ... evidently did not feel he was in a position to marry. His obligatory two years' wait after syphilis had been diagnosed was not over.'[9] What diagnosis? What syphilis? What obligatory wait? Once again, the truth is distorted to fit the fallacious supposition.

It is surprising that Florence Balcombe is reduced to little more than a footnote in most lives of Wilde. Probably this is due to the lack of source material available. Wilde's letters to her have not survived, presumably destroyed at the end of their relationship, so biographers have had little to go on. The paucity of sources has inevitably led to neglect. Yet the few surviving scraps speak volumes. Wilde's letters to her at the end of the relationship and the wretched poems of dejection which her loss wrought from him are enough to make the absence of material a powerful silence. A scream in a vacuum.

It is implicit in the words Wilde places in Florence Balcombe's mouth in his poem 'Her Voice' that she had pledged herself to him:

Sit closer love: it was here I trow
    I made that vow,

Swore that two lives should be like one
    As long as the sea-gull loved the sea,
As long as the sunflower sought the sun, –
    It shall be, I said, for eternity
      'Twixt you and me!

Wilde paints the backdrop to this scene amid bees flitting from flower to flower and poplar trees swaying in the summer air. Again, it is implicit that he has a specific moment in a particular place in mind. The words he places in Florence Balcombe's mouth are not a figment of his imagination but a painful memory of a paradise lost.

Wilde was devastated by Florence Balcombe's rejection of him, and no doubt his vanity was dented by the knowledge that the charms of another were preferred to his own. His letters to her display all the hurt pride of a lover spurned. He requested the return of a gold cross he had given her 'one Christmas morning long ago':

> I need hardly say that I would not ask it from you if it was anything you valued, but worthless though the trinket be, to me it serves as a memory of two sweet years – the sweetest of all the years of my youth – and I should like to have it always with me ...
>
> Though you have not thought it worth while to let me know of your marriage, still I cannot leave Ireland without sending you my wishes that you may be happy; whatever happens I at least cannot be indifferent to your welfare: the currents of our lives flowed too long beside one another for that.
>
> We stand apart now, but the little cross will serve to remind me of the bygone days, and though we shall never meet again, after I leave Ireland, still I shall always remember you at prayer. Adieu and God bless you.[10]

In another letter, probably written a day or so later, he informs Florence that he will return her letters when he returns to Oxford. 'The enclosed scrap I used to carry with me: it was written eighteen months ago: how strange and out of tune it all reads now.'[11]

The final letter before he returned to England is so riven with pain and bitterness that it almost screams between the lines:

As regards the cross, there is nothing 'exceptional' in the trinket except the fact of my name being on it, which of course would have prevented you from wearing it ever, and I am not foolish enough to imagine that you care now for any memento of me. It would have been impossible for you to keep it.

I am sorry that you should appear to think, from your postscript, that I desired any clandestine '*meeting*': after all, I find you know me very little.[12]

The pain that punctuated these lines became Wilde's constant companion after his return to England. In the following months at least five poems were directly inspired by the loss of Florence Balcombe's love. In 'Silentium Amoris' he laments their parting, she 'to some lips of sweeter melody':

> And I to nurse the barren memory
> Of unkissed kisses, and songs never sung.

'Her Voice' speaks of her broken vow, how they had 'lived our lives in a land of dreams', of how 'those times are over and done; Love's web is spun'. 'My Voice' replies:

> Wherefore my cheeks before their time are wan,
>   For very weeping is my gladness fled,
> Sorrow has paled my young mouth's vermilion,
>   And Ruin draws the curtains of my bed.

In 'Taedium Vitae' the self-pity makes way for the anger of despair:

> To stab my youth with desperate knives, to wear
> This paltry age's gaudy livery,
> To let each base hand filch my treasury,
> To mesh my soul within a woman's hair,
> And be mere Fortune's lackeyed groom, – I swear
> I love it not!

Perhaps the most intriguing of the five poems, which taken together could be termed his Florentine verse, is 'Quia Multum Amavi'. In this verse his love for Catholicism and his love for Florence Balcombe are combined; caritas and eros entwined. Both had left him. Yet both had left him with a sense of longing and of loss. The higher and lower loves were both beyond his reach yet he was caught in the webs they wove:

> Dear Heart, I think the young impassioned priest
>> When first he takes from out the hidden shrine
> His God imprisoned in the Eucharist,
>> And eats the bread, and drinks the dreadful wine,
>
> Feels not such awful wonder as I felt
>> When first my smitten eyes beat full on thee,
> And all night long before thy feet I knelt
>> Till thou wert wearied of Idolatry.
>
> Ah! hadst thou liked me less and loved me more,
>> Through all those summer days of joy and rain,
> I had not now been sorrow's heritor,
>> Or stood a lackey in the House of Pain.

In Wilde's art, Florence Balcombe's absence had proved far more potent than her presence. He was fully aware of the paradox and learned the lesson it taught. Thereafter, the paradox of pain and the creativity of sorrow would permeate his life and his work. Yet his life, endured in the still depths from which his art sprang, was still enjoyed on the babbling surface where his public reputation was being moulded.

Early in October 1878, shortly after leaving Ireland, Wilde stayed with his friends the Oswald Sickerts at Neuville near Dieppe. Their fifteen-year-old daughter Helena, whom Wilde called Miss Nelly, remembered Wilde quoting his poem 'Ravenna' to her. He also presented her with a copy of Matthew Arnold's poems. Her two brothers, aged seven and five, found him a delightful playmate. He told them all preposterous stories and when Helena showed scepticism, he replied with feigned sadness: 'You don't believe me, Miss Nelly. I *assure* you ... well, it's as good as true.'[13]

Wilde returned briefly to Oxford, passing his Divinity examination on 22 November and taking his degree of Bachelor of Arts six days later. His mind, however, was on London. 'I have so much to do here,' he wrote to a friend from the St Stephen's Club in Westminster, 'looking for lodgings and making literary friends.'[14] He appears to have found his first lodgings in London towards the end of February 1879 at 13 Salisbury Street, off the Strand. This can be deduced from Wilde's application for a ticket to read at the British Museum Library. The application form, which is dated 24 February 1879, gives his address as 13 Salisbury Street, with Magdalen College crossed out, suggesting that he had moved only recently. Wilde had entered his profession or occupation on the form as 'graduate' and gave his purpose in applying as the 'study of Gk and Latin literature with ref. to university career'.[15]

The desire to pursue an academic career appears to have been Wilde's overriding concern for most of 1879. He applied for a classics fellowship at Trinity College, Oxford and sat a six-hour examination extending over two days. He was not elected. On 28 May he wrote to A.H. Sayce, Oxford Professor of Comparative Philology, whom he had come to know through Mahaffy, hoping that his influence would help secure an archaeological studentship at Oxford which held out the promise of a trip to Athens: 'Can you give me any idea of how the archaeological students ... at Athens are to be assigned as I am anxious to obtain one?'[16] He pursued the matter on 8 December:

> I think it would suit me very well – as I have done a good deal of travelling already – and from my boyhood have been accustomed, through my Father, to visiting and reporting on ancient sites ... it is of course a subject of intense interest to me – and I should give myself to it with a good deal of enthusiasm. Your support would of course be invaluable – I hear there are many competing.[17]

Again, he was unsuccessful.

Parallel with his efforts to find gainful employment, Wilde's principal predilection throughout 1879 was for the artistic and literary life of London. Apart from the 'literary friends' he had alluded to in his letter from the St Stephen's Club, he had manoeuvred his way into the highest thespian circles. He became good friends with Lillie Langtry, tutoring her in Latin and being inspired by her beauty to write 'The New Helen' which was published in *Time* in July. Wilde eulogizes Langtry's charms, 'the white glory of thy loveliness', to such a degree that she is elevated beyond Helen to the Heavenly, so that only epithets borrowed from the Litany of the Blessed Virgin will suffice:

> Lily of love, pure and inviolate!
>> Tower of ivory! red rose of fire!

The Blessed Virgin, with whom his love affair is over, is now no longer worthy of such praise. She is merely the woman 'before whose mouldering shrine / Today at Rome the silent nations kneel':

> Who gat from Love no joyous gladdening,
>> But only Love's intolerable pain,
>> Only a sword to pierce her heart in twain,
> Only the bitterness of child-bearing.

Clearly, Wilde was totally besotted with Lillie Langtry's celebrated charms. The web was spun and he was once again caught. Once again, however, he was to suffer the pain of rejection. The white glory of her loveliness belonged to another. She was the mistress of the Prince of Wales, and Wilde was well aware that he was powerless to woo her away from such an eminent lover.

> So wilt thou fly our evil land and drear,
>> Back to the tower of thine old delight,
> And the red lips of young Euphorion ...

Meanwhile, Wilde was doomed to remain in 'this poisonous garden', 'Crowning my brows with the thorn-crown of pain, / Till all my love-less life shall pass away'.

Langtry was understandably flattered by the poem, even if she had no intentions towards the flatterer, and many years later she published 'The New Helen' in its entirety in her autobiography.

Wilde's new-found role as flatterer to thespian beauties was not limited to the charms of Lillie Langtry alone. On 11 June, only a month before the publication of 'The New Helen' in *Time*, a poem 'To Sarah Bernhardt' was published in *The World*. Later published as

'Phèdre', this verse praised the actress as a Greek beauty. Bernhardt had opened in Racine's *Phèdre* on 2 June and Wilde, as usual, was at the first night. It was 'not until I heard Sarah Bernhardt in *Phèdre* that I absolutely realized the sweetness of the music of Racine', he recalled later.[18]

A month later, Wilde's poem 'Queen Henrietta Maria' was published. It was dedicated to Ellen Terry whose performance as the queen in W.G. Wills's *Charles I* had so impressed Wilde when he had seen the play on 27 June. Purportedly addressed to the play's character, his words were a thinly disguised act of adoration to the actress:

> O Hair of Gold! O Crimson Lips! O Face
> Made for the luring and the love of man!
>   With thee I do forget the toil and stress,
> The loveless road that knows no resting place,
>   Time's straitened pulse, the soul's dread weariness ...

Wilde's poetic acts of homage to London's leading ladies were demonstrably the words of a lovelorn admirer, but they were more than that. He became a valued friend to all three of these objects of his devotion, without any question of their accepting anything from him but platonic friendship. This must have added to the sense of dejection, springing from rejection, which is a recurrent theme in all these poems. Yet their rejection paled into insignificance beside the lingering pain inflicted by his rejection by Florence Balcombe.

Following her marriage, Florence Balcombe had achieved limited success as an actress in her own right. On 3 January 1881 she had a small part alongside Henry Irving, Ellen Terry and William Terriss in Tennyson's verse play *The Cup*, when it opened at the Lyceum. Wilde attended the opening night and the depths of his feelings towards his lost love are evident in the letter he wrote to Ellen Terry before the performance began:

> I send you some flowers – two crowns. Will you accept one of them, whichever you think will suit you best. The other – don't think me treacherous, Nellie – but the other please give to Florrie *from yourself*. I should like to think that she was wearing something of mine the first night she comes on the stage, that anything of mine should touch her.

Of course if you think – but you won't think she will suspect?
How could she? She thinks I never loved her, thinks I forget. My God
how could I![19]

1 President's Notebook entry for 11 June 1878, Magdalen College Archives.
2 President's Notebook entry for 21 June 1878, Magdalen College Archives.
3 Ellmann, *Oscar Wilde*, p. 93.
4 Mikhail, *Interviews and Recollections*, vol. 1, pp. 10–11.
5 Ibid.
6 Hart-Davis, *Letters of Oscar Wilde*, p. 53.
7 President's Notebook entries for 27 October 1878 and 7 November 1878, Magdalen College Archives.
8 Hart-Davis, *Letters of Oscar Wilde*, p. 51.
9 Ellmann, *Oscar Wilde*, p. 99.
10 Hart-Davis, *Letters of Oscar Wilde*, p. 54.
11 Ibid., p. 55.
12 Ibid.
13 Ellmann, *Oscar Wilde*, p. 100.
14 Brief note, undated, to an unidentified recipient, Magdalen College Archives.
15 Application form, 24 February 1879, British Library Department of Manuscripts.
16 Letter to A.H. Sayce, postmarked 28 May 1879, Bodleian Library.
17 Ellmann, *Oscar Wilde*, p. 101.
18 'Literary and Other Notes', *Woman's World*, January 1888, quoted in Ellmann, *Oscar Wilde*, p. 113.
19 Hart-Davis, *Letters of Oscar Wilde*, p. 74.

SEVEN

Courting Controversy

There is only one thing in the world worse than being talked about
and that is not being talked about.

Inspired by his love for the theatre, for the theatrical and for theatrical types, Wilde decided to try his hand as a playwright. Possibly he was also motivated initially by a desire to impress himself upon the thespian sensibilities of Florence Balcombe. Perhaps, more bitterly, he even relished the prospect of becoming a famous playwright as a way of proving himself to her and, in so doing, arousing in her the regret that perhaps, after all, she had married the wrong man.

Whatever his initial motivation, Wilde set about writing his first play in the spring or summer of 1880. By September he had finished it and sent the first copy to Ellen Terry, hoping that she would offer to play the heroine. No offer was forthcoming and Wilde, undeterred, sent further copies to Henry Irving and to the American actress Genevieve Ward. In both cases the response was polite but uncooperative. His new career as a playwright had got off to a faltering start.

The play which had drawn such a lukewarm response from his friends and acquaintances was *Vera; or, The Nihilists*. As the subtitle suggested, Wilde, having dropped both the Church and the freemasons from his affections, had picked up politics as a substitute. Yet even the politics was rooted in negation, itself a revealing reflection of his inner dejection at the time, a dejection deeply at variance with the *joie de vivre* of his public mask. The Nihilist would be defined by Wilde as 'that strange martyr who has no faith, who goes to the stake without enthusiasm, and dies for what he does not believe in ...'[1]

Act I of *Vera* opens with a meeting of the Nihilist conspirators and Wilde draws heavily on his knowledge of masonic ritual to imbue the scene with a sense of subversive secrecy:

PRESIDENT: What is the word?
FIRST CONSPIRATOR: Nabat.
PRESIDENT: The answer?
SECOND CONSPIRATOR: Kalit.
PRESIDENT: What hour is it?
THIRD CONSPIRATOR: The hour to suffer.
PRESIDENT: What day?
FOURTH CONSPIRATOR: The day of oppression.
PRESIDENT: What year?
FIFTH CONSPIRATOR: The year of hope.
PRESIDENT: How many are we in number?
SIXTH CONSPIRATOR: Ten, nine, and three.
PRESIDENT: The Galilaean had less to conquer the world; but what is our mission?
SEVENTH CONSPIRATOR: To give freedom.
PRESIDENT: Our creed?
EIGHTH CONSPIRATOR: To annihilate.
PRESIDENT: Our duty?
NINTH CONSPIRATOR: To obey.
PRESIDENT: Brothers, the questions have been answered well. There are none but Nihilists present. Let us see each other's faces.

The conspirators unmask and one of them recites the oath. Whereas the opening ritual had been based loosely on the 'Opening of a Lodge' in masonic ritual, the oath is borrowed from 'The Catechism of a Revolutionary' by S.C. Nechayev and Mikhail Bakunin. It is the anarchists' dream, or nightmare, 'to stab secretly by night; to drop poison in the glass; to set father against son, and husband against wife; without fear, without hope, without future, to suffer, to annihilate, to revenge'. The oath also demands that the Nihilists are 'neither to love nor to be loved' and in many respects this stricture, and the response of the characters to it, lies at the very heart of the play. Yet if this is the play's moral, its form is that of a dark masquerade, a tragedy of masks. Vera, the heroine, is the most fanatical of all the

Nihilists, intent, at all costs, on assassinating the Czar. Yet she falls in love with a fellow conspirator, Alexis, who, unknown to her, is the Czar's son. When the Czar is murdered, Alexis becomes Czar, and Vera is duty-bound to kill him. As she is about to stab him while he sleeps, he awakes and seizes her by both hands. He then declares his love:

> O God, you think I am a traitor, a liar, a king? I am, for love of you. Vera, it was for you I broke my oath and wear my father's crown. I would lay at your feet this mighty Russia, which you and I have loved so well; would give you this earth as a footstool; set this crown on your head. The people will love us. We will rule them by love, as a father rules his children. There shall be liberty in Russia for every man to think as his heart bids him; liberty for men to speak as they think. I have banished the wolves that preyed on us; I have brought back your brother from Siberia ...

They are reconciled, and Wilde draws deep draughts of Shake-spearean eloquence to crown the consummation of their love. Far from concealing the Shakespearean touch, Wilde brandishes it shame-lessly, making his characters echo, almost word for word, the love scenes of Romeo and Juliet: 'How still it is, and yet methinks the air is full of music. It is some nightingale who, wearying of the south, has come to sing in this bleak north to lovers such as we. It is the nightin-gale. Dost thou not hear it?' Wilde ensures that the fate of Vera and Alexis follows that of Shakespeare's star-crossed lovers, ending in tragedy. There is, however, a twist. Vera kills herself to save her lover's life, throwing the bloodstained dagger from the window as a sign to the Nihilists below that she has killed the Czar. 'What have you done?' pleads Alexis. 'I have saved Russia,' she replies, dying in his arms.

Vera is not particularly important in its own right. It is not, by any stretch of the imagination, one of Wilde's more accomplished plays and Wilde's writing bears all the hallmarks of the beginner cutting his teeth. Yet it is important insofar as it lays the foundations for much of Wilde's future work. Many of the motifs which will characterize later works are put in place and are finding form and expression: the use of dark intellectual forces as a means of conveying the light of morality;

the adoption of iconoclastic characters to illustrate the futility and degradation of iconoclasm; the flirting with decadence to stimulate traditional moral responses. In *Vera*, all the essential ingredients of Wilde's *oeuvre* had been thrown into the creative pot. Mixed up and refashioned they would re-emerge time and again in different guises in future years.

It is ironic, not to say grotesque, that Wilde is popularly perceived as an iconoclast when, artistically and aesthetically speaking, he was the very opposite. No doubt the popular perception has its roots in Wilde's unconventional private life and his provocative table talk, but in his art Wilde is the arch-anti-iconoclast. This is illustrated in 'Libertatis Sacra Fames', a poem published in *The World* in November 1880. It resonates with the political issues which had been at the forefront of Wilde's mind when he was writing *Vera* a few months earlier. He was 'nurtured in democracy' and likes best 'that state republican where every man is Kinglike', yet better the rule of a king

> Than to let clamorous demagogues betray
> Our freedom with the kiss of anarchy.
> Wherefore I love them not whose hands profane
>   Plant the red flag upon the piled-up street
>   For no right cause, beneath whose ignorant reign
> Arts, Culture, Reverence, Honour, all things fade,
>   Save Treason and the dagger of her trade,
> And Murder with his silent bloody feet.

As a work of pre-Orwellian prophecy 'Libertatis Sacra Fames' stands as a timeless monument to perennial wisdom. Predating Lenin, Stalin, Hitler and Mao, this salient verse illustrates Wilde's prescience in the face of what, in the same poem, he calls 'this modern fret for Liberty'. If wisdom is to be judged by its perennial applicability this one poem alone must place Wilde among the Wise.

Wilde's distaste for political revolutionaries, and his disgust for the destruction they cause, did not make him immune from the modern fret for Liberty. 'Ave Imperatrix', published in *The World* in August 1880, had looked towards the birth of the 'young republic'. Sending this to the novelist Mrs Alfred Hunt, wife of the landscape painter, Wilde described the poem as 'my first attempt at political prophecy'.[2]

Wilde also sent a copy of 'Ave Imperatrix' to the painter and sculptor George Frederick Watts. Enclosed with the poem was a short, succinct letter which provides a perfect example of Wilde's aphoristic charm: 'Will you accept from me a copy of a poem I have just published on England, as a very poor mark of homage to one whose pictures are great poems?'[3]

Wilde was very much like his mother in despising the rule of the mob and any excessive display of revolutionary zeal. Lady Wilde had drawn back from nationalism in the wake of the violence of the Fenian uprising, and her son drew back from any form of socialism which called for the manning of the barricades or the destruction of civilized order. Yet his social conscience was certainly genuine. The poet Rennell Rodd recounted how Wilde had taken him to Lambeth in the wake of serious flooding in the area to see if they could help the many people who had been forced out of their houses. There was an old bedridden Irish woman in a tenement whom Wilde so cheered with his stories, and with some money, that she cried after him as he left, 'May the Lord give you a bed in glory.'[4]

Laudable though Wilde's social conscience may have been, he sought, above all, to be lauded by his peers rather than applauded by the proletariat. Socializing would always come before socialism in his order of priorities.

The extent to which Wilde's social standing had improved since his days at Oxford is illustrated by an epigram attributed to the Prince of Wales, 'I do not know Mr Wilde, and not to know Mr Wilde is not to be known.'[5] Hyperbole aside, the statement was confirmation that Wilde was now accepted in the highest circles in the land. The doctor's son from Dublin was finally being noticed by the great and the good, to such an extent that even the heir to the throne paid homage, however lightheartedly.

Presumably, Wilde had made the acquaintance of the Prince of Wales through their mutual friendship with Lillie Langtry. The Prince was known to delight in Wilde's company and, on 4 June 1881, he attended a thought-reading seance at the fashionable house in Tite Street, Chelsea, which Wilde now shared with his friend Frank Miles. One of Wilde's neighbours in Tite Street was the artist James McNeill Whistler. They were to form a vigorous and volatile friendship. 'The most remarkable men I have ever known were Whistler and Wilde,'

Ellen Terry would recall. 'There was something about both of them more instantaneously individual and audacious than it is possible to describe.'[6] When their razor-sharp wits met in combat a firework display of *bons mots* would leave their audience either agape or aghast, but always amused. Some of these exchanges have passed into legend, such as the time when Wilde is said to have remarked of something that Whistler had said, 'How I wish I had said that,' to which Whistler replied, 'You will, Oscar, you will.' The exact source of these legendary exchanges is open to question, but their truth, as an encapsulation of the spirit and wit of the two protagonists, is not in dispute.

By 1881 Whistler and Wilde were two of the most prominent exponents of the aesthetic movement. Wilde, however, was still perceived as a newcomer to aestheticism. For several years before his arrival in London, the creed had been promulgated, in different shades, by those who had been formative influences on Wilde's intellectual and artistic development. The more ethereal aspects of the movement were represented by Rossetti and Pater, its sensuality by Swinburne, and its pseudo-Catholic medievalism by Ruskin. The enmity and diversity of approach between Pater and Ruskin illustrated clearly that the movement was never an homogenous whole and never shared anything other than the broadest and vaguest of aims and aspirations. This had been illustrated even more dramatically in 1877 when Ruskin criticized Whistler's paintings at the Grosvenor Gallery, accusing him of 'flinging a pot of paint in the public's face'. Whistler, always vitriolic and violently tempestuous when crossed, sued Ruskin for libel. The case, one of the most famous libel cases in English legal history, was heard on 25 November 1878. Technically, Whistler won the case. It was, however, a pyrrhic victory serving only to add insult to the artist's injury. He was awarded a farthing damages, with no costs. This led to bankruptcy, forcing him to flee to Venice. He returned to London in November 1880 to find Wilde his neighbour.

In fact, when Whistler returned to Chelsea, he discovered that Wilde was more than a neighbour or a friend. He was a rival. Famous in his own right, Wilde was threatening Whistler's reputation as the wittiest of the aesthetes. By the beginning of 1881 Wilde's aesthetic mannerisms were sufficiently well known for the satirists to take notice. Most notable of these was George du Maurier whose caricatures in *Punch* turned Wilde's affectations into an art form. Du Maurier conceived two aesthetic types, probably modelled on Wilde and Whistler. These were the poet Maudle and the painter Jellaby Postlethwaite. Soon, however, Whistler's caricature was eclipsed by Wilde's with whom du Maurier ran riot satirically. Wilde became Oscuro Wildegoose, Drawit Milde, the Wilde-eyed poet, 'Brother Jonathan' Wilde and Ossian Wilderness in a succession of poses involving his flowing locks, his lilies, his affected Frenchness and his blue china.

Naturally enough, Wilde was not altogether happy with the way he was being depicted in *Punch* but he was aware of the power of publicity and wary of making enemies. As such he made a point of always greeting du Maurier graciously whenever they met. On one occasion, at an exhibition of Whistler's work, Wilde and du Maurier stood talking together when Whistler approached. 'Which of you two discovered the other?' Whistler quipped.[7] The remark was certainly witty and, to a degree, true. Yet it was barbed with jealousy. Increasingly, Whistler would look upon Wilde as an unwelcome *arriviste*, a fact which would sour and finally poison their relationship. In the meantime, Whistler was one of Wilde's ever increasing circle of friends.

Wilde's reputation as an aesthetic dandy was heightened still further on St George's Day 1881 when Gilbert and Sullivan's *Patience* premiered in London. W.S. Gilbert's libretto parodied the aesthetic movement, drawing all its leading figures into the composite characterization of the opera's two aesthetes, Reginald Bunthorne and Archibald Grosvenor. Wilde was, of course, one of the composite parts from which these characters were drawn. Although he benefited from the publicity he was not, it seems, amused by the opera. In *The Importance of Being Earnest* he exacted his revenge in the stage direction which says of Jack and Algernon that 'they whistle some dreadful popular air from a British opera'. It also appears that W.S. Gilbert did not find the real Oscar Wilde as amusing as the parody of him he paraded on stage. At a supper party at the Haymarket Theatre, he became increasingly irritated by Wilde's holding the table with his brilliant talk. At the first opportunity, he interrupted Wilde's flow to say, 'I wish I could talk like you, I'd keep my mouth shut and claim it as a virtue!' He was outgunned. Wilde retorted: 'Ah, that would be selfish! I could deny myself the pleasure of talking, but not to others the pleasure of listening.'[8]

Accounts of Wilde's table talk spread like wildfire around the dinner parties of London, adding to the legend created by the caricaturists and parodists. Yet the legend surrounding him was, like all legends, prone to exaggeration. Wilde was said to have 'walked down Piccadilly with a poppy or a lily in his medieval hand'. When asked by a reporter whether the story was true, Wilde replied that 'To have done it was nothing, but to make people think one had done it was a triumph.'[9] Unfortunately, this flash of brilliance had blinded him from the truth. If people believed the most outlandish things about him, it had at least as much to do with George du Maurier, W.S. Gilbert and others, as it had to do with Wilde himself. These lesser humorists may have been cultivating seeds that Wilde himself had assiduously sown, but the imaginative flowers that grew from the kernel of truth bore little relation to the inner reality of the person portrayed. The danger was obvious. Intoxicated with his new-found celebrity, Wilde began to believe the stories that were circulating about him. What he perceived as a triumph would be the beginning of his downfall. His words would have been truer if he had said: *Not to have done it was nothing, but for people to make one think one had done it was a tragedy.*

In courting controversy Wilde was courting disaster. He was now beginning to wear masks moulded by others which were developing a life of their own. He was no longer in control. The mask was replacing the man.

1 Quoted in Ellmann, *Oscar Wilde*, p. 116.
2 Hart-Davis, *Letters of Oscar Wilde*, p. 68.
3 Ibid.
4 Ellmann, *Oscar Wilde*, p. 116.
5 Ibid., p. 123.
6 Ibid., p. 126.
7 Ibid., p. 130.
8 Ibid., p. 131.
9 *New York World*, 8 January 1882.

EIGHT

Poetry and Pose

Ah! it was easy when the world was young
   To keep one's life free and inviolate,
From our sad lips another song is rung,
   By our hands our heads are desecrate,
Wanderers in drear exile, and dispossessed
Of what should be our own, we can but feed on wild unrest.

In 1881, his first play having faltered, Wilde's creativity continued to find its principal expression in verse. In June, his *Poems* were published, at his own expense, by the small publishing house of David Bogue. Although thirty of the sixty-one poems had appeared previously in a variety of publications, the remaining thirty-one were being published for the first time. Taken as a whole, the collection was a reflection of Wilde's own confusion over the period encompassed by their composition. There are the religious sonnets and verse, inspired by the flirtation with Rome during his days as an undergraduate; there is the 'Florentine verse' exhibiting the desolation he felt after the loss of his first love; and there is the more recent political verse, espousing a moderate republicanism while rejecting the violence and negations of nihilism. Of the previously unpublished verse, the religious sonnets display the dejection which followed his rejection of Rome. Dejection and rejection are in fact the primary components. In his 'Sonnet on Hearing the Dies Irae Sung in the Sistine Chapel' he rejects the pomp of religious ritual and music, declaring that

> white lilies in the spring,
> Sad olive-groves, or silver-breasted dove,
> Teach me more clearly of Thy life and love…

Yet the consolation gleaned from nature is itself akin to desolation, as the 'bird at evening flying to its nest / Tells me of One who had no place of rest'.

Similarly, 'The Burden of Itys' opens with the clarion cry that the English Thames 'is holier far than Rome' and proceeds with a plethora of images comparing the mysteries of religion unfavourably to simple pastoral pleasures. The whole poem reads like an attempt by Wilde to exorcise the power that Catholicism once held over him. Nature is not so much a new love to replace the old, but a noise to drown it out:

> Sing louder yet, why must I still behold
> The wan white face of that deserted Christ,
> Whose bleeding hands my hands did once enfold …

Deserted, the rejected Christ 'sits in his lone dishonoured House and weeps, perchance for me?' Clearly, the exorcism is not successful and Wilde remains haunted by the ghost of his Christian past.

In 'E Tenebris', Wilde cries to Christ as one 'drowning in a stormier sea / Than Simon on thy lake of Galilee':

> The wine of life is spilt upon the sand,
> My heart is as some famine-murdered land
>   Whence all good things have perished utterly,
>   And well I know my soul in Hell must lie
> If I this night before God's throne should stand.

The sonnet ends in the pathetic but passionate hope that 'before the night' he may behold 'the wounded hands, the weary human face'.

Wilde is more successful in exorcising Christianity when it is not Pan but Eros whom he invokes. Whereas his love for nature in 'The Burden of Itys' carries with it the suspicion of disingenuousness, the attractions of the flesh in 'Panthea' are more genuinely tempting:

Nay, let us walk from fire unto fire,
From passionate pain to deadlier delight, –
I am too young to live without desire,
Too young art thou to waste this summer night
Asking those idle questions which of old
Man sought of seer and oracle, and no reply was told.

Losing his faith in religion, Wilde was also, paradoxically, losing his faith in reason. 'Panthea' proclaims that wisdom is barren, 'a childless heritage', and feeling is better than knowledge. Despairing of ever finding the answers, Wilde has ceased to care about the questions:

O we are wearied of this sense of guilt,
Wearied of pleasure's paramour despair,
Wearied of every temple we have built,
Wearied of every right, unanswered prayer,
For man is weak; God sleeps; and heaven is high;
One fiery-coloured moment: one great love; and lo! we die.

Wearying of the sense of guilt, heedless of the sleeping God, Wilde marries his manhood to his weakness and surrenders his conscience to the fiery-coloured moment. In 'Charmides' this logic of lust leads inexorably to a new crucifixion of Christ and the erection of Eros in triumph:

And all his hoarded sweets were hers to kiss,
And all her maidenhood was his to slay,
And limb to limb in long and rapturous bliss
Their passion waxed and waned, – O why essay
To pipe again of love, too venturous reed!
Enough, enough that Eros laughed upon that flowerless mead.

Yet Eros's erection and triumph are transient, a passing lust, and Wilde once again pipes of love. In 'Humanitad', a poem that prefigures *De Profundis* in some respects, the natural, unnatural and supernatural are interwoven in metaphysical speculation. Through nostalgic eyes Wilde remembers the days of grace 'when soul and body seemed to blend in mystic symphonies'. Now, his faith denied, 'the bloom of things has flown':

But we have left those gentle haunts to pass
   With weary feet to the new Calvary,
Where we behold, as one who in a glass
   Sees his own face, self-slain Humanity,
And in the dumb reproach of that sad gaze
Learn what an awful phantom the red hand of man can raise.

O smitten mouth! O forehead crowned with thorn!
   O chalice of all common miseries!
Thou for our sakes that loved thee not hast borne
   An agony of endless centuries,
And we were vain and ignorant nor knew
That when we stabbed thy heart it was our own real hearts
    we slew.

As with *Vera*, his first play, Wilde has revealed himself with candour in these poems. It is, in fact, one of the paradoxes of Wilde's life and art that the true Wilde is to be gleaned from what he says in his art far more than from what he says, or is alleged to have said, in his life. 'Life follows art', one of Wilde's epigrams, is certainly true of Wilde if not of others. This can be readily demonstrated by a comment he is alleged to have made on his tour of the United States in the year after the poems were published. 'My next book may be a perfect contradiction of my first,' he apparently remarked, prompting Ellmann to conclude that 'contradictoriness was his orthodoxy'.[1] Yet Wilde's next book was not a perfect contradiction of his first but, far from it, was a development of the same moral preoccupations which had characterized his poems. Furthermore, Wilde's subsequent works, with the exception of *The Importance of Being Earnest*, would all follow the same consistent pattern. Seen in this light, Wilde's 'contradictoriness' should be greeted cautiously. Where it emerges it is invariably designed to amuse and stimulate his audience. Contradictions are uttered for effect, intended to entertain. Contradictoriness was not Wilde's orthodoxy, it was his pose.

Unfortunately, Wilde's public image, carefully contrived, was so controversial that most critics could not see the poetry for the pose. By 1881 he had polarized opinion about himself to such an extent that few could read his verse without prejudice. Critics in the *Athenaeum*, the *Saturday Review* and the *Spectator* accused Wilde of plagiarism, insincerity and indecency. Of these criticisms only the first related directly to the poems, whereas the charges of insincerity and indecency had more to do with his public posturing. Wilde's poems were indeed highly derivative, hence the inevitable charge of plagiarism, but were executed with an originality borne from personal experience. The charge of insincerity had more to do with Wilde's reputation as an entertainer at dinner parties than with his verse, the critics failing to perceive that the sincerity of the latter stood in marked contrast to the affectation of many of his *bons mots*. The allegations of indecency may have been rooted in the eroticism and sensuality of some of Wilde's verse but the puritanical sensibilities of his critics were no doubt accentuated and inflamed by the author's flouting of Victorian conventions and by his cultivated and mannered 'naughtiness' in public.

On the other hand, *Punch*, the publication that had done more – possibly more than Wilde himself – to invent the image of the aesthetic dandy who had so outraged Victorian values, was a little disappointed that the poems were not more risqué. Whereas other critics were outraged by Wilde, *Punch* expected him to be outrageous. The arch-aesthete, as a media creation, had a duty to his public, a duty to perform. Yet the character that emerged from the poems did not live up to the caricature. According to *Punch*, Wilde had pulled his punches, offering only 'Swinburne and water', adding that 'The poet is Wilde, But his poetry's tame.'[2]

Nowhere was the prejudice provoked by Wilde more evident than in the reception his poetry received from the Oxford Union. The secretary of the Union had written to Wilde requesting a copy of the poems for the library. Respectfully, Wilde inscribed a copy on 27 October 1881 'to the Library of the Oxford Union my first volume of poems'. When the acquisition was announced, Oliver Elton – later a historian of English literature – rose to denounce it in devastating fashion:

> It is not that these poems are thin – and they are thin: it is not that they are immoral – and they are immoral: it is not that they are this or that – and they are all this and all that: it is that they are for the most part not by their putative father at all, but by a number of better-known and more deservedly reputed authors. They are in fact by William Shakespeare, by

Philip Sidney, by John Donne, by Lord Byron, by William Morris, by Algernon Swinburne, and by sixty more, whose works have furnished the list of passages which I hold in my hand at this moment. The Union Library already contains better and fuller editions of all these poets: the volume which we are offered is theirs, not Mr Wilde's: and I move that it be not accepted.[3]

In the spirited debate which followed, no one seems to have employed the obvious riposte to Elton's line of reasoning. If Wilde's poems were merely a 'list of passages' from the works of others, and if the poems were 'immoral', as claimed, which of the great poets were guilty with Wilde of immorality?

Elton's arguments proved persuasive. One hundred and eighty-eight members of the Union voted against the poems being accepted, whereas only 128 voted in their favour. The Librarian requested a poll of the membership and this, though closer, ratified the earlier decision – 180 voting for acceptance and 188 against. The Librarian was left with no option but to return the volume to its author. Wilde wrote in response of his regret that there were still at Oxford 'such a large number of young men who are ready to accept their own ignorance as an index, and their own conceit as a criterion of any imaginative and beautiful work'.[4] In reality, however, it was not the work but its author that had been put on trial. If Wilde's role as chief poseur of the aesthetic movement had not proved so provocative, it is unlikely that anyone would have cared whether his verse was plagiaristic or otherwise.

Nonetheless, provocative posing can be profitable. Towards the end of the year Wilde received a lucrative offer from the producer Richard D'Oyly Carte to travel to the United States for a lecture tour. Carte would cover Wilde's expenses and would share equally with him the net profits. Wilde agreed. The final arrangements were made by W.F. Morse who managed the lectures on Carte's behalf. Writing to a booking agent in Philadelphia, Morse promised much public interest in Wilde's exposition of aestheticism which he described as 'this latest form of fashionable madness'.[5]

Wilde crossed the Atlantic on the SS Arizona, docking in New York on the evening of 2 January 1882. He was besieged by reporters who noted every item of his dress in meticulous detail. He was in a green coat that hung down almost to his feet; the collar and cuffs were trimmed with seal or otter, as was the round cap on his head which was variously described as a smoking cap or a turban. Beneath the coat the reporters discerned a shirt with a wide Lord Byron collar and a sky-blue necktie. Wilde had become an icon of chic eccentricity, an arbiter of sartorial grandiloquence. The press hung on his every word as much as on every thread of his attire. The reporter from the *New York Tribune* was astonished to find that Wilde's voice was anything but feminine, in fact rather burly. Another journalist thought Wilde spoke in hexameters while the representative from the *New York World* heard him accentuating every fourth syllable in a kind of singsong: 'I came from *Eng*land because I *thought* America was the best *place* to see.'[6]

When asked what he had thought of the crossing, Wilde merely responded that it had been uninteresting. The response was itself too uninteresting for the sensation-seeking journalists and they sought second opinions from several other passengers. One told them that Wilde had remarked during the voyage that 'I am not exactly pleased with the Atlantic. It is not so majestic as I expected. The sea seems tame to me. The roaring ocean does not roar.' These were words more worthy of the wit they had expected. Even if received only second-hand it was what the headlines demanded. It was what Wilde *should* have said. The comments, suitably amended, were translated into large type and cabled to England: 'Mr Wilde Disappointed with the Atlantic'. As a news story it was too good to miss. The *Pall Mall Gazette* printed a poem, 'The Disappointed Deep', and a letter printed in *Truth* began, 'I am disappointed in Mr Wilde,' and was signed, The Atlantic Ocean. It was the stuff of which Wilde's legend was made. What did it matter that he may never, in fact, have said the words? In similar fashion, he was reputed to have said when passing through customs that 'I have nothing to declare except my genius'. No contemporary account records Wilde saying anything of the kind. As he would no doubt have quipped if pressed on the subject, *to have said such a thing was nothing, but to make people think one had said it was a triumph.*

The triumph of Wilde's arrival in the United States was short-lived. The American media refused to take his aestheticism seriously and reverted to the sort of lampoons which characterized his treatment by the press in England. The *New York Tribune* dismissed Wilde as 'a penny Ruskin' and a pretentious fraud. The *Washington Post*, on its front page of 21 January, juxtaposed a drawing of Wilde holding a sunflower with one of a 'citizen of Borneo' holding a coconut.[7] When W.F. Morse protested to the paper about the 'gratuitous malice' of their approach the *Post* responded with a smirking editorial claiming that their comparison was justified. Such was the hostility Wilde had engendered that some Chicago papers announced that the whole affair in the *Washington Post* had been contrived by Wilde as a publicity stunt, even suggesting that Wilde had corrected the original proofs of the attack on himself and that he had passed the caricature of himself and the 'citizen of Borneo' for publication. Perhaps it was not surprising that Wilde began to take a jaundiced view of the press. 'If you survive yellow journalism,' he told the *New York Times*, 'you need not be afraid of yellow fever.'[8]

Wilde's ten-month tour of the United States and Canada involved an exhausting itinerary, including almost daily lectures, punctuated by ceaseless travel across the vastness of the continent. From January until the middle of March he lectured in the east, beginning and ending in New York. He then set out for the west which, in 1882, was still in its infancy. Stopping off in Omaha en route to San Francisco, Wilde's first impressions of western cities were conveyed to a local journalist. There was, he said, 'less prejudice and more simple and sane people' in the west, an obvious reference to his treatment at the hands of eastern newspapers.

Wilde, evidently relaxed in the presence of the pleasant and unsophisticated provincial journalist, laughed merrily when asked about his plans for the future. 'Well, I'm a very ambitious young man. I want to do everything in the world. I cannot conceive of anything that I do not want to do. I want to write a great deal more poetry. I want to study painting more than I've been able to. I want to write a great many more plays, and I want to make this artistic movement the basis for a new civilization.' He was also more earnest and less esoteric than usual when questioned about the aesthetic movement. 'It is indeed to become a part of the people's life. It must begin not in the scholar's study – not even in the studio of the great artist, but with the handicraftsman always. And by handicraftsman I mean a man who works with his hands; and not with his hands merely, but with his head and his heart. The evil that machinery is doing is not merely in the consequences of its work but in the fact that it makes men themselves machines also. Whereas, we wish them to be artists, that is to say men.'[9] In this eloquently disarming exposition of the aesthetic movement, Wilde's practical approach prophesies the creed of the distributists several decades later. His words could very easily be the utterances of Eric Gill, G.K. Chesterton, Hilaire Belloc or Father Vincent McNabb.

Arriving in San Francisco, Wilde repeated his preference for the west. 'The further West one comes the more there is to like. The Western people are much more social than those in the East, and I fancy I shall be greatly pleased with California.' Yet he appeared to contradict his earlier exposition of aestheticism when he complained that there were too many 'amateurs' in America, declaring that 'amateur art is worse than no art'. He was, however, more disarmingly modest when asked by a reporter whether his admirers believed he had created a new school of poetry. 'They certainly should not – that is if I have any admirers.' He explained that he belonged to the Pre-Raphaelite school which owed its origin to Keats more than to anyone else. Keats was to the Pre-Raphaelites what Pheidias was to Grecian art, and Dante was to 'the intensity, passion and colour of Italian painting'. Burne-Jones in painting and Morris, Rossetti and Swinburne in poetry, represented 'the fruit of which Keats was the blossom'.[10]

At his lectures in San Francisco Wilde fulfilled his billing as an arbiter of aesthetic sensibilities, discoursing on household decoration, old china and the ugliness of grand pianos. His wit was evident in his directions for the hanging of pictures. 'They should be hung upon the eye-line. The habit in America of hanging them up near the cornice struck me as irrational at first. It was not until I saw how bad the pictures were that I realized the advantage of the custom.'[11]

At the end of one of the lectures a reporter declared that he had seen a 'giddy blonde aesthete of thirty, whose soul was languishing in the atmosphere of poesy', bargaining with an usher to convey to Wilde 'a tender missive in the old Italian style and a yellow envelope' which read:

The vierlet is for faithfulness,
Which in me shall abide
Hopeing likewise from your hart
You will not let it slide.

Clearly, regardless of his words of modesty when he arrived in San Francisco, Wilde was not without admirers.

It was not only lovelorn ladies who were vying for Wilde's attention. In the exiled eyes of San Francisco's Irish émigrés, Wilde's mother was a heroine of Irish nationalism and Wilde a hero by association. As such, the city's sizeable Irish population sought him out as the son of Speranza. He was beseeched to deliver an extra lecture on 5 April on 'Irish Poets of the Nineteenth Century'. The offer was too good to refuse. Whereas, according to the local press, his lectures on aestheticism were being delivered to halls which were only half-full, the Irish lecture was added 'in obedience to a numerously signed requisition'. A packed and patriotic audience assured, Wilde rose to the occasion and delivered a homily on Irish nationalism.

Wilde began his lecture by telling his audience how he had opened a book at random in a San Francisco bookshop and discovered a poem which charmed and fascinated him by its sweet simplicity and concluded that no one but an Irishman could have written it. Turning to the title page he noted that it had been written by Father Ryan of Mobile, Alabama, known as the 'Poet-Priest of the South'. He went on to discourse on the beauties of Irish art, adding that 'the English conquest destroyed art, but could not destroy the poetry of the Celtic people, as that was something beyond the reach of the sword and vandal hand of the conquering Saxon'. Art, he claimed, sickens in slavery, grows languid in luxury, but reaches its full fruition under the fostering care of liberty. In consequence, art dies when the chains of slavery rust on people's limbs. 'The poetry of the Irish people', he said, 'ever kept alive the fires of patriotism in the hearts of the Irish people.'[12]

Indeed the poetic genius of the Celtic race never flags or wearies. It is as sweet by the groves of California as by the groves of Ireland, as strong in foreign lands as in the land which gave it birth. And indeed I do not know anything more wonderful, or more characteristic of the Celtic genius, than the quick artistic spirit in which we adapted ourselves to the English tongue. The Saxon took our lands from us and left them desolate. We took their language and added new beauties to it.[13]

Not surprisingly, Wilde gave pride of place in his lecture to his mother. His references to her, and his reading of two of her poems, drew great applause from the audience and caused a young lady to rush up to the platform with a bouquet of flowers. As Wilde accepted the gift the audience once more burst into applause and Oscar bowed in gratitude. It was all a far cry from the beauty of Keats and the ugliness of grand pianos.

This was not the first time that Wilde had been lauded as the son of Speranza during his American tour. On St Patrick's Day he had been in St Paul, Minnesota, and was introduced by a Father Shanley who called him the son 'of one of Ireland's noblest daughters – of a daughter who in the troublous times of 1848 by the works of her pen and her noble example did much to keep the fire of patriotism burning brightly'.[14]

Much had changed in Ireland since the troublous times of 1848. Wilde and his mother had grown disillusioned with the violent twist in events and were not the full-blown nationalists that his Irish-American audience imagined. Yet Wilde perceived that the subtler distinctions of Irish politics would be lost on the children of exile. For Irish-Americans, the 'forty shades of green' referred only to the fields of their homeland, not to the nuances of political opinion which divided it. Patriotism was measured by expatriates in the crude simplicity of black and white, or rather Green and the Rest. Wisely, or at least pragmatically, Wilde gave his audience what they wanted and told them what they wished to hear. The result, at times, verged on disingenuous jingoism, punctuated with genuine insight. It was akin to the language of the demagogue that Wilde had censured so savagely in his poem 'Libertatis Sacra Fames'. Yet if he was a hypocrite, he was a happy one, enjoying the intoxication of hero-worship.

A month later, Wilde was forced to face the grim reality of Irish politics when he heard that Lord Frederick Cavendish had been murdered in Phoenix Park in Dublin by a group calling itself the Invincibles. The anachronistic nature of his, and his mother's, position was highlighted by the fact that Lord Frederick was a friend of the family who had dined with them at their home in Merrion Square. 'When liberty comes with hands dabbled in blood it is hard to shake hands with her,' he told a reporter who had asked his attitude to the murder. He added, however, that England was partially to blame:

'She is reaping the fruit of seven centuries of injustice.'[15] The principles of his mother's nationalism remained, even if he, like her,
abhorred the violent way it was being practised. In fact, his own position was even more confused because, psychologically speaking, he
considered himself at least partially English – though presumably not
the part responsible for the problems in Ireland. In his letter to the
Oxford Union following the rejection of his poems he had referred to
himself as a poet and writer 'of England'.[16] He also believed that
Ireland should remain a part of, and loyal to, the British Empire.
Wilde, if not an Englishman, was certainly a singular sort of Irishman
whose nationalist mask revealed only half the truth.

Following his Irish lecture, Wilde was taken to the Bohemian Club
where several of the members had decided to wine and dine him.
Then, according to legend, some of the more robustly masculine of his
hosts, considering their aesthetic guest to be 'a Miss Nancy' specializing in 'woman-talk', decided that it would be fun to get him drunk. It
was all carefully planned. They would start drinking before dinner,
wine their guest through the meal and finish him off afterwards. As
the night wore on, Wilde plied them with his wit while they plied him
with their drinks. Slowly the uproarious laughter subsided as, one by
one, the hard-drinking Irish-Americans slumped beneath the table.
When the last had collapsed Wilde is said to have risen slowly to his
feet and sauntered off into the sunrise to his rooms at the Palace Hotel.

Word of Wilde's drinking feat passed through the city during the
day. Having sartorially seduced the women he had succeeded in
wooing the men with whiskey. Those who had previously held the
aesthete in contempt now treated him with the respect and reverence
due to 'a three-bottle man'.[17] The legend grew, aided and abetted by
the local press, so that Wilde was soon a wild west hero – Oscar Wilde
transformed into Wild Oscar – who, according to another legend,
excelled in poker as well as whiskey. It was said that he had been
invited by some hardened gamblers to a game of 'dollar ante', to
which he was said to have replied 'What is dollar ante?' The gamblers
explained the rules, expecting Wilde to prove easy pickings, and he
agreed to join them in a game. Later, sweeping his winnings from the
table, Wilde rose and remarked casually, 'Now that I remember it,
gentlemen, we used to indulge in this little recreation at Oxford.'[18]
It is, of course, difficult to ascertain whether these stories contain any

more than a grain of truth. Perhaps, however, it is significant that they arose in the state which would soon spawn Hollywood.

Leaving California at the beginning of April, Wilde experienced the real west, still untainted by future Hollywood fantasies. At Leadville in Colorado he was lowered in a bucket into a silver mine, describing in a letter to a friend the 'long galleries of silver-ore, the miners all at work, looking so picturesque in the dim light as they swung the hammers and cleft the stone'.[19] He spent most of the night deep in the heart of the earth, talking to the miners, before being brought down the mountain by a special train at half past four in the morning. He proceeded to Kansas and then to St Joseph in Missouri where the legendary outlaw Jesse James had just been murdered by one of his own followers. Wilde was fascinated to find that the whole town was mourning over him and buying relics of his house:

> His door-knocker and dust-bin went for fabulous prices, two speculators absolutely came to pistol-shots as to who was to have his hearthbrush, the unsuccessful one being, however, consoled by being allowed to purchase the water-butt for the income of an English bishop, while his sole work of art, a chromo-lithograph of the most dreadful kind, of course was sold at a price which in Europe only a Mantegna or an undoubted Titian can command![20]

On 24 April, after giving a talk in the morning to the undergraduates at the State University in Lincoln, Nebraska, Wilde was taken to visit a large prison nearby. His view of the prison and its occupants was vividly portrayed in a letter to a friend:

> Poor odd types of humanity in hideous striped dresses making bricks in the sun, and all mean-looking, which consoled me, for I should hate to see a criminal with a noble face. Little whitewashed cells, so tragically tidy, but with books in them. In one I found a translation of Dante, and a Shelley. Strange and beautiful it seemed to me that the sorrow of a single Florentine in exile should, hundreds of years afterwards, lighten the sorrow of some common prisoner in a modern gaol, and one murderer with melancholy eyes – to be hung they told me in three weeks – spending that interval in reading novels, a bad preparation for facing either God or Nothing.[21]

It is tempting to see a connection between this incident, recounted by Wilde only a day after it happened, and a story he recounted to a journalist shortly before his death. Discussing his time in the west, Wilde remarked that a cowboy had galloped past him who, he was told, had 'painted the town red' the previous night. Wilde was struck by the slang phrase. He had not heard it before in common usage but it sounded familiar. 'Where had I heard it? I could not remember, but the same afternoon ... I was shown a condemned cell where a prisoner, who had been sentenced to death, was calmly smoking a cigarette and reading *The Divine Comedy* of Dante in the original.'[22] It was then that Wilde remembered the words of Francesca da Rimini in Dante's *Inferno*: 'We are those who painted the world red with our sin.' Is it possible that two such similar incidents were witnessed by Wilde during his American tour, or is it more likely that the contemporary account is the accurate version and the latter a romantic embellishment?

Wilde's tour continued apace, in fact at a lightning pace. From Kansas and Missouri he proceeded to Nebraska, Iowa, Ohio, Pennsylvania and New Jersey, before continuing, via New York and Virginia, across the border into Canada. Lecturing almost daily at diverse venues during the two weeks north of the border, Wilde returned to the United States at the beginning of June. He then proceeded south through Tennessee into Louisiana and then to Texas. Towards the end of June he began the long journey north again, lecturing in towns and cities throughout Alabama, Georgia, South Carolina, Delaware, Virginia and Rhode Island, before arriving back in New York on 17 July. Throughout August he lectured in and around New York and New Jersey, rested in September, then crossed again into Canada for a final series of lectures in October. From 14 October until 27 December Wilde resided in New York, recovering from a truly gruelling year.

Wilde's impressions of America were manifold and multi-faceted. Periodically they would furnish his writing as he drew inspiration from the new experiences which his sojourn into uncharted cultural waters had afforded him. There was, however, one aspect of his experience in the United States which continually repelled him. His eyes, and his aesthetic sensibilities, had been assaulted wherever he went by billboard advertising which he considered both ugly and vulgar. It is difficult to perceive what Wilde would have made of its omnipresence in a multitude of media a century later. Certainly his definition of a cynic as someone who knows the price of everything and the value of nothing is at least as relevant today as it was in his own day.

Whatever Wilde's view of American advertising, his American tour was a remarkable feat of self-advertisement. His poems were being pirated and sold at ten cents a copy and he had become the inspiration for several popular songs, including the 'Oscar Wilde Forget-Me-Not Waltzes', 'The Flippity Flop Young Man' and 'Oscar Dear'. Young women posed with sunflowers in their hats or sang 'Twenty lovesick maidens we' as he approached. The writer and humorist Eugene Field dressed up as Wilde and drove through Denver on 15 April in an open carriage, lily in hand and gazing languidly at a book. When Wilde was informed of the stunt he was said to have remarked that it was a 'splendid advertisement' for his lecture in the city.[23]

While Wilde was conquering America, he was not being forgotten at home. As a letter from his mother on 18 September made clear, news of his American conquests had enhanced his reputation in England. 'You are still the talk of London – the cabmen ask me if I am anything to Oscar Wilde – the milkman has bought your picture! and in fact nothing seems celebrated in London but you. I think you will be mobbed when you come back by eager crowds and will be obliged to shelter in cabs.'[24]

With the new level of fame came an enlargement of the legend. Wilde was no longer merely the dandified object of fun depicted in *Punch*, nor was he only a wild west hero, whether Wild Oscar the Drinker or Jokers Wilde the Gambler. In the eyes of many young artists and poets, he was a god – a fact he relayed with relish to a friend.[25] Encouraged in his vanity by his mother, Wilde was stagestruck. More than ever, his conscience-inspired muse would have to struggle with the godlike image he had created for himself, or, more dangerously, which had been created for him by others. The pose and the poet were at war.

1 Ellmann, *Oscar Wilde*, p. 137.

2 *Punch*, 23 July and 12 November 1881.

3 Henry Newbolt, *My World as in My Time*, 1932, pp. 96–7; quoted in Ellmann, *Oscar Wilde*, p. 140.

4 Hart-Davis, *More Letters of Oscar Wilde*, p. 102.
5 Ellmann, *Oscar Wilde*, p. 145.
6 *New York World*, 3 January 1882.
7 *Washington Post*, 21 January 1882.
8 *New York Times*, 23 January 1882.
9 *Omaha Weekly Herald*, 24 March 1882.
10 *Daily Examiner* (San Francisco), 27 March 1882.
11 Lloyd Lewis and Henry Justin Smith, *Oscar Wilde Discovers America*, New York: Benjamin Blom, 1967, p. 254.
12 Hyde, *Annotated Oscar Wilde*, p. 373.
13 Ibid., p. 378.
14 Ellmann, *Oscar Wilde*, p. 186.
15 Ibid.
16 Hart-Davis, *More Letters of Oscar Wilde*, p. 102.
17 Lewis and Smith, *Oscar Wilde Discovers America*, pp. 255–6.
18 Ibid., pp. 256–7.
19 Hart-Davis, *Letters of Oscar Wilde*, p. 114.
20 Ibid., p. 115.
21 Ibid.
22 Chris Healy, *Confessions of a Journalist*, London: Chatto & Windus, 1904, pp. 132–4.
23 Ellmann, *Oscar Wilde*, p. 182.
24 Ibid., p. 181.
25 Ibid., p. 182.

NINE

Courting Constance

DUCHESS: I see when men love women
They give them but a little of their lives,
But women when they love give everything ...

The conflict between Wilde's art and his artistic theories was exemplified by a discussion he had with George E. Woodberry, a young academic at the University of Nebraska. Wilde had begun to promote the idea that art should dissociate itself from morality, freeing itself from ethical constraints and conventions. 'Poetry', he insisted, 'should be neither intellectual nor emotional,' that is, neither didactic nor autobiographical. Woodberry pointed out that Wilde's own poems did not conform to these principles. 'Well,' Wilde replied defensively, 'those poems are not the best.'

Woodberry's perceptive incision into the contradictions at the heart of Wilde's life and art were expressed succinctly in a letter to the American author Charles Eliot Norton. 'I have seen no man whose charm stole on me so secretly, so rapidly, and with such entire sweetness. His poems are better than his theories, and he better than his poems.'[1]

Wilde sailed home from New York on 27 December 1882. After two or three weeks in London he departed for Paris where he spent three months consuming the remainder of the money he had earned on the American tour. In Paris he met many doyens of French literature, including Paul Verlaine, Victor Hugo, Stéphane Mallarmé, Emile Zola, Edmond de Goncourt and Alphonse Daudet, as well as the artist Edgar Degas. After the virginal delights of the New World, Wilde sampled Paris *en pleine décadence*, enjoying the company of a sensuous avant garde who were picking over the bones of the *ancien régime*. 'Je suis l'Empire à la fin de la Décadence,' Verlaine had written in his poem 'Langueur'.

Wilde paid homage to Verlaine's decadent credentials but was not about to emulate the decadence of Verlaine's seedy appearance. Wilde's own decadence was altogether more refined. He had his hair curled in imitation of a bust of Nero in the Louvre and always dressed in the height of fashion. His decadent pose required a certain air of worldly cynicism and a subversive approach to moral conventions. This found expression in the advice he offered his friend Robert Sherard who was contemplating marriage. Wilde informed Sherard that the infidelity of wives was almost universal. 'Act dishonourably, Robert. It's what soon or later she'll certainly do to you.' As they passed a statue of Henri IV he offered the historical evidence for his sweeping assertion, ruminating on a subject he would later discuss with Louis Latourette. Henri IV was 'another great Frenchman who was a cuckold':

All the great men of France were cuckolds. Haven't you observed this? All! In every period. By their wives or by their mistresses. Villon, Molière, Louis XIV, Napoleon, Victor Hugo, Musset, Balzac, kings, generals, poets! Those I mention, a thousand more that I could name, were all cuckolds. Do you know what that means? I will tell you. Great men, in France, have loved women too much. Women don't like that. They take advantage of this weakness. In England, great men love nothing, neither art, nor wealth, nor glory ... nor women. It's an advantage, you can be sure.[2]

There was, however, a conflict between the affectations on the cynical surface and the clinging conscience of the inner self. This was particularly evident in the disgust Wilde felt after using the services of a well-known Paris prostitute. Confessing his act to Robert Sherard the following day, he exhibited the self-loathing which would surface throughout his life. 'What animals we all are, Robert,' he exclaimed. The disgust also surfaced in his poems. 'You wake in me each bestial sense, you make me what I would not be', he had written in 'The Sphinx'. In 'The Harlot's House' the bestial sense is replaced by a specifically Christian sense of sin. The imagery passes from the physical to the metaphysical so that the bestial becomes demonic. Lust is a metaphysical murderer that kills the soul: 'The dead are dancing with the dead, / The dust is whirling with the dust.' Since 'The Harlot's House' wasn't written until possibly as late as 1885, the poem serves as a revealing illustration of Wilde's residual faith and its endurance long after his public renunciation of Christianity. It also illustrates the struggle at the heart of the man. Wilde's cynicism dances on the surface of his psyche, whereas desolation and despair lurk in the depths. The cynical shallows, the shadows of decadence, were for show, but the spiritual well was carefully concealed, smothered, shielding from public scrutiny the real Oscar Wilde. 'The Oscar of the first period is dead,' Wilde declared at this time.[3] In fact, he wasn't so much dead as buried.

As ever, the real Oscar Wilde emerges in his art. During the three months in Paris at the beginning of 1883 he was writing his second play, *The Duchess of Padua*, an Italian tragedy set in the sixteenth century. The eponymous character is the play's heroine, whereas its villain is her husband, the duke. It is, therefore, a revelation that the duke is typecast as a worldly wit who comes out with the sort of iconoclastic *bons mots* which Wilde had made his own speciality. Thus the duke tells the cardinal that he is weary of his wife: 'Why, she is worse than ugly, she is good.' Then, when the duchess brings a delegation of destitute citizens to the palace and beseeches the duke to help them, his contempt finds voice in a string of witty ripostes reminiscent of Wilde's table talk with Whistler and others. The citizens complain that their bread is made of nothing but chaff; the duke responds: 'And very good food too, I give it to my horses.' To the complaint of the citizens that their drinking water is stagnant, the duke replies: 'They should drink wine; water is quite unwholesome.' The citizens reply that their taxes are so high that they can't afford wine. 'Then you should bless the taxes which make you temperate,' he responds. The duchess intercedes on the citizens' behalf, informing her husband that the wretched poverty on the streets is leading to fever and death. The duke is unmoved: 'They should thank me for sending them to Heaven, if they are wretched here.'

At this stage the cardinal enters the fray, counselling the duke that he has no right to wash his hands of the misery of his subjects. 'True,' he begins, 'it is Christian to bear misery, for out of misery God bringeth good,

Yet it is Christian also to be kind,
To feed the hungry, and to heal the sick,
And there seem many evils in this town,
Which in your wisdom might your Grace reform.

'Reform, Lord Cardinal,' the duke replies, 'did *you* say reform?' He reminds the cardinal that he had denounced Luther as a heretic for his calls for reform of the Church. Luther, the cardinal replies, rising from his seat in indignation, 'would have led the sheep out of the fold, we do but ask of you to feed the sheep.'

Against the duke's Machiavellian misanthropy is set the duchess's Christian faith. She reminds her husband that 'those who forget what honour is, forget all things'. Then, after the duke's exit, she ponders a woman's state within marriage in terms that are the antidote to Wilde's expressed cynicism on the subject. She also alludes to an unknown prostitute, an unmistakable echo of the author's guilt:

I know it is the general lot of women,
Each miserably mated to some man
Wrecks her own life upon his selfishness:
That it is general makes it not less bitter.
I think I never heard a woman laugh,
Laugh for pure merriment, except one woman,
That was at night time, in the public streets.
Poor soul, she walked with painted lips, and wore
The mask of pleasure: I would not laugh like her;
No, death were better.

After these words of desolation the duchess throws herself down before a picture of the Madonna, a prayer of pleading on her lips: 'Mother of God, have you no help for me?'

The play's other principal protagonist, Guido, is described by Wilde as 'impulsive, ready to take oaths, to forget the past, to realize the moment only: full of noble ideas but "Fortune's fool".'[4] Guido is governed by Pateresque principles, living each moment with flame-like intensity, and, as a result, is doomed to echo Romeo's words and Romeo's fate. He is 'fortune's fool' condemned by his own moral myopia to a tragic end. It is, therefore, more than coincidental that the love scene between Guido and the duchess resonates with hints of Shakespeare's *Romeo and Juliet* in much the same way as had the love scene in *Vera*.

> GUIDO: Methinks I am bold to look upon you thus:
> The gentle violet hides beneath its leaf
> And is afraid to look at the great sun
> For fear of too much splendour, but my eyes,
> O daring eyes! are grown so venturous
> That like fixed stars they stand, gazing at you,
> And surfeit sense with beauty.
> DUCHESS: Dear love, I would
> You could look upon me for ever, for your eyes
> Are polished mirrors, and when I peer
> Into those mirrors I can see myself,
> And so I know my image lives in you.

The parallels with *Romeo and Juliet* are unmistakable, arguably too much so. Sometimes it seems that the Shakespearean shades are daubed on so heavily that the Wildean touch is almost smothered completely. The lesser talent is being offered in sacrifice to the greater. Yet when the Wildean touch emerges it does so with brilliance. Guido's short exposition of the nature, or rather the supernature, of love contains deep theology, in which grace is seen as paramount in both life and art:

> without love
> Life is no better than the unhewn stone
> Which in the quarry lies, before the sculptor
> Has set the God within it.

For one who had distanced himself from orthodox Christianity, Wilde conveys a decidedly orthodox view of life and art. Implicit in this short exposition is the belief that art is sub-creation drawn from Creation. The creativity of the creature is the image of the Creator within him.

The fourth key player in *The Duchess of Padua* is the hate-filled figure of Moranzone, the incarnation of Revenge. Moranzone pours scorn on Guido's love for the duchess, declaring him a 'weak fool, to let love in upon your life, save as a plaything'. Guido responds that age had dimmed Moranzone's perceptions and hardened his heart. The old man retorts contemptuously that he has been in love and knows what love is.

Oh, in my time, boy, I have walked i' the moon.
Swore I would live on kisses and on blisses,
Swore I would die for love, and did not die,
Wrote love bad verses; ay, and sung them badly,
Like all true lovers: Oh, I have done the tricks!
I know the partings and the chamberings;
We are all animals at best, and love
Is merely passion with a holy name.

Guido interprets Moranzone's bitterness as indicative that he has not really loved at all. If he had truly loved, Guido insists, he would know that 'love is the sacrament of life':

The days are over when God walked with men,
But Love, which is His image, holds His place.
When a man loves a woman, then he knows
God's secret, and the secret of the world.
There is no house so lowly or so mean,
Which, if their hearts be pure who live in it,
Love will not enter; but if bloody murder
Knock at the Palace gate and is let in,
Love like a wounded thing creeps out and dies.
This is the punishment God sets on sin.
The wicked cannot love.

The dialogue between Moranzone and Guido is significant on several levels. It is crucial to the play itself because the plot pivots on the conflict between love and hate, reconciliation and revenge. It is crucial to an understanding of Wilde's art because the concept under discussion forms the principal motif in much of his work. Repeatedly, Wilde re-enacts Calvary in his works, most of which are passion plays in various poses, depicting the wounding of love by the wicked. Lastly, it is important as a means of understanding Wilde's own life and personality. The dialogue between Moranzone and Guido is an expression of the conflict between Wilde's worldly mask and his inner self.

The tragedy of *The Duchess of Padua* centres on Moranzone's success. He had sought the duke's death and urged Guido to murder him in revenge for the duke's earlier betrayal of Guido's father. In the event, however, it is the duchess who murders the duke. Guido and the duchess are the instruments of Moranzone's revenge and their sin poisons their love for each other. 'Sure it is the guilty, who, being very wretched, need love most,' says the duchess. 'There is no love where there is any guilt,' Guido replies.

'I see when men love women they give but a little of their lives,' says the duchess, 'but women when they love give everything.'

> Dear Christ! how little pity
> We women get in this untimely world;
> Men lure us to some dreadful precipice,
> And, when we fall, they leave us.

Love, once poisoned, seeks revenge and the original sin is repeated. The duchess, her love for Guido hardened into hatred, contrives to have him condemned for the murder she has committed. The Shakespearean twists are flavoured with hints of Dante's *Divine Comedy*. Perhaps, indeed, it is no coincidence that the duchess's name is Beatrice. After Guido is condemned to death, the cardinal reminds him that his repentance will save him from Hell, secure him a place in Purgatory, from which, aided by the prayers of the Church, he will eventually reach Paradise.

> For the great power of our mother Church,
> Ends not with this poor bubble of a world,
> Of which we are but dust, as Jerome saith,
> For if the sinner doth repentant die,
> Our prayers and holy masses much avail
> To bring the guilty soul from purgatory.

Too late to avert the doom that awaits them, Guido and the duchess are reconciled. Full of remorse, she tells him that she is not worthy of his love, 'for I have stained the innocent hands of love with spilt-out blood'. Seeking to comfort her, Guido suggests that it was not she who committed the sin but some devil which tempted her. 'No, no,' she cries, 'we are each our own devil, and we make this world our hell.'

For the play's tragic climax Wilde reverts to *Romeo and Juliet*. The parallels with Shakespeare's tragedy are so potently obvious that they are patently intentional. Even the instruments of suicide are identical, although Wilde has his hero use the dagger and his heroine the poison. To assuage any doubt that Wilde's drama was intended as a morality play, the final stage directions are explicit: *The Lord Justice rushes forward and drags the cloak off the Duchess, whose face is now the marble image of peace, the sign of God's forgiveness.*

In a letter written shortly after he had completed *The Duchess of Padua* Wilde was quite candid about the Shakespearean influence on the play. Guido's soliloquy at the close of Act III was, he said, necessary because 'suspense is immensely important for the audience: Macbeth must hesitate at the door of Duncan's room, and Hamlet behind the praying King, and Romeo before Juliet's body'. Suspense, he continued, 'is the essence of situation, and surprise its climax ... it ·produces on the audience the most tragical effect in the world: the effect of his speaking *too late*: the effect of Juliet waking *too late*'.[5] Unfortunately, the derivativeness of *The Duchess of Padua* has devalued it in the eyes of the critics. A work which owes so much to another, which cannot claim to be original, is seen as relatively worthless. Yet if *The Duchess of Padua* is an imitation of Shakespeare, it is a very good imitation. Wilde was imitating his master but he had at least mastered his master's style. Furthermore, the play deserves to be seen as something beyond mere imitation. Embedded in the Shakespearean blank verse are gems of Wildean wisdom and wit which are woven into the fabric of a dramatic tour de force. The neglect of *The Duchess of Padua* has left the world's theatre-goers so much the poorer.

In the summer of 1883, Wilde's first play, *Vera*, opened in New York. On 2 August Wilde sailed to the United States on the *SS Britannic* to oversee its production. Rehearsals began on 13 August and the play opened to a packed house a week later. It was greeted with mixed reviews but the balance of critical opinion was negative. The *New York Times* was the most scathing, describing Wilde as 'very much of a charlatan and wholly an amateur' whose play was valueless. These words, published on 28 August, came too late to have any adverse effect on the play's prospects. By this time, only eight days after it had opened, *Vera* was already doomed to failure. Box office returns had fallen off sharply and the theatre was too expensive to keep open at a loss. On the very day the *New York Times* declared that it was valueless, *Vera* was withdrawn. It was taken on tour, beginning 15 October, but this was cold comfort for the crestfallen author whose hopes had been dashed on the rocks of public indifference.

Returning to England, Wilde gave a series of lectures on his 'Impressions of America', beginning at Wandsworth Town Hall in South London on 24 September. His views, seen with the wisdom of more than a century's hindsight, seem marked with the wisdom of foresight which is the mark of prophecy. What was 'particularly noticeable' about America, Wilde remarked, was that 'everybody seems in a hurry to catch a train'.

> This is a state of things which is not favourable to poetry or romance. Had Romeo or Juliet been in a constant state of anxiety about trains, or had their minds been agitated by the question of return-tickets, Shakespeare could not have given us those lovely balcony scenes which are so full of poetry and pathos.

America, complained Wilde, was 'the noisiest country that ever existed'. One was awakened in the morning not by the nightingale but by the steam whistle. He wondered why the Americans did not take measures to 'reduce this intolerable noise'. The continual turmoil was destructive of the delicate sensibilities required by all art.

Apart from the restlessness and the noise, the other negative impression concerned size. 'One is impressed in America, but not favourably impressed, by the inordinate size of everything. The country seems to try to bully one into a belief in its power by its impressive bigness.'[6]

Two months later, Wilde's lecture tour took him to Dublin. On 22 November he talked on 'The House Beautiful' at the city's Gaiety Theatre, and the next day delivered his 'Impressions of America'. During his stay he renewed his acquaintance with a young woman named Constance Mary Lloyd whom he had first met in London two years earlier. She was three years younger than Wilde, born on

2 January 1858, and had made an instant impression at their first meeting in May 1881. Physically this was scarcely surprising. She was strikingly beautiful; tall and slim with long, wavy chestnut hair and large alluring deep-blue eyes. Yet there was more to her than physical beauty. She liked music, painting, embroidery, and could (and did) read Dante in Italian. Wilde paid her marked attention and allegedly informed his mother as they were leaving that he thought of marrying her some day. It appears that Constance was equally struck by her suitor. When Wilde came to visit on 6 June she wrote excitedly to her brother that he had arrived at five thirty, 'by which time I was shaking with fright!' He stayed for half an hour and begged her to come and see his mother again soon. 'I can't help liking him, because when he's talking to me alone he's never a bit affected, and speaks naturally, excepting that he uses better language than most people.'[7]

Constance's father had died in 1874. She did not live with her remarried mother, with whom her relationship had been strained since childhood, but with her grandfather, a Queen's Counsel named John Horatio Lloyd who owned a mansion in Lancaster Gate in London. It was here that the relationship between Constance and Oscar developed during the second half of 1881. Wilde was a frequent visitor, gaining the approval of both her grandfather and brother. The embryonic courtship was interrupted by Wilde's year in America during 1882 and by the three months he spent in Paris at the beginning of 1883. While Wilde was away, Constance attended art school and adopted an aesthetic style of dress. Whether this was a result of Wilde's influence or simply a calculated attempt by Constance to influence Wilde in her direction is not clear. Either way, their respective relatives did their best to encourage the relationship. One of Constance's relatives visited Lady Wilde in December 1882 and 'praised Constance immensely'. Since it was Constance herself who had given her relative Lady Wilde's address it seems likely that Constance had instigated the visit personally. Lady Wilde wrote suggestively to her son in America that she had nearly made it known that she would like Constance for a daughter-in-law, but refrained from doing so. 'I thought the visit looked encouraging,' she added, suggesting that she and Oscar had already discussed the possibility of his future marriage.[8] For her part, Lady Wilde invited Constance and her brother to an at-home on 28 February 1883, and sang the praises of her son.

As soon as Wilde returned from Paris their relationship resumed, at first falteringly but then with intensity. On 6 July Lady Wilde reproved her son for devoting himself to Constance to the impolite exclusion of her other guests. Thus admonished, Wilde circulated dutifully but it was noticed that he kept following Constance with his eyes. A week later he beseeched her to come to see him as it would be their last opportunity to meet before his trip to New York to oversee preparations for the opening of *Vera*.

In mid-October Wilde came to London between lectures, and Lady Wilde invited Constance to her reception so they could meet. Constance informed him that she was about to depart for Dublin on a visit. She was pleased to learn that her stay would coincide with two lectures in Dublin by Wilde. It was, they agreed, a pleasant coincidence.

When Wilde checked in at the Shelbourne Hotel in Dublin on 21 November, he found a note requesting him to visit Constance at her grandmother's house in Ely Place. Constance informed her brother that when Wilde arrived at Ely Place he was 'decidedly extra affected, I suppose partly from nervousness'. Yet 'he made himself very pleasant'.[9] On the following afternoon Constance was an admiring member of the audience as Wilde gave his lecture on 'The House Beautiful'. After the lecture Wilde again visited Ely Place for four o'clock tea before proceeding to a dinner appointment with the Fellows of Trinity College. Constance attended Wilde's American lecture on 23 November but found it less interesting than the former one. The next day she wrote to her brother informing him that one of her friends was teasing her terribly about her feelings for Wilde, adding bashfully that it was 'such stupid nonsense'.[10] Two days later she wrote once more to her brother. 'My dearest Otho, Prepare Yourself for an astounding piece of news! I am engaged to Oscar Wilde and perfectly and insanely happy.' Upon receipt of the news Otho wrote to Wilde that he was 'pleased indeed'. 'I am sure that for my own part I welcome you as a new brother ... if Constance makes as good a wife as she has been a good sister to me your happiness is certain; she is staunch and true.'[11]

Lady Wilde was equally delighted, concluding her letter to him in her own inimitable style. 'May the Divine Intelligence that rules the world, give you happiness and peace and joy in your beloved.' She signed herself 'La Madre'.[12]

It seems from a letter that Constance wrote to Wilde at this time that he had confessed his previous relationship with Florence Balcombe. 'I don't think I shall ever be jealous,' she wrote. 'Certainly I am not jealous now of anyone: I trust in you for the present: I am content to let the past be buried, it does not belong to me: for the future trust and faith will come, and when I have you for my husband, I will hold you fast with chains of love.'[13] Richard Ellmann comments that Wilde's confession was only partial. 'Syphilis was not mentioned, for Wilde thought himself cured.'[14] Wilde, no doubt, would have been as surprised as Constance to discover that he was cured of a disease that he had never contracted.

In the middle of December, Wilde wrote to Lillie Langtry, ostensibly to congratulate her on her triumphant American tour but taking the opportunity to inform her of his engagement.

> I am going to be married to a beautiful girl called Constance Lloyd, a grave, slight, violet-eyed little Artemis, with great coils of heavy brown hair which make her flower-like head droop like a blossom, and wonderful ivory hands which draw music from the piano so sweet that the birds stop singing to listen to her. We are to be married in April ...
>
> I am hard at work lecturing and getting rich, though it is horrid being so much away from her, but we telegraph to each other twice a day, and I rush back suddenly from the uttermost parts of the earth to see her for an hour, and do all the foolish things that wise lovers do.[15]

On 21 December Constance, now returned to London, wrote to Nellie Hutchinson, her brother's future wife. 'I am with Oscar when he is in town, and I am too miserable to do anything while he is away.' She informed her future sister-in-law that she was lunching with Wilde later that day in Norwood before his lecture at the Crystal Palace, 'and after that he has a week's holiday, which will be much joy for me'.[16] At around this time she wrote passionately to Wilde, reassuring him of her unfailing devotion. 'I am so cold and undemonstrative outwardly: you must read my heart and not my outward semblance if you wish to know how passionately I worship and love you.' At times her worship of him approached the idolatrous. He was 'my hero and my god' before whom she was 'not worthy'.[17]

News of the engagement soon roused the attentions of the press. On 26 December 1883 *The World* announced that Whistler's last Sunday breakfast of the year had been given 'in honour of two happy couples, Lord Garmoyle and his fairy queen, and Oscar and the lady whom he has chosen to be the *châtelaine* of the House Beautiful'.

Wilde and Whistler were themselves perceived as a happy couple in the eyes of the press, inextricably linked in endless jocular jousting. The previous month, Wilde had sent a telegram to Whistler, referring to an article about them in *Punch*. '*Punch* too ridiculous. When you and I are together we never talk about anything except ourselves.' Whistler replied, also by telegram: 'No, no, Oscar, you forget. When you and I are together, we never talk about anything except me.' Both telegrams were published in *The World* of 14 November, and subsequently republished by Whistler in his book *The Gentle Art of Making Enemies*.

Perhaps it is not surprising that Constance found Whistler's company abrasively overpowering. For one as reserved as she, Whistler's egocentric *bons mots* would have seemed barbed beyond toleration, especially if she had herself become the object of his bullish and bullying brilliance. Wilde wrote whimsically to the American sculptor Waldo Story on 22 January 1884 that Constance was 'quite perfect except that she does not think Jimmy [i.e. Whistler] the only painter that ever really existed'.[18]

Wilde's letter to Story was a repetition, in lighter vein, of his letter to Lillie Langtry a month earlier:

Her name is Constance and she is quite young, very grave, and mystical, with wonderful eyes, and dark brown coils of hair ... We are, of course, desperately in love. I have been obliged to be away nearly all the time since our engagement, civilizing the provinces by my remarkable lectures, but we telegraph to each other twice a day, and the telegraph clerks have become quite romantic in consequence.[19]

He informed Story that the wedding was planned for April and that they planned to honeymoon in Paris and possibly Rome.

It is clear from such correspondence that Wilde was in love with his bride-to-be. Yet it is equally clear that her love was the more intense and the more dependent. After their week together at Christmas,

Constance broke down in tears when Wilde once again departed on his lecture tour of the provinces. Later she wrote to apologize for her weakness. In January Wilde sent Constance a marmoset which he had dubbed 'Jimmy' for its whistling. The monkey died soon afterwards leaving Constance in some distress. 'Is it my fault that everything you give me has an untimely end?' she wrote, evidently recalling an earlier ill-fated gift. Her misery was compounded when Wilde misaddressed a telegram to her. 'How much do you think of me that you did not even remember that I was not at home? Your telegram was forwarded to me this morning ... I am too gloomy to write.'[20] Little did she know that the forgetfulness and the long absences from home would become a hallmark of their future marriage.

Oscar and Constance were married at 2.30 p.m. on 29 May 1884 at St James's Church, Sussex Gardens. Whistler, unprepared to be upstaged by Wilde even on his wedding day, sent a telegram. 'Fear I may not be able to reach you in time for the ceremony. Don't wait.'[21] After the wedding a small group of friends saw the newlyweds off at Charing Cross. They were bound for Paris where they would spend three weeks at the Hôtel Wagram on Rue de Rivoli. Any plans to proceed to Rome had been dropped.

For Constance the honeymoon was a foretaste of their future life together. It was dominated by a succession of aesthetic pursuits and an endless round of social gatherings, presumably organized by her husband. Wilde was addicted to his place of honour in the social mêlée and was thoroughly at home at the dinner tables of London, Dublin, New York, San Francisco and, of course, Paris. Even the delights of his new wife could not keep him from the company of his Parisian friends. He and Constance went to art exhibitions, to the opera and to see Sarah Bernhardt in *Macbeth*. They went to breakfast with Henrietta Reubell, a wealthy American spinster who kept a salon in Paris and was a good friend of Whistler's. On several occasions they met the young sculptor John Donoghue, whom Constance described as having a 'very handsome Roman face but with Irish blue eyes'.[22] They regularly met Robert Sherard, who reminded Constance of Thomas Chatterton. On 4 June they hosted a dinner party at their hotel at which the American artist John Singer Sargent was present, as was the French novelist and critic Paul Bourget. Henrietta Reubell and John Donoghue also attended. Constance made a strong impression on

Bourget in particular. A few days later he remarked to the writer Vernon Lee, *'J'aime cette femme – j'aime la femme annulée et tendre'*.[23] Two days later, Oscar and Constance lunched with Bourget and Sargent again, this time at the latter's house. At other times Wilde would go out to meet friends by himself, leaving his bride alone in the hotel. Constance seemed not to mind. She was basking in the post-marital afterglow. 'Of course I need not tell you that I am very happy,' she wrote to her brother on one occasion when Wilde had left her in the hotel, adding that she was enjoying her liberty enormously.[24]

Once, with Constance safely and happily ensconced in the hotel, Wilde had gone for a walk with Robert Sherard and had proceeded to divulge the secrets of the marriage bed. He got as far as 'It's so wonderful when a young virgin ...' before Sherard steered him away from the subject.[25] This was on the second day of their honeymoon. It hadn't taken Wilde long to betray his wife for the first time. It would not be the last.

In many respects, the words of the duchess in Wilde's play were an augury of his wife's future fate:

> ... it is the general lot of women,
> Each miserably mated to some man
> Wrecks her own life upon his selfishness ...

1 Ellmann, *Oscar Wilde*, p. 192.
2 Ibid., pp. 205–6.
3 Hart-Davis, *Letters of Oscar Wilde*, p. 135.
4 Ibid., p. 137.
5 Ibid., p. 141.
6 Hyde, *Annotated Oscar Wilde*, p. 379.
7 Hart-Davis, *Letters of Oscar Wilde*, p. 152.
8 Ellmann, *Oscar Wilde*, p. 222.
9 Hart-Davis, *Letters of Oscar Wilde*, p. 152.
10 Ibid., p. 153.
11 Ibid.
12 Ellmann, *Oscar Wilde*, p. 234.
13 Ibid., p. 231.
14 Ibid.
15 Hart-Davis, *Letters of Oscar Wilde*, p. 154.
16 Ibid.
17 Ellmann, *Oscar Wilde*, p. 232.
18 Hart-Davis, *Letters of Oscar Wilde*, p. 155.
19 Ibid.

20 Ellmann, *Oscar Wilde*, pp. 232–3.
21 Ibid., p. 234.
22 Hart-Davis, *Letters of Oscar Wilde*, p. 157.
23 Ibid., pp. 157–8.
24 Ibid., p. 157.
25 Robert Sherard, letter to A.J.A. Symonds; quoted in Ellmann, *Oscar Wilde*, p. 235.

TEN

The French Connection

There is no modern literature outside France.

On 9 June 1884 a reporter from the *Morning News* knocked on the door of Wilde's hotel room at the Hôtel Wagram. Speculatively, he hoped to be granted an interview with the newly married writer. Wilde had not expected to be harassed by journalists on his honeymoon and declared that he was 'too happy to be interviewed'. Nonetheless the reporter was allowed in. He discovered that Wilde had been on a bibliophilic spending spree in Parisian bookshops and was in the midst of reading a heap of novels. 'There is no modern literature outside France,' Wilde declared to the writer Catulle Mendès at breakfast a few days later,[1] and he was evidently soaking up as much of it as possible while he had time on his hands in Paris. He told the *Morning News* reporter that he was particularly impressed by *A Rebours*, a new novel by J.K. Huysmans which had been published only a couple of weeks earlier, in mid-May. 'This last book of Huysmans is one of the best I have ever seen,' he enthused.[2] It was much more than that. Huysmans' novel would prove to be one of the most potent and poisonous influences on Wilde's future life.

A Rebours was being reviewed everywhere as the handbook of decadence. A few years later the poet Paul Valéry would declare it his 'Bible and bedside book' and it would not be an exaggeration to say that it was held in similar reverence by Wilde. Its enormous influence surfaced a few years later in Wilde's novel *The Picture of Dorian Gray*. Wilde admitted that the 'yellow book' which had such . pernicious effect on Dorian Gray in his novel was based on Huysmans' *A Rebours*. The impact of the 'yellow book' on Dorian Gray was similar to Wilde's own reaction when he had first read Huysmans' novel in the Paris hotel room: 'After a few minutes he became absorbed. It was the strangest book that he had ever read. It seemed to him that in exquisite raiment, and to the delicate sound of flutes, the sins of the world were passing in dumb show before him. Things that he had dimly dreamed of were suddenly made real to him. Things of which he had never dreamed were gradually revealed.' The novel's hero, a young Parisian, des Esseintes, sought new experiences, both moral and immoral, 'loving for their mere artificiality those renunciations that men have unwisely called virtue, as much as those natural rebellions that wise men still call sin'. At times it was difficult to discern in the pages of the novel 'whether one was reading the spiritual ecstasies of some mediaeval saint or the morbid confessions of a modern sinner. It was a poisonous book. The heavy odour of incense seemed to cling about its pages and to trouble the brain.' It was a strange book to be reading on honeymoon, and even more strange that it should have such a morbidly unsettling influence on one so recently married.

Throughout the following years *A Rebours* would hang over Wilde like an ominously dark cloud, or lurk within him like a shadow of his darker self: 'For years, Dorian Gray could not free himself from the influence of this book. Or perhaps it would be more accurate to say that he never sought to free himself from it. He procured from Paris no less than nine large paper copies of the first edition ... The hero, the wonderful young Parisian ... became to him a kind of pre-figuring type of himself. And, indeed, the whole book seemed to contain the story of his own life, written before he had lived it.'

Wilde would never be the same again. 'Dorian Gray had been poisoned by a book. There were moments when he looked on evil simply as a mode through which he could realize his conception of the beautiful.'

The 'young Parisian', des Esseintes, would become more than the archetype of Wilde's Dorian Gray. To a degree, he would become the archetype of Wilde himself. 'I am mad just like des Esseintes,' he would remark regularly in the company of friends such as Gomez Carrillo.[3] The 'madness' of des Esseintes was particularly evident in the two chapters in *A Rebours* dedicated to a study of contemporary writers.

According to des Esseintes, writers had hitherto confined themselves
to exploring the surface of the soul, or such underground passages as
were easily accessible and well-lit ... Baudelaire had gone further; he
had descended to the bottom of the inexhaustible mine, had picked his
way along abandoned or unexplored galleries, and had finally reached
those districts of the soul where the monstrous vegetations of the
sick mind flourish. There, near the breeding ground of intellectual
aberrations and diseases of the mind – the mystical tetanus, the burning fever of lust, the typhoids and yellow fevers of crime – he had
found, hatching in the dismal forcing-house of *ennui*, the frightening
middle-age of thoughts and emotions. He had laid bare the morbid
psychology of the mind ...[4]

This was deliciously dangerous new territory for Wilde. Baudelaire
was not new to him. He had read and admired his verse long before
reading *A Rebours*. The novelty was in the way that Huysmans had
arranged Baudelaire's *fleurs du mal* in an enticingly lurid fashion. He
was seeing them afresh or, more accurately, he was seeing them for
the first time in the fullness of their decay. He was seeing them
through the eyes of des Esseintes who believed Baudelaire had gone
beyond the trivial causes of unhappiness such as unrequited love, or
the jealousies caused by adultery. Instead, he had twisted the knife in
those 'deeper, deadlier, longer-lasting wounds that are inflicted by
satiety, disillusion, and contempt upon souls tortured by the present,
disgusted with the past, terrified and despairing of the future'.[5] For
one as tormented by self-loathing as Wilde such a vision was alluring.
Temperamentally tempted to despair he saw Baudelaire and Huysmans as kindred spirits. They were seeking enlightenment from the
depths of their own inner darkness. He was trying to do the same.

Wilde's plunging into the depths with the decadents was to have
some surprising consequences. Far from vanquishing the religious
question from his life it would bring it back to the centre. Despair
was, after all, a religious concept. It was not a physical but a metaphysical reality. It was the denial of hope. Furthermore, despair was
distinct from desolation. The former was the denial of hope, the latter
the hunger for it. A desolate soul does not seek suicide, it seeks consolation. Ultimately, the hunger for hope engenders a hunger for faith.

This was the deeper reality at the heart of the decadent movement in France. In the final chapter of *A Rebours*, des Esseintes discovers that his lustful appetites have not satisfied his inner hunger. In his hour of anguish he realizes that 'the arguments of pessimism were powerless to console him, and the only possible cure for his misery was the impossible belief in a future life'. At the very last, utterly desolate, des Esseintes breaks into a faltering prayer:

Ah! but my courage fails me, and my heart is sick within me! – Lord, take pity on the Christian who doubts, on the sceptic who would fain believe, on the galley-slave of life who puts out to sea alone, in the darkness of night, beneath a firmament no longer illumined by the beacon-fires of the ancient hope![6]

The similarity between this *cri de coeur* and those in Wilde's poems scarcely needs elucidating. It is safe to assume, therefore, that Wilde was as moved by the novel's climax, its moral, as he was by the various immoral acts, 'the sins of the world', that had passed 'in dumb show' before him in the novel's earlier chapters.

On 14 June 1884, while Wilde was still honeymooning in Paris, Léon Bloy wrote a poignant review of *A Rebours* in *Le Chat Noir*, the leading journal of the emerging decadent movement. Bloy maintained that Huysmans' supreme achievement in *A Rebours* was to demonstrate that man's pleasures were finite, his needs infinite. The choice that Huysmans had placed before his readers was 'whether to guzzle like the beasts of the field or to look upon the face of God'.

I know of no contemporary work which puts this alternative in a more definitive or a more terrifying form than *A Rebours*. There is not a single page in this book where the reader can enjoy a breathing-space and relax in some semblance of security; the author allows him no respite. In this kaleidoscope review of all that can possibly interest the modern mind, there is nothing that is not flouted, stigmatized, vilified, and anathematized by this misanthrope who refuses to regard the ignoble creatures of our time as the fulfilment of human destiny, and who clamours distractedly for a God. With the exception of Pascal, no one has ever uttered such penetrating lamentations ...

A month later, *Le Constitutionnel* and *Le Pays* published an article on *A Rebours* which Huysmans' biographer considered 'among the most outstanding reviews written in the last century'.[7] It was by the ageing Romantic writer Jules Barbey d'Aurévilly. Like Bloy, Barbey emphasized that 'behind the hero's boredom and his futile efforts to conquer it, there is a spiritual affliction which does even more to exalt the book than the author's considerable talent'. He went on to draw a suggestive parallel between *A Rebours* and Baudelaire's *Les Fleurs du mal*; and finally, with extraordinary prescience, predicted Huysmans' eventual conversion.

> Baudelaire, the satanic Baudelaire, who died a Christian, must surely be one of M. Huysmans' favourite authors, for one can feel his presence, like a glowing fire, behind the finest pages M. Huysmans has written. Well, one day, I defied Baudelaire to begin *Les Fleurs du mal* over again, or to go any further in his blasphemies. I might well offer the same challenge to the author of *A Rebours*. 'After *Les Fleurs du mal*,' I told Baudelaire, 'it only remains for you to choose between the muzzle of a pistol and the foot of the Cross.' Baudelaire chose the foot of the Cross. But will the author of *A Rebours* make the same choice?[8]

At the time these words were published there seemed little likelihood that Huysmans would ever take the road to Rome. He knew no practising Catholics, never had occasion to meet a priest, and had not set foot in a church for many years. Twelve years later, after he had been received into the Church, he recalled Barbey's review: 'Strange! But that man was the only one who saw things clearly in my case, after he had read *A Rebours* ... He wrote an article which contained these last prophetic words: "There only remains for you to commit suicide or become a Catholic."'[9]

After the publication of *A Rebours* the new writers of Montmartre were quickly branded as '*les décadents*'. The term was popularized by Maurice Barres in a long essay on the influence of Baudelaire on modern literature published in November and December 1884. Yet if Baudelaire was the father of decadence and Huysmans his first-born, the leaders of the 'decadent school', post-*A Rebours*, were Stéphane Mallarmé and Paul Verlaine.

Wilde's admiration for Mallarmé was unrestrained. The awe he felt in his presence was evident in a letter to him in February 1891.

Referring to Mallarmé as the 'Master', Wilde paid homage to Mallarmé's translation of Poe's 'The Raven', describing it as a 'magnificent symphony in prose'. In England, he continued, 'we have prose and we have poetry, but French prose and poetry become in the hands of such a master as you one and the same thing'.[10]

In many respects, the excesses of Paul Verlaine's life prefigured Wilde's in fact, in much the same way as des Esseintes had prefigured it in fiction. In 1873 Verlaine shot his homosexual lover, the poet Arthur Rimbaud, after Rimbaud, who was ten years his junior, had threatened to terminate their tempestuous relationship. Verlaine was arrested for attempted murder and sentenced to two years' hard labour. On 24 April 1874, while Verlaine was serving his sentence in Belgium, his estranged wife, who had been deserted for Rimbaud, obtained a judicial separation and legal custody of her son. The prison governor took a copy of the decree to Verlaine in his cell at Mons. Devastated, the poet wept bitterly and an hour or two later requested to see the prison chaplain. His conversion to Catholicism inspired much of his future work, most notably *Sagesse*, published in 1881, and *Parallèlement*, published eight years later, both of which are filled with a spirit of penitential introspection. On release from prison he unsuccessfully attempted to enter a monastery. His subsequent life was characterized by repeated cycles of relapse and repentance.

There are, of course, notable differences between Verlaine's life and Wilde's. Yet the similarities are remarkable. Furthermore, the similarities go deeper than the purely biographical. On an artistic level, within the context of the Catholic literary revival, Wilde belongs with Verlaine, Baudelaire and Huysmans more than he does with his English contemporaries. He stands, in fact, as the French connection between the parallel revivals in both countries.

Obviously Wilde was influenced by the Catholic literary revival in England which rose phoenix-like out of the ashes of the Oxford Movement under Newman's patronage and inspiration. Ultimately, however, he had little in common with many of the converts who had followed Newman's example. Coventry Patmore, Robert Stephen Hawker, F.W. Faber and Gerard Manley Hopkins were all deeply religious men before their entry into the Church. Their conversions were theologically driven. They found the fullness of an already existent faith in Catholic dogma. They had never tried naturalism as a way of life as had Baudelaire, Verlaine, Huysmans, Maurice Barres and Paul Bourget. Consequently, while the two revivals enjoyed a parallel existence, they derived their sustenance from a widely differing intellectual and ethical soil.

There were among the English literary converts no penitent souls weighed down with the burden of sin, no disillusioned agnostics convinced by bitter experience of the emptiness of life on the naturalistic level. In this sense, Wilde belongs with the 'sinners' of the French revival rather than the 'saints' of its English counterpart. Furthermore, he can be seen as the father of the English decadence in much the same way as Baudelaire was father of the French. He stands in relation to later decadent converts to Catholicism, such as Ernest Dowson and Aubrey Beardsley, in much the same way that Baudelaire stands in relation to Verlaine and Huysmans. The parallel, however, must not be overstated. Whereas Baudelaire's approach was genuinely innovative, Wilde's was very much derivative. Wilde, never an original sinner, had picked up the taste for decadence as a French fashion accessory, flaunting it with provocative affectation in the face of Victorian convention.

'One had, in the late eighties and early nineties, to be preposterously French,' complained Victor Plarr, Ernest Dowson's biographer, 'and to spectators of this psychological aberration, especially to genuine French spectators ... the sight of young Englishmen discovering an unworthy side of France would have been disgusting had it not been mainly comic.'[11] In Wilde's case it would be mainly tragic.

1 *Life*, 19 June 1884; quoted in Ellmann, *Oscar Wilde*, p. 237.
2 *Morning News*, 20 June 1884.
3 Mikhail, *Interviews and Recollections*, vol. 1, p. 195.
4 Robert Baldick, *The Life of J.K. Huysmans*, Oxford: Clarendon Press, 1955, pp. 85–6.
5 Ibid., p. 86.
6 Ibid.
7 Ibid., p. 91.
8 Ibid.
9 Barbara Beaumont (ed.), *The Road from Decadence, From Brothel to Cloister: Selected Letters of J.K. Huysmans*, London: Athlone Press, 1989, p. 166.
10 Hart-Davis, *Letters of Oscar Wilde*, pp. 287–8.
11 Victor Plarr, *Ernest Dowson*, London: Elkin Mathews, 1914, pp. 22–3.

ELEVEN

Truth and Masks

Be warned in time, James; and remain, as I do, incomprehensible: to be great is to be misunderstood.

Oscar and Constance had barely become accustomed to married life in London when Wilde embarked on another major lecture tour of the provinces. Throughout the final months of 1884 he enlightened his audiences on the higher aesthetics in places as diverse as York, Ealing, Bristol, Stoke-on-Trent and Leeds. His subjects included 'The Value of Art in Modern Life' and 'Beauty, Taste and Ugliness in Dress'. He spoke on both these themes in Edinburgh on 20 December; on 'Dress' at 3 p.m. and on 'Art' at 8 p.m. Yet his considerable fame did not guarantee packed houses. The *Scotsman* reported 'a meagre attendance' for the second of the lectures.

It was from Edinburgh that Wilde wrote to his 'dear and beloved' Constance, lamenting the fact that the lecture tour was keeping their lips from kissing, 'though our souls are one'. Even in his wife's absence, Wilde took consolation in the fresh memories of nuptial pleasures. 'I feel your fingers in my hair, and your cheek brushing mine. The air is full of the music of your voice, my soul and body seem no longer mine, but mingled in some exquisite ecstasy with yours. I feel incomplete without you. Ever and ever yours.'[1] Unfortunately, this is one of a mere handful of Wilde's letters to Constance which is known to have survived. The rest were almost certainly destroyed by Constance or her family. Although such destruction is perfectly understandable, posterity is sadly impoverished, and deprived of any in-depth understanding of the nature of their love and their married life. Instead, all too often, all that remains is hearsay evidence from unreliable sources.

When Wilde wrote this letter to Constance she was already in the early months of pregnancy. According to Frank Harris, a less than trustworthy source, Wilde was not enamoured with the sight of his wife's swollen body. In fact, if Harris is to be believed, Wilde found Constance's pregnant body repulsive. Habitually, Harris invented in hindsight, though allegedly from memory, speeches which Wilde was said to have related to him personally. Such speeches often fail to ring true but these words are more plausible than some:

> When I married, my wife was a beautiful girl, white and slim as a lily, with dancing eyes and gay rippling laughter like music. In a year or so the flowerlike grace had all vanished; she became heavy, shapeless, deformed. She dragged herself about the house in uncouth misery with drawn blotched face and hideous body, sick at heart because of our love. It was dreadful. I tried to be kind to her; forced myself to touch and kiss her; but she was sick always, and – oh! I cannot recall it, it is all loathsome ... I used to wash my mouth and open the window to cleanse my lips in the pure air.[2]

The contrast between this sense of loathing and the love expressed so eloquently in the letter is astonishing. If both accounts are truthful expressions of what Wilde was feeling in 1885 he was evidently in a state of some confusion. Either he was telling a lie, to Constance or to Frank Harris, or he was living a lie.

Constance gave birth to their first son, Cyril, on 5 June 1885. Within eight months she was pregnant again, their second son, Vyvyan, being born in November 1886.

Meanwhile, the contradictions inherent in Wilde's character were finding wilder and wilder expression in his art criticism. In May 1885 his essay 'The Truth of Masks' was published in *The Nineteenth Century*. Its conclusion was not only baffling but was deliberately designed to baffle. Drama critics were required to 'cultivate a sense of beauty', he wrote, adding a sentence or so later that drama should have 'the illusion of truth for its method, and the illusion of beauty for its result'. Was the sense of beauty to be cultivated only an illusion? Was beauty itself an illusion? Was truth an illusion? And if truth was an illusion, a mask, could there be a 'truth of masks'? How could masks be true if truth was only an illusion? None of these questions were addressed, but merely fudged with the trite dismissal that 'a Truth in art is that whose contradictory is also true'. Possibly to cover his retreat from the logically untenable position, Wilde was also careful to include a disclaimer in his conclusion. 'Not that I agree with everything that I have said in this essay. There is much with which I entirely disagree.' Ultimately *what* he had said did not really matter anyway. It was the *way* he had said it: 'in aesthetic criticism attitude is everything'.

Wilde's attitudes fluctuated as often as his opinions. On 14 January 1885 he had written that 'Keats's grave is a hillock of green grass with a plain headstone, and is to me the holiest place in Rome'.[3] Yet in implicitly anti-Keatsian mood he told Margot Asquith that 'I hate views – they are only made for bad painters ... Let us go in – the sound of a cuckoo makes me sick.'[4]

There were also indications that Wilde's attitude to aestheticism was changing. After the novel excitements of French decadence, his own aesthetic views appeared boring by comparison. His views on the beauties of Shakespearean costume, or women's dress, or the ugliness of grand pianos, could not compete with the sick flowers of Baudelaire or the beautiful sins of Huysmans.

Wilde's boredom with his old-style aestheticism surfaced in a letter to T.H. Escott, editor of *The World*, early in 1885. After considering Escott's proposal that he should write an essay on aestheticism, Wilde replied that he was 'a little in doubt about the subject'. He had said everything he wanted to say already, particularly in his lectures. Instead, he expressed a desire to write about 'Impressionism in Literature'.[5] Wilde's reticence may also have been linked to a recent attack on his aestheticism by his friend James McNeill Whistler. On 20 February 1885 Whistler had delivered his famous Ten O'Clock lecture on art in the Prince's Hall, London. Much of it was a scathing and scarcely disguised attack on Wilde. 'The voice of the aesthete is heard in the land,' he declared with distaste, adding categorically that he was not to be identified with aestheticism. Without naming Wilde directly, Whistler attacked the position Wilde had taken on his recent lecture tours. Beginning with dilettantism about dress reform, he said the aesthete wanted costume, but 'costume is not dress'.

Wilde was in the audience and must have been stung by Whistler's attacks, yet his account of the lecture, published in the following day's edition of the *Pall Mall Gazette*, was restrained and charitable. Wilde praised Whistler's 'really marvellous eloquence', describing the lecture as a masterpiece and the lecturer, alliteratively, as 'a miniature Mephistopheles, mocking the majority'. Nonetheless, he begged to differ with some of Whistler's strictures on art:

> That an artist will find beauty in ugliness, *le beau dans l'horrible*, is now a commonplace of the schools ... but I strongly deny that charming people should be condemned to live with magenta ottomans and Albert blue curtains in their rooms in order that some painter may observe the side lights on the one and the values of the other. Nor do I accept the dictum that only a painter is a judge of painting. I say that only an artist is a judge of art; there is a wide difference ... For there are not many arts, but one art merely: poem, picture and Parthenon, sonnet and statue – all are in their essence the same, and he who knows one knows all. But the poet is the supreme artist, for he is the master of colour and of form, and the real musician besides, and is lord over all life and all arts; and so to the poet beyond all others are these mysteries known; to Edgar Allan Poe and to Baudelaire, not to Benjamin West and Paul Delaroche.

Wilde's comments about the supremacy of the poet were barbed and intended to strike home. Even if his overall tone had been restrained this one riposte was an act of revenge. Whistler, never one to let an opponent have the last word, wrote Wilde a reply which was published in *The World* on 25 February.

> I have read your exquisite article in the *Pall Mall*. Nothing is more delicate, in the flattery of 'the Poet' to 'the Painter', than the *naïveté* of 'the Poet' in the choice of his Painters – Benjamin West and Paul Delaroche!
>
> You have pointed out that 'the Painter's' mission is to find '*le beau dans l'horrible*', and have left to 'the Poet' the discovery of '*l'horrible* dans '*le beau*'!

Wilde's response, also published in *The World*, stated sarcastically that the greatest mistake of Benjamin West and Paul Delaroche was that they 'recklessly took to lecturing on Art': 'As of their works nothing at all remains, I conclude that they explained themselves away. Be warned in time, James; and remain, as I do, incomprehensible: to be great is to be misunderstood.'[6]

Such a *pas de deux* in public by two of society's most celebrated wits was delightful entertainment for readers of *The World*. Offstage, however, the interchange had soured their relationship. Wilde was not as vituperative or as vindictive as Whistler and, initially, he was saddened by the cooling of their friendship. He was also a little nervous of further attacks in the future. 'There is an ominous silence from "Jimmy",' he wrote to T.H. Escott, 'if he sends any letter to the *World* I wish you would not publish it till I can write my answer. There is no delight unless both guns go off together.'[7] In the event the ominous silence continued for more than a year. Whistler, however, was simmering, waiting for the appropriate moment to launch his next attack. It came in November 1886 when Whistler heard that the Committee of the National Art Exhibition had invited Wilde to become one of its members. On 17 November *The World* dutifully published his letter to the Committee in which he declared that Wilde's membership was a 'farce' which would bring upon the Committee the 'scorn and ridicule of your *confrères* in Europe'.

> What has Oscar in common with Art? except that he dines at our tables and picks from our platters the plums for the pudding he peddles in the provinces. Oscar – the amiable, irresponsible, esurient Oscar – with no more sense of a picture than of the fit of a coat, has the courage of the opinions – of others!

Wilde countered in *The World* on 24 November: 'this is very sad! With our James "vulgarity begins at home", and should be allowed to stay there.' Whistler was unimpressed, replying privately to Wilde: ' "A poor thing", Oscar – but, for once, I suppose, "your own"!'[8]

A few years later Wilde gave Whistler an irresistible opportunity to renew his attacks when he unwisely, and presumably inadvertently, used Whistler's joke concerning the courage of the opinion of others in his essay 'The Decay of Lying'. In doing so he had stolen his own scalp, Whistler chortled. On 2 January 1890, *Truth* published a caustic letter from Whistler on the subject of Wilde's alleged plagiarism.

Among your ruthless exposures of the shams of today, nothing, I confess, have I enjoyed with keener relish than your late tilt at that arch-impostor and pest of the period – the all-pervading plagiarist!

... How was it that, in your list of culprits, you omitted that fattest of offenders – our own Oscar?

Wilde's defence, published the following week, showed none of the restraint of his earlier ripostes. This was Wilde emulating Whistler not in terms of his art criticism or his wit, but in terms of the bitterness of his invective:

I can hardly imagine that the public are in the very smallest degree interested in the shrill shrieks of 'Plagiarism' that proceed from time to time out of the lips of silly vanity or incompetent mediocrity.

However, as Mr James Whistler has had the impertinence to attack me with both venom and vulgarity in your columns, I hope you will allow me to state that the assertions contained in his letter are as deliberately untrue as they are deliberately offensive.

The definition of a disciple as one who has the courage of the opinions of his master is really too old even for Mr Whistler to be allowed to claim it, and as for borrowing Mr Whistler's ideas about art, the only thoroughly original ideas I have ever heard him express have had reference to his own superiority over painters greater than himself.

It is a trouble for any gentleman to have to notice the lucubrations of so ill-bred and ignorant a person as Mr Whistler, but your publication of his insolent letter left me no option in the matter.

Whistler replied a week later, determined, as ever, to have the last word. In mock humility he apologized for being responsible for 'the incarnation – Oscar Wilde'. Later in the year Wilde took one last sideswipe in Whistler's direction in his essay 'The Critic as Artist', where he wrote that accusations of plagiarism 'proceed either from the thin colourless lips of impotence, or from the grotesque mouths of those who, possessing nothing of their own, fancy that they can gain a reputation for wealth by crying out that they have been robbed'. Thus, in an acrid and acrimonious atmosphere, the friendly rivalry between Wilde and Whistler was finally vanquished by bitter enmity.

Meanwhile the strange duality in Wilde's feelings towards Constance continued. An intriguing insight into their relationship in July 1886 was provided by Anna, Comtesse de Brémont, an American who had first met Wilde in New York during his lecture tour four years earlier. The Comtesse's first impressions of Constance were both favourable and effusive:

Constance Wilde! As I write a vision of her sweet face and graceful personality seems to arise in the vista of the past. A face whose loveliness was derived more from the expression and exquisite colouring than from any claim to the regular lines that constitute beauty. Sympathy, sensitiveness and shyness were expressed in that charming womanly face, and revealed a character intensely feminine.

She was wearing an 'exquisite Greek costume of cowslip yellow and apple leaf green' and her hair, 'a thick mass of ruddy brown, was wonderfully set off by bands of yellow ribbon'. These impressions were gained at a reception at the Wildes' house in Tite Street. As Wilde introduced the Comtesse to his wife, Constance exhibited 'an air of shy self-consciousness and restraint':

'My wife,' said Oscar Wilde, as we paused before her. Then he whispered, but not too low for me to hear:

'You are looking lovely, Constance – not a bit too tired with all these people.'

I saw her sweet face light up, and all the shyness and nervousness melt out of her eyes under those words of approval from her husband and teacher.[9]

Perhaps Wilde's concern for Constance was related to the fact that she was five months pregnant with their second child. Indeed, it is likely that the loose and flowing folds of Constance's 'exquisite Greek costume' had been devised to conceal the signs of her impending maternity.

In spite of Constance's evident delight at her husband's praise, the Comtesse still detected that she seemed 'bored and overwrought by the part she was playing before all those people – the aesthetic pose that she was not fitted to take'. Soon afterwards, the Comtesse recalled, Wilde dominated proceedings with a brilliant display of intellectual fireworks. Constance, who had probably heard it all before, and more than once, subsided into the background, 'completely forgotten and eclipsed by the brilliant glow of her husband's eloquence'. When the Comtesse looked about for her, she caught sight of her beyond the doorway, in the crush of people in the hall, 'a rapt expression of love and pride on her face, while her eyes were fixed, as one magnetized, on her husband's inspired features'. Trusting the evidence of her own eyes, Anna, Comtesse de Brémont, had no doubt that Oscar Wilde and his wife were still 'fondly devoted to one another'. 'A son had been born to them,' she wrote, 'and the future was all rose-coloured.'[10]

The problem was that Wilde no longer saw life as rose-coloured. He was developing an altogether darker vision which would plague both him and his wife in the years ahead.

A glimpse of the emerging differences between Wilde and Constance can be gleaned from the poet Richard Le Gallienne. He recalled that Constance was 'evangelically religious' and had a particular interest in missionaries. 'Missionaries, my dear!' Wilde remarked to his wife when the subject came up at a dinner party. 'Don't you realize that missionaries are the divinely provided food for destitute and underfed cannibals? Whenever they are on the brink of starvation, Heaven, in its infinite mercy, sends them a nice plump missionary.' 'Oh, Oscar!' Constance exclaimed with a shocked expression. 'You surely cannot be in earnest. You can only be joking!'[11] Wilde was, of course, joking, but the humour exposed his prurience as surely as Constance's response had exposed her puritanism.

The prurience of Wilde's darker vision was the legacy of his time in Paris. Its flavour was distinctly French, spiced with the exotic sins of Huysmans and scented with the sickly odour of Baudelaire. It was evident in a letter to a friend early in 1886. There was, he declared, 'no such thing as a romantic experience; there are romantic memories, and there is the desire of romance – that is all'. Romance, like truth, was only a mask and therefore, ultimately, an illusion. Furthermore, since everything was illusory, the only thing that remained 'infinitely fascinating' was 'the mystery of moods'. 'To be master of these moods is exquisite, to be mastered by them more exquisite still. Sometimes I think that the artistic life is a long and lovely suicide, and am not sorry that it is so ... There is an unknown land full of strange flowers and subtle perfumes, a land of which it is joy of all joys to dream, a land where all things are perfect and poisonous.' Immediately, as though by way of recantation, he added that he had been reading Walter Scott during the previous week and urged his correspondent to do likewise: 'you too should read him, for there is nothing of all this in him'. It was almost as if the romance of Scott was an antidote, a cure, for the narcotic decadence that he was finding ever harder to resist. 'I myself would sacrifice everything for a new experience, and I know there is no such thing as a new experience at all.'[12]

Wilde was now ripe for the new experience he craved. It would take him a little longer to confirm the truth of the afterthought – that there was no such thing as a new experience. The 'new' experiences were merely old sins wearing masks.

In 1886 Wilde approached the edge of the abyss. All that was needed for his long and lovely suicide was to take one step forward.

1 Hart-Davis, *Letters of Oscar Wilde*, p. 165.
2 Frank Harris, *Oscar Wilde, His Life and Confessions* (1930), quoted in Ellmann, *Oscar Wilde*, p. 250.
3 Hart-Davis, *Letters of Oscar Wilde*, p. 169.
4 Ellmann, *Oscar Wilde*, p. 131.
5 Oscar Wilde, letter to T.H. Escott, undated (early 1885), Manuscripts Department, British Library.
6 Hart-Davis, *Letters of Oscar Wilde*, pp. 170–1.
7 Oscar Wilde, letter to T.H. Escott, undated (1885?), Manuscripts Department, British Library.
8 Hart-Davis, *Letters of Oscar Wilde*, p. 191.
9 Ervine, *Oscar Wilde: A Present Time Appraisal*, pp. 47–8.
10 Ibid., pp. 48–9.
11 Hyde, *Annotated Oscar Wilde*, pp. 12–13.
12 Hart-Davis, *Letters of Oscar Wilde*, p. 185.

TWELVE

Purity and Passion

Being ourselves the sowers and the seeds,
  The night that covers and the lights that fade,
The spear that pierces and the side that bleeds,
  The lips betraying and the life betrayed;
The deep hath calm: the moon hath rest: but we
Lords of the natural world are yet our own dread enemy.

In 1886 Wilde met a precocious seventeen-year-old, Robert Baldwin Ross, a Canadian of Ulster descent whose grandfather had been the first Prime Minister of Upper Canada and whose father had been Attorney-General in the Upper Canada Government. When Ross was first introduced to Wilde, he was studying to go up to King's College, Cambridge where his undergraduate career would be cut short by a nervous breakdown and other troubles. Ross was a great admirer of Wilde's poetry and adopted many of Wilde's aesthetic affectations as his own. A homosexual, he was determined from the outset to seduce his hero. Ultimately he was successful, the master succumbing to the advances of the disciple. Although it is generally accepted that Ross was responsible for introducing Wilde to homosexual practices, it is not certain when he actually succeeded in doing so. Ross told Frank Harris that he was 'the first boy Oscar ever had' and he made a similar admission to Arthur Ransome.[1] It is likely that sexual relations began fairly soon after their first meeting and it is certain that such a relationship existed by the following year when Ross stayed with Wilde for a two-month period.[2]

Apparently, Constance remained blissfully ignorant of Wilde's sexual activities. Nonetheless, their impact was felt within the marriage.

Conjugal relations ceased at around this time, and Wilde began to absent himself from the family home for ever longer periods.

The sexual subterfuge which now became an integral part of Wilde's life is evident in a curious episode recounted by Charles Hirsch, a bookseller who had moved from Paris to London to open a bookshop specializing in the sale of French literature. Wilde was one of Hirsch's earliest and most valued customers, buying the works of contemporary French authors such as Zola and Maupassant. Shortly after he had been initiated into homosexual activity by Ross, Wilde began to order 'certain licentious works of a special *genre*', which he euphemistically described as 'socratic'. Wilde trusted in Hirsch's discretion, taking him into his confidence, and the bookseller obtained these titles for him 'not without difficulty'.

One day in 1890, Wilde came into the bookshop carrying a small package, which was carefully wrapped up and sealed. He gave instructions for it to be passed on to a certain person who would call in to collect it. The person would show Wilde's card as a means of establishing his credentials. A few days later, the package was collected. When it was returned, carefully wrapped, Hirsch was given instructions for it to be passed on to another caller. The procedure was repeated three times. The last borrower, more careless than the others, returned the manuscript unwrapped and simply tied round with a piece of ribbon. The bookseller, his curiosity aroused by the furtive transactions, could not resist the temptation to open the manuscript and read it. On the greyish paper cover which held together the pages there was a single word, 'Teleny'. That evening Hirsch read the manuscript and discovered that it was a homoerotic novel about a rich Parisian and his relationship with a young boy.[3]

The contradictions at the heart of Wilde's personality, its complexities and perplexities, were exacerbated by the increasing respectability of his public position. It was ironic that Wilde's adoption of homosexuality in private coincided with his new image in public as a respectable married man. Whistler had dubbed Wilde contemptuously as '*le bourgeois malgré lui*'[4] and the *Pall Mall Gazette*, on 16 September 1887, reported wryly that 'Oscar's star has been low in the horizon since he cut his hair and became "Benedick the married man".' The respectable married persona was emphasized still further in April 1887 when Wilde agreed to become editor of *Woman's World*. Throughout the summer of 1887 much of his time was taken up with writing letters to numerous literary ladies, beseeching them to contribute articles to the magazine. Typical of these was a letter he wrote to Minnie Simpson, the socialite and writer, informing her of his appointment to *Woman's World*. He was, he wrote, 'anxious to make it an organ through which women of culture and position will be able to give expression to their views'. To illustrate the point, he listed several women of culture and position who had already agreed to write for the magazine, stating by way of added incentive that 'the honorarium will be a guinea a page' and requesting an article 'on some literary subject – some woman of letters for instance – or some salon in Paris'. At present the magazine could not accept fiction. Her article would be illustrated if she so desired, as he believed 'that illustrations always give a charm to an article, though I dislike them in a novel'.[5] His efforts, in the case of Minnie Simpson, proved successful as later correspondence testifies.

Wilde's increasingly respectable reputation was bolstered in February 1887 by the publication of *The Canterville Ghost* in *The Court and Society Review*. In many respects this story, which weaves the tale of the hapless ghost's unsuccessful efforts to haunt a stately home, is the most charming of all Wilde's works. The humour rolls through the story with ease, an echo of the charm and wit with which its author beguiled the dinner tables of London. Yet, as with so much of Wilde's work, *The Canterville Ghost* is ultimately a tale of morality. The mirth is only a means to an end, and the end is unequivocally moral. The ghost is condemned, through the sins he committed in his earthly life, to continue haunting the house until the prophecy on the library window is fulfilled:

When a golden girl can win
Prayer from out the lips of sin,
When the barren almond bears,
And a little child gives away its tears,
Then shall all the house be still
And peace come to Canterville.

The ghost is befriended by Virginia, the fifteen-year-old daughter of the house, who takes pity on him. The ghost realizes that she is both the golden girl and the little child in the prophecy who can free him from the centuries-old curse. Desiring the peace that reigns in the Garden of Death, he pleads with Virginia to help him. 'To forget time, to forgive life, to be at peace. You can help me. You can open for me the portals of Death's house, for Love is always with you, and Love is stronger than Death is.' He explains the meaning of the words of prophecy:

> 'They mean ... that you must weep for me for my sins, because I have no tears, and pray with me for my soul, because I have no faith, and then, if you have always been sweet, and good, and gentle, the Angel of Death will have mercy on me. You will see fearful shapes in darkness, and wicked voices will whisper in your ear, but they will not harm you, for against the purity of a little child the powers of Hell cannot prevail.'

Virginia overcomes her fear and agrees to go with him into the unknown. 'I am not afraid ... and I will ask the Angel to have mercy on you.'

The whole episode, which forms the crux and the pivotal moment in the story, resonates with scarcely shrouded allusions to the Annunciation. The purity of the child, her faith and her love, are essential to the ghost's deliverance and it is surely no coincidence that Wilde chooses to call his heroine Virginia. At the story's conclusion Virginia expresses her debt to the Canterville Ghost in terms which encapsulate the moral of the tale. 'He made me see what Life is, and what Death signifies, and why Love is stronger than both.'

The Canterville Ghost may have reiterated the moral theme of much of Wilde's earlier work but it also marked a significant change in literary form and direction. For the next few years he would largely neglect the composition of verse in favour of writing short stories. In May 1887 *The Sphinx without a Secret* was published in *The World* and a month later the same periodical published Wilde's *The Model Millionaire. Lord Arthur Savile's Crime* was published in *The Court and Society Review* before the end of the year. Yet it was the publication of *The Happy Prince and Other Tales* in May 1888 which really established Wilde's reputation as an author. The *Athenaeum* compared Wilde to Hans Christian Andersen, an accolade which was a far cry from his earlier reputation as the doyen of decadence, but it was the praise of Walter Pater which most pleased Wilde. On 12 June Pater had written to Wilde from Brasenose College, Oxford, enthusing over the 'delightful' stories in the book. He couldn't decide whether he admired most the 'wise wit' of 'The Remarkable Rocket' or the 'beauty and tenderness' of 'The Selfish Giant', adding that 'the latter certainly is perfect in its kind'. Pater reserved his most eloquent tribute for last, claiming that 'the whole, too brief, book abounds with delicate touches and pure English'.[6] Wilde's delight on receipt of Pater's comments was evident in a letter he wrote to the publisher, Alfred Nutt, a day or so later. 'Mr Pater has written me a wonderful letter about my prose, so I am in high spirits.'[7]

Like *The Canterville Ghost*, the stories in *The Happy Prince and Other Tales* abound with Christian imagery and mysticism. Love and sacrifice are interwoven in the central thread that runs through all the tales. Ellmann writes that 'Wilde presents the stories like sacraments of a lost faith'.[8] Yet faith is not lost in the stories but found, rediscovered. However much Wilde may have been struggling with his own faith, it always emerges triumphant in the stories. It is almost as though he is using his art to escape from the wretchedness of his life. As Ellmann admits, the tales 'often begin with disfigurement and end ... in transfiguration'.[9] This was quite literally the theme of 'The Happy Prince'. The eponymous character is a beautiful statue who stands on a tall column overlooking the city. He is 'gilded all over with thin leaves of fine gold' and his eyes are sapphires. He is befriended by a swallow who must shortly depart for Africa before the arrival of winter. Saddened by all the suffering he sees in the city, the Prince insists that the swallow strip him of all his jewelled finery and deliver it to the poor. At the Prince's insistence, the swallow removes the sapphires from his eyes and carries them off to give to a poor student and a match-girl. 'You are blind now,' the swallow tells the Prince, 'so I will stay with you always.' When winter arrives, the swallow dies at the Prince's feet and, simultaneously, the Prince's leaden heart snaps in two. The town councillors are horrified by the dilapidated state of the statue. 'How shabby, indeed!' they agree in unison.

'The ruby has fallen out of his sword, his eyes are gone, and he is golden no longer,' said the Mayor; 'in fact, he is little better than a beggar!'

'Little better than a beggar,' said the Town Councillors.

'And here is actually a dead bird at his feet!' continued the Mayor.

'We must really issue a proclamation that birds are not to be allowed to die here.'

The statue of the Happy Prince is unceremoniously demolished and the metal melted down.

'What a strange thing!' said the overseer of the workmen at the foundry. 'This broken lead heart will not melt in the furnace. We must throw it away.' So they threw it on a dust-heap where the dead Swallow was also lying.

'Bring me the two most precious things in the city,' said God to one of His Angels; and the Angel brought Him the leaden heart and the dead bird.

'You have rightly chosen,' said God, 'for in my garden of Paradise this little bird shall sing for evermore, and in my city of gold the Happy Prince shall praise me.'

In the story of 'The Happy Prince' Wilde had moved from the implicit morality of his earlier poetry and prose to the realm of outright Christian parable. This is continued in 'The Selfish Giant' where the Giant, cured of his selfishness by the love of a child, is infuriated to see that the child has the prints of nails on his hands and his feet. The child quells his anger, insisting that 'these are the wounds of Love'. In 'The Nightingale and the Rose' a more subtle approach is adopted. The message is nonetheless clear. The Nightingale embodies the spirit of sacrificial love, ultimately even unto death, but the gift of the Rose, for which she lays down her life, is rejected by the lovers for whom it is intended. When the student presents the Rose to the professor's daughter she frowns. 'I am afraid it will not go with my dress ... and, besides, the Chamberlain's nephew has sent me some real jewels, and everyone knows that jewels cost far more than flowers.' Incensed at her ingratitude, the student throws the Rose into the street, where it falls into the gutter and is run over by a cartwheel.

The charm and wit of Wilde's table manner are more to the fore in the other two stories in the collection. 'The Remarkable Rocket' is a satire on vanity which may have been aimed at Whistler, but was surely as applicable to the public image which Wilde had sought to project of himself. 'You should be thinking about others,' said the

Rocket. 'In fact, you should be thinking about me. I am always thinking about myself, and I expect everybody else to do the same.' On
another occasion, referring disingenuously to a tragedy in someone
else's life, the Rocket remarks that 'I certainly am very much affected'.

'You certainly are!' cries the Bengal Light. 'In fact, you are the most
affected person I ever met.'

Clearly, such an exchange could have been intended as a gibe
against Whistler but it is difficult to conceive that it wasn't also
intended as an act of self-criticism or self-ridicule aimed at his own
public posturing. It is a display of his own humanity and humility
and illustrates his disarming ability to laugh at himself.

A similar tongue-in-cheek approach was apparent in 'The Devoted
Friend'. The story, recounted by the Linnet to the Water-rat, is a parable on friendship in which the selflessness of one long-suffering
friend is compared with the selfishness of the other. Yet the real
genius of the story resides not so much in the parable as in the postscript to the story which contains a parable about the parable, or a
moral about the moral.

> 'I am afraid you don't quite see the moral of the story,' remarked the
> Linnet.
>
> 'The what?' screamed the Water-rat.
>
> 'The moral.'
>
> 'Do you mean that the story has a moral?'
>
> 'Certainly,' said the Linnet.
>
> 'Well, really,' said the Water-rat, in a very angry manner, 'I think you
> should have told me that before you began. If you had done so, I
> certainly would not have listened to you; in fact, I should have said
> "Pooh", like the critic. However, I can say it now'; so he shouted out
> 'Pooh', at the top of his voice, gave a whisk of his tail, and went back
> into his hole.

The parenthetical conclusion to Wilde's story also serves as the
paradoxical conclusion that Wilde may have been coming to about
himself. It was almost as though the dialogue between the Linnet and
the Water-rat was a battle between the two halves of the author's own
character, between the romantic moralist and the amoral cynic. The
Linnet sang of sacrifice and love, of purity and passion; the Water-rat

sacrificed love for cynicism, and poisoned the passion with impurity. Wilde, more than ever, was at war with himself.

1 Hyde, *Oscar Wilde*, p. 185.
2 Hart-Davis, *Letters of Oscar Wilde*, p. 862.
3 Hyde, *Oscar Wilde*, p. 185.
4 Quoted in Ellmann, *Oscar Wilde*, p. 259.
5 Oscar Wilde, letter to Minnie Simpson, 1887 (June?), unpublished manuscript in the National Library of Wales, Aberystwyth.
6 Lawrence Evans (ed.), *Letters of Walter Pater*, Oxford: Clarendon Press, 1970, p. 85.
7 Hart-Davis, *Letters of Oscar Wilde*, p. 219.
8 Ellmann, *Oscar Wilde*, p. 282.
9 Ibid.

THIRTEEN

Poison and Passion

There is an unknown land full of strange flowers and subtle perfumes
... a land where all things are perfect and poisonous.

In June 1888, even as Wilde was being lauded for the morality of the
stories in the newly published *The Happy Prince*, the secretive side
of his alter ego was surfacing in another casual homosexual liaison.
This time his partner was the young poet Richard Le Gallienne, who
was, like Ross, a disciple of Wilde's. It is not known whether Wilde
was seducer or seduced on this occasion but the seduction appears to
have happened when Le Gallienne was staying with the Wildes at
Tite Street. During his stay, and presumably while Constance was
otherwise engaged, Wilde presented Le Gallienne with a copy of
his *Poems* inscribed 'To Richard Le Gallienne, poet and lover, from
Oscar Wilde. A summer day in June '88.' Le Gallienne responded with
a poem entitled 'With Oscar Wilde, A Summer-Day in June '88'.
Attached to the verse was a further inscription: 'This copy of verse I
have made for my friend Oscar Wilde, as a love-token, and in secret
memory of a summer day in June '88.' It appears that Le Gallienne
soon regretted the secret memory, remarking to a friend later in the
year that two letters from Wilde were 'very rich'.[1] Wilde, however,
continued to hope for a renewal of their intimacy, writing as late as
1 December 1890 that 'I want so much to see you', adding that he
hoped 'the laurels are not too thick across your brow for me to kiss
your eyelids'.[2]

Wilde, having been introduced to the strange flowers and subtle
perfumes of homosexuality by Robert Ross, was developing an insatiable promiscuity. New experiences demanded new partners. The

strange land he was now exploring could be pleasant but never satis-factory. On the contrary, the appetite for his new-found sexuality only served to feed an unmercifully demanding addiction. Furthermore, the addiction demanded duplicity. From now on he would be con-demned to a double life, deceiving his wife on a daily basis.

Wilde's subterranean sexuality was, at this stage, as carefully con-cealed from the public as it was from Constance. He lived a seemingly conventional life, accompanying Constance to an endless array of dinner parties and literary at-homes. 'It will give my wife and myself great pleasure to come to you on Friday,' he wrote in response to one such invitation from the poet and novelist Beatrice May Allhusen.[3] He also shared with Constance an enthusiasm for the emerging socialist movement. They had become friends with the controversial Member of Parliament R.B. Cunninghame Graham, and his wife, the Chilean poetess Gabriela de la Balmondière. In or around 1888 Wilde wrote to Cunninghame Graham, requesting a ticket for a Parliamentary Com-mission which Constance was 'very anxious' to attend.[4]

Cunninghame Graham was a colourful character and was described by Rupert Hart-Davis as 'the most picturesque Scot of his time, traveller, horseman, writer and Socialist campaigner'.[5] On 13 November 1887, the original 'Bloody Sunday', he had taken part in the riot at Trafalgar Square, after which he and the Scottish poet John Barlas were arrested and imprisoned. Wilde was also a friend of Bar-las, who received severe head injuries after being struck by a police-man's truncheon on 'Bloody Sunday'. His reason adversely affected by the injury, he discharged the contents of a revolver outside the Speaker's House in the Palace of Westminster on New Year's Eve 1891, declaring: 'I am an anarchist. What I have done is to show my contempt for the House of Commons.' On 16 January 1892, after a remand in custody and a medical report saying he was not in his right mind, Barlas was bound over to keep the peace in the sum of £200, half of which was guaranteed by Wilde. Barlas wrote to thank Wilde for his help to which Wilde replied that he had done 'merely what you would have done for me', adding that 'we poets and dreamers are all brothers'.[6] Sadly, Barlas, who published eight volumes of verse between 1884 and 1893 and counted among his friends William Morris as well as Wilde, never recovered from his injuries. He died in a lunatic asylum in 1914.

In many respects, Gabriela de la Balmondière, Cunninghame Graham's wife, was as picturesque as her husband. She had eloped with him in 1879, at the age of eighteen, when he was living the life of an adventurer in Argentina. When her husband succeeded to the family estates in 1883 she returned with him to Scotland and London, where she published poems, stories and translations. She shared her husband's enthusiasm for socialism, preaching a potent mixture of socialism and Roman Catholicism. She insisted on the complete political emancipation of women, but her Christian-inspired attacks on liberalism and dialectical materialism incurred the wrath and vociferous opposition of Karl Marx's daughter, Eleanor Marx Aveling. When she lectured to the Bloomsbury Socialist Club on her 'Ideals of Socialism' on 2 July 1889, Wilde's response to her theme indicated his own changing beliefs. Although he found her subject 'most interesting' he had severe reservations: 'what is to become of an indolent hedonist like myself if Socialism and the Church join forces against me? I want to stand apart, and look on, being neither for God nor for his enemies.'[7] Wilde concluded his letter with a request that Mrs Cunninghame Graham remember him to her 'delightful and dangerous husband'.

Wilde's drift into agnosticism was probably genuine enough, but his claim in the same letter to Mrs Cunninghame Graham that he sought a reconciliation of socialism with science seemed disingenuous. Everything he had written previously had sought to counter the claims of science, or scientism, to any meaningful role in life or art. One of the few recurring themes in Wilde's art and criticism was the distaste for rationalism and materialism, either in its philosophical or its scientific form. He had reviewed D.G. Ritchie's *Darwinism and Politics* in the May 1889 issue of *Woman's World*, finding it shallow and unconvincing. It is true that he appears to have developed a fascination for Darwinism at around this time, but only insofar as it fired his artistic imagination as a creed, not insofar as it convinced him of its practical applicability to politics or life. As ever, Wilde's contradictions pose a conundrum. Were they the result of muddle-headed inconsistency or evidence of deliberate evasiveness, a desire to remain intellectually incognito?

Wilde's growing antagonism towards Roman Catholicism was apparent in a letter he wrote in 1888 to the author and journalist Alice Corkran, who had offered to write an article for *Woman's World* on a retreat which she had recently undertaken. 'I suppose it was in a Protestant or an English Catholic convent?' he asked. 'A *Roman* Catholic convent will hardly do.'[8] The gratuitous sectarianism masked a deeper aversion to Christianity in general. He wrote that a retreat for literary people should not be religious but merely a retirement from the world for a short period. To illustrate the point he cited the example of Wordsworth's escape to the Lakes and the idea of standing aloof from practical life which was a recurring feature of Greek philosophy. Such sentiments sat uneasily beside the overt Christian morality which had infused the stories in *The Happy Prince* earlier in the year and were plainly contradicted at the end of the year by 'The Young King', a story published in the Christmas edition of *The Lady's Pictorial*.

'The Young King' was nothing less than a romantic evocation of the socialism and Roman Catholicism advocated by Mrs Cunninghame Graham which Wilde had rejected in his letter to her. Once again, not for the first or the last time, Wilde's art was a blatant contradiction of his public mask.

The eponymous hero of Wilde's tale is afforded a series of visions on the eve of his coronation which reveal the injustices at the heart of the kingdom he is about to inherit. Transformed by the experience, the king emulates St Francis of Assisi. Refusing to wear the gold coronation robe, which he says has been woven on 'the loom of sorrow' and by 'the white hands of Pain', he dresses instead in a shepherd's clothing, takes a rude shepherd's staff, and places a circlet of wild thorns upon his head. He is mocked by the nobles and by the people as he rides to the cathedral for the coronation. Climbing the steps of the altar, he kneels before the image of Christ ...

And suddenly a wild tumult came from the street outside, and in entered the nobles with drawn swords and nodding plumes, and shields of polished steel. 'Where is this dreamer of dreams?' they cried. 'Where is this King, who is apparelled like a beggar – this boy who brings shame upon our state? Surely we will slay him, for he is unworthy to rule over us.'

And the young King bowed his head again, and prayed, and when he had finished his prayer he rose up, and turning round he looked at them sadly.

And lo! through the painted windows came the sunlight streaming upon him, and the sunbeams wove round him a tissued robe that was fairer than the robe that had been fashioned for his pleasure. The dead staff blossomed, and bare lilies that were whiter than pearls. The dry thorn blossomed, and bare roses that were redder than rubies. Whiter than fine pearls were the lilies, and their stems were of bright silver. Redder than male rubies were the roses, and their leaves were of beaten gold.

He stood there in the raiment of a king, and the gates of the jewelled shrine flew open and from the crystal of the many-rayed monstrance shone a marvellous and mystical light. He stood there in a king's raiment, and the Glory of God filled the place, and the saints in their carven niches seemed to move. In the fair raiment of a king he stood before them, and the organ pealed out its music, and the trumpeters blew upon their trumpets, and the singing boys sang.

And the people fell upon their knees in awe, and the nobles sheathed their swords and did homage, and the Bishop's face grew pale, and his hands trembled. 'A greater than I hath crowned thee,' he cried, and he knelt before him.

And the young King came down from the high altar, and passed home through the midst of the people. But no man dared look upon his face, for it was like the face of an angel.

The contradictions at the heart of Wilde's psyche were brought to the fore dramatically within days of the publication of 'The Young King'. In January 1889 his critical essay 'The Decay of Lying' was published in *The Nineteenth Century*. Written in the form of a dialogue, 'The Decay of Lying' replaces the simplicity of the Christian vision in 'The Young King' with a myriad of critical contortions characterized by the author's own inner confusion. At the heart of the confusion is Wilde's inability to differentiate between fact, which is physical, and truth, which is metaphysical. Physical fact and metaphysical truth are continually confused one with the other, so that Wilde does not see art as a conveyer of transcendent truth but as a means of telling a beautiful lie. Art, on the physical level, does not tell the truth but merely distorts the facts. Such a view is a surrender to the scientific materialism which Wilde so evidently despises, and which he attacks in the same essay as 'the prison-house of realism'. At the same time, understood on the metaphysical level, he is repeating the words of Pilate,

'What is Truth?', and dismissing the question with the *reductio ad absurdum* that 'truth is a lie'.

The tragedy at the core of the contortions, and the key which untwists them, is that Wilde had ceased to believe in metaphysical truth while remaining in love with it. 'As for the Church,' says Vivien, Wilde's protagonist in 'The Decay of Lying', 'I cannot conceive anything better for the culture of a country than the presence in it of a body of men whose duty it is to believe in the supernatural, to perform daily miracles, and to keep alive that mythopoeic faculty which is so essential for the imagination. But in the English Church a man succeeds, not through his capacity for belief, but through his capacity for disbelief. Ours is the only Church where the sceptic stands at the altar, and where St Thomas is regarded as the ideal apostle.'

The paradox of Wilde's position is that he believes in the capacity for belief but only possesses the capacity for disbelief. He is in love with the Church but finds himself exiled with the unbelievers. He desires metaphysical truth but can only see it as a beautiful lie.

The rest of Wilde's artistic vision follows on inexorably. Since Truth does not exist, art, the means by which truth is conveyed, ceases to be a means to an unbelievable end but becomes an end in itself. Art for art's sake is only an agnostic substitute for art for God's sake. It is a falling away from a higher truth to a lesser one; or, as Wilde puts it in 'The Decay of Lying', it is like 'the Blue Bird singing of beautiful and impossible things, of things that are lovely and that never happen, of things that are not and that should be'.

Wilde's final twist is an ugly one which poisons the rest of his vision. Since Truth does not exist he insists that 'we must cultivate the lost art of Lying'. The harmful psychological effects of putting such a principle into practice are easy to discern. He who tells the truth, or *believes* he is telling the truth, is worthy of respect and attains self-respect. He who tells lies, and is discovered to be a liar, is always treated with contempt and is prone to self-contempt. Embittered by his own incapacity for belief, Wilde was slowly and self-deceitfully poisoning himself.

In the same month that 'The Decay of Lying' was published in *The Nineteenth Century*, another critical essay, entitled 'Pen, Pencil and Poison', was published in *The Fortnightly Review*. This was a memoir of Thomas Griffiths Wainewright, the art critic and painter, who became notorious as both a perpetrator of fraud and as a mass murderer who poisoned his victims. Heavily in debt, Wainewright committed forgery in 1822 and 1824. In 1828 he probably poisoned his uncle, and two years later his mother-in-law and sister-in-law. Before she was poisoned the sister-in-law had been fraudulently insured for £16,000. It is thought that Wainewright may also have poisoned others but he was never convicted of any of the murders. He was sentenced to life transportation to Australia for the forgery offences and served out the last years of his life painting portraits and eating opium.

It is interesting, perhaps suggestive, that Wilde should find inspiration in such a figure, and even more so when Wilde makes it clear that Wainewright's work has little artistic value: 'it may be partly admitted that, if we set aside his achievements in the sphere of poison, what he has actually left to us hardly justifies his reputation'. It soon becomes clear, since his art does not merit much attention, that Wilde is attracted to Wainewright in his capacity as a liar, a cheat, a forger and, most seductively, a poisoner. 'This young dandy sought to be somebody, rather than to do something. He recognized that Life itself is an art, and has its modes of style no less than the arts that seek to express it.'

Wainewright was attractive to Wilde because he had cultivated the lost art of Lying to a singular degree. He was a 'strange and fascinating figure' whose life as a serial killer and a professional deceiver was itself a work of art and, as such, was above moral strictures. 'I know that there are many historians, or at least writers on historical subjects, who still think it is necessary to apply moral judgments to history ... this, however, is a foolish habit ...' The Artist is not as foolish as the historian. He is able to pay tribute to Wainewright without the constraints of convention. 'Art has not forgotten him. He is the hero of Dickens's *Hunted Down*, the Varney of Bulwer's *Lucretia*, and it is gratifying to note that fiction has paid some homage to one who was so powerful with "pen, pencil and poison". To be suggestive for fiction is to be of more importance than a fact.'

Wilde's pen remained impassioned but was dipped in poison. 'Pen, Pencil and Poison' and 'The Decay of Lying' marked further significant milestones on Wilde's road to ruin, his long and lovely suicide.

1 Ellmann, *Oscar Wilde*, p. 267.
2 Hart-Davis, *Letters of Oscar Wilde*, p. 277.
3 Oscar Wilde, letter to Mrs Allhusen, undated (pre-1890?), British Library, Department of Modern Manuscripts.
4 Oscar Wilde, letter to R.B. Cunninghame Graham, undated (1888?), British Library, Department of Modern Manuscripts.
5 Hart-Davis, *More Letters of Oscar Wilde*, p. 165.
6 Ibid., p. 108.
7 Ibid., p. 84.
8 Ibid., p. 79.

FOURTEEN

Unhappy Hypocrite

I hope you have not been leading a double life, pretending to be wicked
and being really good all the time. That would be hypocrisy.

Throughout the final months of 1888 Wilde was touting his poem
'Symphony in Yellow' to the editors of sundry publications in an
endeavour to get it published. Initially, he met with little success. 'I
am so sorry that on second thoughts you could not print my *Sym-
phonie en jaune*,' he wrote to T.H. Escott, 'second thoughts are very
dangerous as they are usually good: However, *il n'y a pas de rancure*,
and I enclose two little "impressions" of the children flying balloons
in the Tuilery [*sic*] gardens, which perhaps you may like: I admire
them both very much myself.'[1]

'Symphony in Yellow', an attempt to evoke the spirit of the impres-
sionists in verse, would eventually be published in February 1889 by
the *Centennial Magazine* in Sydney. The other verse to which Wilde
refers was presumably 'Le Jardin des Tuileries', which is a joyous evocation of children at play. Its concluding imagery is reminiscent of the
moment in Wilde's story 'The Selfish Giant' when the trees break into
blossom in the midst of winter for sheer joy that the children had
climbed them. 'And the trees were so glad to have the children back
again that they had covered themselves with blossoms, and were
waving their arms gently above the children's heads.'

The genuine nature of Wilde's love for children should be clear
enough from these examples in his art. Yet the best example, in this
case at least, is not drawn from art but life. His younger son, Vyvyan,
remembered golden days spent with his father in the nursery. 'Most
parents in those days were far too solemn and pompous with their

children,' he recalled, 'insisting on a vast amount of usually unde-served respect. My own father was quite different; he had so much of the child in his own nature that he delighted in playing our games.' Vyvyan had vivid and happy memories of his father going down on all fours on the nursery floor, being in turn a lion, a wolf, a horse, 'caring nothing for his usually immaculate appearance'. On one occa-sion Wilde brought home a toy milk-cart drawn by a horse with real hair on it. Dispensing with his usual distaste for realism, he went downstairs and returned with a jug of milk and proceeded to fill the toy churns in the cart. He and the children then had great fun tearing round the nursery, spilling milk all over the place, until the arrival of the nurse put an end to the game.

Vyvyan also remembered that his father spent most of one after-noon repairing a wooden fort that his children had demolished in the course of various wars. 'When he had finished he insisted upon everyone in the house coming to see how well he had done it and to give him a little praise ...'

When he wasn't playing with Cyril and Vyvyan he would tell them fairy stories, or tales of adventure, 'of which he had a never-ending supply'. He was a great admirer of Jules Verne, Robert Louis Steven-son and Rudyard Kipling. He presented Vyvyan with *Treasure Island* and Jules Verne's *Five Weeks in a Balloon*, and the last present he ever gave him before their tragic separation was *The Jungle Book*. Wilde also told his sons all his own written fairy stories. Cyril once asked him why he had tears in his eyes when he told them the story of 'The Selfish Giant', and he replied that really beautiful things always made him cry.[2]

Vyvyan's recollections of his father suggest that it was Wilde's role as paterfamilias which had prompted the switch from verse to fairy stories as his mode of literary expression. This was confirmed in a dis-cussion with Richard Le Gallienne shortly before the publication of *The Happy Prince and Other Tales*. 'It is the duty of every father to write fairy tales for his children,' he began. 'But the mind of a child is a great mystery. It is incalculable, and who shall divine it, or bring to it his own peculiar delights? You humbly spread before it the treasures of your imagination, and they are as dross.' Wilde then presented Le Gallienne with an example to illustrate his point:

...a day or two ago, Cyril yonder came to me with the question, 'Father, do you ever dream?' 'Why of course, my darling. It is the first duty of a gentleman to dream.' 'And what do you dream of?' asked Cyril, with a child's disgusting appetite for facts. Then I, believing, of course, that something picturesque would be expected of me, spoke of magnificent things: 'What do I dream of? Oh, I dream of dragons with gold and silver scales, and scarlet things coming out of their mouths, of eagles with eyes made of diamonds that can see over the whole world at once, of lions with yellow manes, and voices like thunder, of elephants with little houses on their backs, and tigers and zebras with barred and spotted coats ...' So I laboured on with my fancy, till, observing that Cyril was entirely unimpressed, and indeed quite undisguisedly bored, I came to a humiliating stop, and, turning to my son there, I said: 'But tell me, what do you dream of, Cyril?' His answer was like a divine revelation: 'I dream of *pigs*,' he said.[3]

Wilde would also tell his children about Moytura, the house his father had built on Lough Corrib in Ireland. Weaving a spell of Celtic magic, he told them of the 'great melancholy carp' that never moved from the bottom of the lough unless he called them with the Irish songs he had learned from his father. He would sing these songs to the children. Vyvyan remembered one song in particular. It began, '*Atha me in mu codladh, is ne duishe me*' – 'I am asleep, do not wake me.'[4]

There is more than a suspicion that the real Oscar Wilde emerges from the shadows of himself in these unguarded, unobserved moments, alone with his children. The figure who emerges from the nursery is far removed from the decadent debauchee who performs in public. Which is the true Wilde? Is one true and the other a lie? Or are they both true, separate parts of the same personality like the Jekyll and Hyde in Stevenson's story? Has Wilde's secret, hidden from the pharisees and hypocrites, been revealed to little children? Is he open to Cecily's reproach to Algernon in *The Importance of Being Earnest*? 'I hope you have not been leading a double life, pretending to be wicked and being really good all the time. That would be hypocrisy.'

Wilde was acutely aware of the discrepancy between the two worlds in which he moved. Decadence and domesticity did not make good bedfellows and he did his best to keep them apart. The American writer Edgar Saltus observed during a visit to Tite Street that Wilde was a little embarrassed by the bourgeois trappings of his Chelsea home. The two writers had last met when Wilde was in America and Saltus couldn't help noticing the change in Wilde since he had last seen him.

> In appearance and mode of life he had become entirely conventional. The long hair, the knee-breeches, the lilies, the velvet, all the mountebank trappings had gone. He was married, he was a father, and in his house in Tite Street he seemed a bit bourgeois. Of that he may have been conscious. I remember one of his children running and calling at him: 'My good papa!' and I remember Wilde patting the boy and saying: 'Don't call me that, it sounds so respectable.'[5]

The difference in Wilde's attitude to his children when he was being observed by one of his peers adds to the suspicion that his public face was little more than a pose.

During his visit Saltus met Constance, recalling her 'blue eyes, fair hair, chapped lips, and a look of constant bewilderment'. She asked him to sign the visitors' book and as he flicked through the pages one particular entry caught his eye: 'From a poet to a poem ... Robert Browning.' Saltus observed wryly that Wilde 'helped himself to that line', placing it in a poem entitled 'To My Wife with a copy of my poems'. The poem in question, which would not be published until 1893, speaks of Wilde's continuing love for Constance:

> I can write no stately proem
>   As a prelude to my lay;
> From a poet to a poem
>   I would dare to say.
>
> For if of these fallen petals
>   One to you seem fair,
> Love will waft it till it settles
>   On your hair.
>
> And when wind and winter harden
>   All the loveless land,

It will whisper of the garden,
   You will understand.

In July 1889 the illness of one of his sons forced Wilde to put off a visit to Cambridge, where he had arranged to meet Robert Ross and his old friend Oscar Browning. It is evident from Wilde's letter of apology to Browning that he was deeply disappointed. He explained that Constance was 'very nervous' over the state of Cyril, who was suffering from a bad bout of measles, and that she had begged him not to leave town. 'You are so fond of children that I am sure you will understand how one feels about things of this kind, and I think it would be rather horrid of me to go away.'[6] To Robert Ross, he explained that 'terror for Cyril kept me away'.[7] On this occasion, parental duty triumphed over the pursuit of pleasure. It would not always be the case.

At around this time, a new young man entered Wilde's life who, for a time, would eclipse Robert Ross in his affections. This was John Gray, a fascinating figure who warrants more than the status of a footnote in the life of Wilde that posterity has placed upon him. He was the model for the physical beauty of Dorian Gray in Wilde's novel but not, as some writers have implied, for the corrupted character that Dorian Gray becomes as the book progresses. The distinction is crucial.

Dorian Gray is first described in the novel as 'a young man of extraordinary personal beauty'. Wilde told John Gray that he had been the model for this character and Gray, understandably flattered, took to signing himself 'Dorian' in his letters to Wilde. It is, therefore, perhaps not too fanciful to quote the extract from Wilde's novel describing Basil Hallward's first impressions of Dorian Gray as a description of Wilde's first impressions of John Gray.

Well, after I had been in the room about ten minutes, talking to huge overdressed dowagers and tedious Academicians, I suddenly became conscious that some one was looking at me. I turned half-way round, and saw Dorian Gray for the first time. When our eyes met, I felt that I was growing pale. A curious sensation of terror came over me. I knew that I had come face to face with some one whose mere personality was so fascinating that, if I allowed it to do so, it would absorb my whole nature, my whole soul, my very art itself. I did not want any external influence in my life. You know yourself, Harry, how independent I am by nature. I have always been my own master; had at least always been so, till I met Dorian Gray.

When Wilde and Gray first met, probably some time in the summer of 1889, Gray was twenty-three years old. Born on 10 March 1866, he was the eldest of nine children. His father was a journeyman carpenter and wheelwright employed in the Woolwich Dockyard. The family were poor which necessitated Gray's entering full-time employment as soon as possible. Consequently his formal education ended at the age of thirteen. In his spare time, after finishing work as a metal-turner at the Woolwich Arsenal, he took up the study of languages, mastering Latin, French and German. He also taught himself to play the violin. Seeking an escape from the repetitive drudgery of his manual employment, he began to study for the entrance examinations for the Civil Service. In 1884, at the age of eighteen, he passed a competitive examination and gained employment before the end of the year with the post office. In June 1887 he was awarded the London University Matriculation; and in November 1888 he was transferred to the Foreign Office where he worked as a librarian.

Gray's achievement in extricating himself from the bondage of poverty in Victorian London was phenomenal. The considerable obstacles to social mobility in the nineteenth century meant that only the most talented and determined could rise above their allotted station in life. Gray was both, to such a degree that he was dissatisfied with his material successes. Spiritually and aesthetically he remained unfulfilled.

Aesthetically, Gray was a disciple of Wilde which makes it all the more likely that Wilde's first awareness of him was as described in *The Picture of Dorian Gray*. The writer Frank Liebich was at a dinner party in 1889 at which Wilde and Gray were present, and it is conceivable that this was the gathering at which the two men first met. Gray had assiduously exorcised any traces of his working-class accent in order to gain access to these literary soirées, and it is easy to imagine him staring in awe at Wilde until the master noticed the presence of his disciple. In August 1889 the full extent of Gray's discipleship was evident in a fairy-tale he wrote in Wilde's manner, entitled 'The Great Worm', which was published in the *Dial*.

Wilde took full advantage of the master–disciple relationship, setting out to seduce his young admirer. Gray, no doubt still in awe at

the heady heights in which he was now moving, appears to have succumbed readily. Again, an insight into their early friendship can perhaps be gleaned from *The Picture of Dorian Gray* in Basil Hallward's
description of his relationship with Dorian.

'I know he likes me. Of course I flatter him dreadfully. I find a strange
pleasure in saying things to him that I know I shall be sorry for having
said. As a rule, he is charming to me, and we sit in the studio and talk
of a thousand things. Now and then, however, he is horribly thought-
less, and seems to take a real delight in giving me pain. Then I feel,
Harry, that I have given away my soul to some one who treats it as if it
were a flower to put in his coat, a bit of decoration to charm his vanity,
an ornament for a summer's day.'

It is likely that Gray's occasional coolness towards Wilde had less to
do with the charming of his vanity than with the easing of his conscience. Gray's aesthetic, and presumably sexual, attraction to Wilde
coincided almost exactly with his spiritual attraction to Catholicism.
His conversion took place in the summer of 1889, almost simultaneously with his meeting with Wilde. The battle between the two
conflicting passions raged in the depths of Gray's being throughout
the duration of their relationship.

The strength of Gray's religious sensibilities at the time of his conversion, and the stress this must have caused in his relations with
Wilde, are illumined by Gray's own account of the events leading up
to his acceptance of the Catholic faith. He had been invited by a
Catholic friend, Marmaduke Langdale, to stay with him and his family at the Breton fishing village of St Quay-Portrieux. His experience
of life with Langdale's profoundly Catholic family and his admiration
for the simple faith of the Breton peasants were instrumental in his
own decision to join the Communion they shared. Early one morning
he found himself at Mass in a small wayside chapel with half a dozen
peasant women. It was an untidy, neglected place, and the priest, an
unshaven, dishevelled figure, went about his business at the altar in a
slovenly and matter-of-fact manner. It was then that Gray reached a
decision as if by revelation, saying to himself, 'here is the real thing'.[8]

On his return from Brittany, Gray received instruction and was
received into the Church on 10 March 1890. Consequently, it seems

that Wilde's seduction of Gray coincided exactly with Gray's efforts to reform his life. Wilde must have been aware of this and it is possible that he revelled in the perversion of his friend's conversion. The ebb and flow of their relationship would have been closely linked to Gray's efforts to conform his life to the requirements of his faith. Whenever loyalty or love for the Church got the upper hand Wilde's affair with Gray inevitably suffered. Thus, in a perverse inversion of his earlier religious trials, Wilde once again found himself struggling with the Church, though in very different circumstances from those of fifteen years earlier. In fact, since Robert Ross was also becoming increasingly attracted to Rome, Wilde must have felt that the Scarlet Woman of his youth had returned to haunt him. For the time being, however, she held little attraction for him. Insatiably attracted to new experiences, he had no intention of returning to old loves.

The new loves, however, were in love with her even if he wasn't. Through them, she remained as a ghost of his past and an unwanted guest in his present. There was no escape. In his religious conversations with Gray and Ross she would return to probe his heart and to prod accusingly at his conscience. All the time, in spite of the protestations of his friends, he typecast himself in the role of devil's advocate. Even though the Scarlet Woman refused to leave him in peace, he continued to insist that she was an illusion, a figment of his, and their, imagination. A Beautiful Lie.

It was a paradoxical irony in Wilde's life that his disciples were remaining true to his vision while he was betraying it. They were faithfully seeking and honestly attracted by the highest common factors in life – the aesthetic heights of beauty, love and romance – whereas he was becoming ever more attracted to life's lowest common denominators – its lusts and not its loves. The paradox, set against the backdrop of his relationship with Gray, was the motive force behind the writing of *The Picture of Dorian Gray*. Wilde's novel was the confession of an unhappy hypocrite. Years later he wrote from prison to Lord Alfred Douglas in words of bitter regret: 'When I compare my friendship with you to my friendship with such still younger men as John Gray and Pierre Louÿs I feel ashamed. My real life, my higher life was with them and such as they.'

1 Oscar Wilde, letter to T.H. Escott, undated, British Library, Department of Modern Manuscripts.
2 Hyde, *Oscar Wilde*, p. 106.
3 Ibid., p. 107.
4 Ibid.
5 Edgar Saltus, *Oscar Wilde: An Idler's Impression*, Chicago: Brothers of the Book, 1917, p. 14.
6 Hart-Davis, *Letters of Oscar Wilde*, p. 247.
7 Ibid.
8 Brocard Sewell, *Footnote to the Nineties: A memoir of John Gray and André Raffalovich*, London: Cecil and Amelia Woolf, 1968, p. 5.

FIFTEEN

Malice through the Looking Glass

This portrait would be to him the most magical of mirrors. As it had revealed to him his own body, so it would reveal to him his own soul.

The curiously carved mirror that Lord Henry had given to him, so many years ago now, was standing on the table ... He took it up, as he had done on that night of horror, when he had first noted the change in the fatal picture, and with wild, tear-dimmed eyes looked into its polished shield ... Then he loathed his own beauty, and, flinging the mirror on the floor, crushed it into splinters beneath his heel. It was his beauty that had ruined him, his beauty and the youth that he had prayed for. But for those two things, his life might have been free from stain. His beauty had been to him but a mask, his youth but a mockery.

The most quoted aphorism from Wilde's *The Picture of Dorian Gray* is probably the stricture that 'there is no such thing as a moral or an immoral book. Books are well written, or badly written. That is all.' It is, therefore, ironic that Wilde's first and only novel was itself a living contradiction of the maxim. It was condemned as an immoral book when in fact its sole purpose was explicitly and unmistakably moral.

The Picture of Dorian Gray was first published in *Lippincott's Magazine* in 1890, and was published in book form with additional chapters and a preface in the following year. Its principal protagonists are Lord Henry Wotton and Dorian Gray, the former being the cause of the latter's corruption. Lord Henry at first confuses and then converts the youthful Gray to his gospel of decadence. With urbane eloquence he flatters Dorian's vanity, urging him to self-indulgence.

'The mutilation of the savage has its tragic survival in the self-denial that mars our lives. We are punished for our refusals. Every impulse that we strive to strangle broods in the mind, and poisons us. The body sins once, and has done with its sin, for action is a mode of purification. Nothing remains then but the recollection of a pleasure, or the luxury of a regret. The only way to get rid of a temptation is to yield to it.'

Poisoned by Lord Henry's flattery and philosophy, Dorian's vanity verges on the insanity which will ultimately cause both suicide and murder. 'I know, now,' he exclaims to Basil Hallward, the artist who has painted his portrait, 'that when one loses one's good looks ... one loses everything. Your picture has taught me that. Lord Henry Wotton is perfectly right. Youth is the only thing worth having. When I find that I am growing old, I shall kill myself.'

'I am jealous of everything whose beauty does not die. I am jealous of the portrait you have painted of me. Why should it keep what I must lose? Every moment that passes takes something from me, and gives something to it. Oh, if it were only the other way! If the picture could change, and I could be always what I am now! Why did you paint it? It will mock me some day – mock me horribly!'

This is the catastrophic point upon which the whole novel rests. The moment of truth. Significantly Wilde suggests a supernatural element. As soon as these words are spoken, Dorian throws himself on to the divan, burying his face in the cushions, 'as though he was praying'. Thus, with hints of either the divine or the diabolical, Dorian's wish receives added power. Whether from prayer to God or through a pact with the devil his wish will be granted. The portents of doom are suggested in the prophetic nature of Dorian's final words. The picture will indeed mock him horribly one day, but only because it has fulfilled his desire that it change while he remains the same.

Dorian's desire for eternal youth keeps him outwardly beautiful but the price he pays is an inner corruption. The picture grows increasingly ugly with every act of cruelty that Gray commits. When he commits murder the hands of the picture drip with blood. Dorian Gray's physical beauty is but a mask, ultimately superficial. The metaphysical reality is to be found in the portrait which becomes the mirror of his soul, the ugly truth staring him uncomfortably in the face.

Throughout the novel, Dorian Gray is guided along the path of corruption by the influence of Lord Henry who sets about moulding his young protégé in his own image. 'He would seek to dominate him – had already, indeed, half done so. He would make that wonderful spirit his own.' In some respects Lord Henry is modelled on Pater, whose influence on Wilde had been, according to Wilde's own estimation, poisonous. Yet it is clear that Wilde saw an element of Lord Henry in himself, in the role he was beginning to play in the wilful corruption of young impressionable disciples such as John Gray. As autobiography, therefore, *The Picture of Dorian Gray* can be read on two distinct levels. Wilde is both Dorian Gray, corrupted by the pernicious influence of some of his mentors, and Lord Henry Wotton, the corrupter of disciples. Seen in this light, there is a particular poignancy in Basil Hallward's rebuke to Lord Henry, after the latter had expressed a desire to see Dorian Gray's descent into decadence: 'You don't mean a single word of all that, Harry; you know you don't. If Dorian Gray's life were spoiled, no one would be sorrier than yourself. You are much better than you pretend to be.'

The autobiographical element is extended in Dorian's reading of a book which Wilde later confessed was based on Huysmans' *A Rebours*. The influence of this book on Dorian Gray paralleled the impact which Huysmans' novel had on Wilde six years earlier.

Autobiography was also evident in a description of Dorian Gray's earlier attraction to the Catholic liturgy:

It was rumoured of him once that he was about to join the Roman Catholic communion; and certainly the Roman ritual had always a great attraction for him. The daily sacrifice, more awful really than all the sacrifices of the antique world, stirred him as much by its superb rejection of the evidence of the senses as by the primitive simplicity of its elements and the eternal pathos of the human tragedy that it sought to symbolize. He loved to kneel down on the cold marble pavement, and watch the priest, in his stiff flowered vestment, slowly and with white hands moving aside the veil of the tabernacle, or raising aloft the jewelled lantern-shaped monstrance with that pallid wafer that at times, one would fain think, is indeed the '*panis caelestis*', the bread of angels, or, robed in the garments of the Passion of Christ, breaking the Host into the chalice, and smiting his breast for his sins.

Dorian Gray had renounced his earlier attraction to the Christian faith, believing that any formal acceptance of creed or system would arrest his intellectual development. Subsequently, he passed through mysticism to the materialism of the Darwinists where he discovered 'a curious pleasure in tracing the thoughts and passions of men to some pearly cell in the brain, or some white nerve in the body, delighting in the conception of the absolute dependence of the spirit on certain physical conditions, morbid or healthy, normal or diseased'. Finally he rejected philosophical Darwinism also, concluding that all intellectual speculation was barren. Henceforth he sought only action and experiment, knowing that 'the senses, no less than the soul, have their spiritual mysteries to reveal'. The parallels with Wilde's own position at the time of his writing *The Picture of Dorian Gray* are striking. He too had become fascinated by the philosophical speculation arising out of Darwin's theory even though there is little evidence that he ever accepted any of the new philosophies as a creed. It is clear also that Dorian's idolatry of the senses was Wilde's own fetish at the time the novel was written.

Possibly the most remarkable aspect of *The Picture of Dorian Gray* is Wilde's prescience. The plot unfurls like a parable, illuminating the grave spiritual dangers involved in a life of immoral action and experiment. The novel's ante-climax – the lesser climax which precedes its ultimate moral – is an angry exchange between Dorian Gray and Basil Hallward. The artist, still as in love with Dorian as he had been when he painted the portrait, beseeches his friend to deny all the horrible stories that are circulating about him. Dorian smiles contemptuously and decides to show Hallward the hideously deformed painting which he has locked away from prying eyes in an upstairs room. 'Come upstairs, Basil ... I keep a diary of my life from day to day, and it never leaves the room in which it is written. I shall show it to you if you come with me.'

'So you think that it is only God who sees the soul, Basil?' Dorian asks before revealing the picture.

An exclamation of horror broke from the painter's lips as he saw in the dim light the hideous face on the canvas grinning at him. There was something in its expression that filled him with disgust and loathing. Good heavens! It was Dorian Gray's own face that he was looking at!

Even though Hallward is horrified by the ugly cruelty of the portrait's features he still recognizes his own brush strokes on the canvas. 'It was some foul parody, some infamous, ignoble satire. He had never done that. Still, it was his own picture! He knew it ... His own picture! What did it mean? Why had it altered?' In explanation Dorian Gray reminds him of the scene in his studio many years earlier.

'Years ago, when I was a boy ... you met me, flattered me, and taught me to be vain of my good looks. One day you introduced me to a friend of yours, who explained to me the wonder of youth, and you finished the portrait of me that revealed to me the wonder of beauty. In a mad moment, that, even now, I don't know whether I regret or not, I made a wish, perhaps you would call it a prayer ...'

Hallward complains that there was never anything evil or shameful in his original painting whereas the deformed portrait had the face of a satyr and the eyes of a devil. 'It is the face of my soul,' Dorian replies.

'Each of us has Heaven and Hell in him, Basil,' cried Dorian, with a wild gesture of despair.

Hallward turned again to the portrait, and gazed at it. 'My God! If it is true,' he exclaimed, 'and this is what you have done with your life, why, you must be worse even than those who talk against you fancy you to be!' He held the light up again to the canvas, and examined it. The surface seemed to be quite undisturbed, and as he had left it. It was from within, apparently, that the foulness and horror had come. Through some strange quickening of inner life the leprosies of sin were slowly eating the thing away. The rotting of a corpse in a watery grave was not so fearful ...

'Good God, Dorian, what a lesson! What an awful lesson!' There was no answer, but he could hear the young man sobbing at the window. 'Pray, Dorian, pray,' he murmured. 'What is it that one was taught to say in one's boyhood? "Lead us not into temptation. Forgive us our sins. Wash away our iniquities." Let us say that together. The prayer of your pride has been answered. The prayer of your repentance will be answered also. I worshipped you too much. We are both punished.'

Dorian Gray turned slowly around, and looked at him with tear-dimmed eyes. 'It is too late, Basil,' he faltered.

'It is never too late, Dorian. Let us kneel down and try if we cannot remember a prayer. Isn't there a verse somewhere, "Though your sins be as scarlet, yet I will make them as white as snow?"'

'Those words mean nothing to me now.'

'Hush! Don't say that. You have done enough evil in your life. My God! Don't you see that accursed thing leering at us?'

Dorian Gray glanced at the picture, and suddenly an uncontrollable feeling of hatred for Basil Hallward came over him, as though it had been suggested to him by the image on the canvas, whispered into his ear by those grinning lips.

Dorian grabs a knife and stabs Basil Hallward repeatedly in the neck until he is dead. In committing murder, he adds yet another new experience to his list of sensual experiments.

The wretchedness of Dorian's life becomes ever more pronounced as the novel approaches its climax. When a prostitute whose services he had used regularly calls him 'the devil's bargain' he reacts angrily as if stabbed by the truth of the words: 'Curse you!,' he answers, 'don't call me that.' Finally, the novel's moral, implicit throughout, is stated explicitly in Dorian's last conversation with Lord Henry. 'By the way, Dorian,' Lord Henry asks, no doubt intent on observing his quarry's reaction, 'what does it profit a man if he gain the whole world and lose his own soul?' Dorian is startled by the question and stares in horror at his friend: 'Why do you ask me that, Harry?'

'My dear fellow,' says Lord Henry, elevating his eyebrows in surprise, 'I asked you because I thought you might be able to give me an answer. That is all ...'

Lord Henry proceeds to mock the whole concept of the soul's existence. In the provocative language which Wilde often adopted in his critical essays, he proclaims that Art has a soul but man has not. Dorian disagrees. 'The soul is a terrible reality,' he counters. 'It can be bought, and sold, and bartered away. It can be poisoned, or made perfect. There is a soul in each one of us. I know it.'

With his own sin, and Lord Henry's cynicism, weighing heavily on his conscience, Dorian feels 'a wild longing for the unstained purity of his boyhood'. He compares his own wretchedness with the innocence of the latest woman whom 'he had lured to love him'. 'What a laugh she had! – just like a thrush singing. And how pretty she had been in her cotton dress and her large hats! She knew nothing, but she had everything that he had lost.'

He knew that he had tarnished himself, filled his mind with corruption, and given horror to his fancy; that he had been an evil influence to others, and had experienced a terrible joy in being so; and that, of the lives that had crossed his own, it had been the fairest and the most full of promise that he had brought to shame. But was it all irretrievable? Was there no hope for him?

Ah! in what a monstrous moment of pride and passion he had prayed that the portrait should bear the burden of his days, and he keep the unsullied splendour of eternal youth! All his failure had been due to that. Better for him that each sin of his life had brought its sure, swift penalty along with it. There was purification in punishment. Not 'Forgive us our sins,' but 'Smite us for our iniquities,' should be the prayer of a man to a most just God.

Such contemplation brings Dorian to the brink of repentance but, at the last, he feels unable to confess his sins, unwilling to accept the consequences of his crimes. If he cannot cleanse his soul from sin, he must be rid of the conscience which has made his sins a burden to him. Liberated from any trace of conscience he can once more enjoy his sinful life. Convinced that the hideous portrait is to blame, he decides upon its destruction. 'It had been like conscience to him. Yes, it had been conscience. He would destroy it.' In the novel's final climactic moments Dorian takes the knife with which he had killed the artist and stabs the picture with it. There is a hideous cry which wakes the servants. When they gain entry to the room they find a beautiful portrait hanging on the wall and a withered, wrinkled old man, 'loathsome of visage', lying on the floor with a knife in his heart.

In spite of Wilde's insistence in the Preface to *The Picture of Dorian Gray* that there was no such thing as a moral book, there can be little doubt that the novel was itself a contradiction of the statement. Few novels have been more obviously moral in extent and intent than this cautionary tale of a soul's betrayal of itself and others. Yet it was widely condemned as an immoral book by the critics, principally because of the hints of homosexuality that surface at times in its pages. To the charge of immorality, Wilde responded that, on the contrary, *Dorian Gray* was too moral, itself a contradiction of the maxim in his Preface. He pointed out that 'in his attempt to kill conscience Dorian Gray kills himself', a moral for which he claimed an 'ethical beauty'.

On 26 June 1890 Wilde wrote to the editor of the *St James's Gazette* in an endeavour to defend his novel from charges of immorality. His letter was published on the following day.

> The poor public, hearing, from an authority so high as your own, that this is a wicked book that should be coerced and suppressed by a Tory Government, will, no doubt, rush to it and read it. But, alas! they will find that it is a story with a moral. And the moral is this: All excess, as well as all renunciation, brings its own punishment. The painter, Basil Hallward, worshipping physical beauty far too much, as most painters do, dies by the hand of one in whose soul he has created a monstrous and absurd vanity. Dorian Gray, having led a life of mere sensation and pleasure, tries to kill conscience, and at that moment kills himself. Lord Henry Wotton seeks to be merely the spectator of life. He finds that those who reject the battle are more deeply wounded than those who take part in it. Yes; there is a terrible moral in *Dorian Gray* – a moral which the prurient will not be able to find in it, but which will be revealed to all whose minds are healthy.

Four days later, Wilde was again forced to defend his novel from charges of indecency. This time the critical review was published in the *Daily Chronicle*. Describing *The Picture of Dorian Gray* as 'dirt' and 'unclean', the reviewer wrote that it was 'a tale spawned from the leprous literature of the French *Décadents* – a poisonous book, the atmosphere of which is heavy with the mephitic odours of moral and spiritual putrefaction'. Dorian Gray was a 'cool, calculating, conscienceless character' and the point of the story seemed to be that when a man feels himself becoming 'too angelic' he should rush out and make a 'beast of himself'. Wilde's reply, published on 2 July, insisted that Dorian Gray is haunted by 'an exaggerated sense of conscience' and repeated that the novel, far from being immoral, was, if anything, the very opposite:

> ...the real trouble I experienced in writing the story was that of keeping the extremely obvious moral subordinate to the artistic and dramatic effect.
>
> When I first conceived the idea of a young man selling his soul in exchange for eternal youth – an idea that is old in the history of literature, but to which I have given new form – I felt that, from an aesthetic point of view, it would be difficult to keep the moral in its proper secondary place; and even now I do not feel quite sure that I have been able to do so. I think the moral too apparent.

On 5 July a reviewer in the *Scots Observer* wrote that Wilde's story dealt with matters 'only fitted for the Criminal Investigation Department', adding that if Wilde could 'write for none but outlawed noblemen and perverted telegraph-boys, the sooner he takes to tailoring (or some other decent trade) the better for his own reputation and the public morals'. The reference to noblemen and telegraph-boys was an allusion to the Cleveland Street scandal of the previous year which forced Lord Arthur Somerset to leave the country after alleged offences with telegraph-boys at a homosexual brothel.

Amid the condemnation of many secular critics, a few eyebrows were raised by the praise which Wilde's novel elicited from several Christian publications. *Christian Leader* and the *Christian World* referred to it as an ethical parable, and *Light*, a journal of Christian mysticism, regarded it as 'a work of high spiritual import'. The critic in the *Scots Observer* who had attacked the novel so scathingly, commented sarcastically that it must have been 'particularly painful' for Wilde to discover that his work was being praised by Christian publications on both sides of the Atlantic. Wilde, however, appeared to be pleased by Christian approval of the morality in *Dorian Gray*. On 2 August the *Scots Observer* published a letter from him in which he insisted that he had 'no hesitation in saying that I regard such criticisms as a very gratifying tribute to my story'.

> For if a work of art is rich, and vital, and complete, those who have artistic instincts will see its beauty, and those to whom ethics appeal more strongly than aesthetics will see its moral lesson. It will fill the cowardly with terror, and the unclean will see in it their own shame. It will be to each man what he is himself. It is the spectator, and not life, that art really mirrors.

Wilde offered a particularly candid appraisal of his own ethical approach to *Dorian Gray* in a letter to Arthur Fish, who had been his assistant editor on *Woman's World* until Wilde had relinquished the editorship a year earlier. On hearing in July 1890 that Fish was to be married, Wilde wrote him a congratulatory note, assuring him that Lord Henry Wotton's views on marriage in *The Picture of Dorian Gray* were 'quite monstrous', adding that he 'highly disapproved of them'. Expressing his delight that Fish had enjoyed his novel he wrote that 'it has been attacked on ridiculous grounds, but I think it will be ultimately recognized as a real work of art with a strong ethical lesson inherent in it'.[1]

In spite of Wilde's protestations to the contrary, many people continued to see *The Picture of Dorian Gray* as further evidence of its author's immorality. One result was the shunning of Wilde by certain erstwhile friends. The change of attitude was felt acutely by Constance who remarked that 'since Oscar wrote *Dorian Gray* no one will speak to us'.[2] Needless to say, Lady Wilde was effusively fawning in her praise for her son's work. 'It is the most wonderful piece of writing in all the fiction of the day,' she gushed, before adding with customary hyperbole that she had 'nearly fainted at the last scene'.[3] More significantly, *Dorian Gray* was praised warmly by Pater in the *Bookman*, and W.B. Yeats wrote that 'with all its faults' it was a 'wonderful book'.[4] Such views were those of a dissident minority. The consensus condemned Wilde and his novel as an affront to civilized values. W.H. Smith refused to sell the book on the grounds that it was 'filthy' and the scandal surrounding its publication further tarnished Wilde's already suspect reputation.

Ironically, one of the most poignant appraisals of *The Picture of*

Dorian Gray was to be made by Lord Alfred Douglas, whose relationship with Wilde would tarnish the writer's reputation far more conclusively than any of his books. In his memoirs, published many years after Wilde's death, Douglas attacked those critics who condemned *Dorian Gray* for being immoral as well as the later generations of critics who attacked its morality.

> It is the foolish fashion to run it down now, but the truth is that it is a work of great genius. The objection brought against it in the present time is that it is melodramatic ... whereas at the time when I read it it was attacked in a section of the Press because it was supposed to be immoral, and a very wicked book. As a matter of fact the book is entirely moral, and that is probably why the feeble and sheep-like critics of today affect to despise it. Any book or play with a moral is what they call melodramatic. The pose nowadays of the 'Intellectuals', as they choose to call themselves, is that it is *bourgeois* ever to be shocked by anything, while on the other hand a really immoral or wicked book is exactly what delights them and commands their admiration. What they do not like about *Dorian Gray* is precisely that it is the moral story of a man who destroys his own conscience and thereby comes to a terrible end. If Dorian Gray had been presented as triumphant and 'happy' to the last, they would probably hail it as a great work of art, whereas Oscar Wilde, just like Shakespeare or any first-rate writer, knew that a play or a novel without a moral is, from the artistic point of view, a monstrosity.
>
> I once said in the witness-box ... that while *Dorian Gray* was on the surface a moral book, there was in it 'an undercurrent of immorality and corruption'. I said that out of the bitterness of my heart, but it was not a fair criticism, because the 'undercurrent' is part of the legitimate atmosphere which the author creates for his story.[5]

These words, written almost fifty years after the novel's publication, suggest that Wilde's stricture in the Preface to *Dorian Gray* that there was no such thing as a moral or an immoral book had fallen on deaf ears. The issue of morality was as central to critical conceptions and misconceptions of the book as it had been to the author's own conception of it. His own attitude to the critics was best summarized in a lesser known but more profound aphorism from the Preface: 'Those who find ugly meanings in beautiful things are corrupt without being charming. This is a fault. Those who find beautiful meanings in beautiful things are the cultivated. For these there is hope.'

1 Arthur Fish, 'Memories of Oscar Wilde', *Cassell's Weekly*, 2 May 1923.
2 Ellmann, *Oscar Wilde*, p. 302.
3 Ibid.
4 *United Ireland*, 26 September 1891; quoted in Hart-Davis, *Letters of Oscar Wilde*, p. 270.
5 Lord Alfred Douglas, *Without Apology*, London: Martin Secker, 1938, pp. 41–3.

SIXTEEN

Critic or Artist

'You cut life to pieces with your epigrams.'

'You would sacrifice anybody, Harry, for the sake of an epigram.'

In Wilde's novel, Dorian Gray grows increasingly tired of Lord Henry's iconoclastic cynicism, rebuking him for cutting life to pieces with his epigrams. It is tempting to see an element of self-reproach on Wilde's part in such dialogue, not least because Wilde continued to play the role of iconoclast in many of his critical essays. If his art continued to express themes of moral intensity, his criticism toyed with immorality to such an extent that, like Lord Henry, he would sacrifice anybody or anything for an epigram.

In July and September 1890, even as Wilde was robustly defending the morality of his novel from the attacks of the critics, his essay 'The Critic as Artist' was published. Written in the form of a dialogue it serves as a contradiction and refutation of the moral message in *The Picture of Dorian Gray*. In the novel Lord Henry's *bons mots* were balanced and checked by the counterpoise provided by Basil Hallward's moral objections and by the disastrous consequences of Dorian's decadence. In 'The Critic as Artist' no such balance is present. 'Gilbert', the chief protagonist in the essay, is a literary clone of Lord Henry Wotton, a pseudonymous substitute. Yet he has no opposition to counter his views because 'Ernest', the other protagonist, is a purely passive partner who serves merely as a foil to Gilbert's brilliance. As such Gilbert is allowed free rhetorical rein, reeling off an endless stream of epigrams.

This is Wilde at his most self-consciously poisonous. 'If we lived long enough to see the results of our actions it may be that those who call themselves good would be sickened with a dull remorse, and those whom the world calls evil stirred by a noble joy.' The machine of life may grind virtues to powder, making them worthless, or transform sins into elements of a new civilization. Sin is essential to progress and conscience merely a sign of our imperfect development. Religion was both *passé* and an impasse. 'The courts of the city of God are not open to us now. Its gates are guarded by Ignorance, and to pass them we have to surrender all that in our nature is most divine. It is enough that our fathers believed. They have exhausted the faith-faculty of the species. Their legacy to us is the scepticism of which they were afraid ... We cannot go back to the saint. There is far more to be learned from the sinner.'

Gilbert's insistence on the superiority of sin may have been linked psychologically to Wilde's adoption of a sexually licentious lifestyle. If, like Dorian Gray, Wilde was determined to continue sinning, it was far easier and more psychologically comforting to scoff at the concept of sin than to admit that he was a sinner. Stubbornly unwilling to amend his life, it became necessary to amend his critical approach to morality. If conventional morality did not conform with the self-image, it must be reinvented in the image of the self. If repentance was undesirable, sin must be sanctified. If innocence was thought to be impossible, guilt must be abolished. Wilde, like Dorian Gray, had nothing but his conscience to overcome and this singular essay may have been an attempt to achieve this.

The singular approach, once adopted, produced some singularly peculiar results. Art, Gilbert insists, is a passion and, as such, cannot be narrowed into a theological dogma. Yet the passively compliant Ernest does not come back with the obvious riposte that it is impossible to understand or fully appreciate religious art – its passion – without understanding the dogma that underpins and inspires it. (In fact, the same is true of all art, not just the religious. All art is the product of metaphysical presuppositions on the part of the artist, though expressed sub-consciously.) Similarly, Gilbert maintains, 'There is nothing sane about the worship of beauty. It is too splendid to be sane.' He then declares that Art and Ethics must be kept absolutely distinct and separate. 'When they are confused, Chaos has come again.' Yet if insanity is splendid, what is wrong with Chaos? Again, the question remains unasked and therefore conveniently unanswered. 'There is no sin except stupidity,' says Gilbert, and one longs in vain for Ernest's reply, 'No, there is no stupidity except sin.' The ensuing debate would have been of considerable interest but the lamentable reticence of Gilbert's disciple ensures the stultification of further stimulating discussion.

Throughout this curiously contorted essay Wilde is not so much grappling, in the sense of one who is wrestling with or for the truth, as groping, in the sense of one trying to find the light in a darkened room, or as one clutching at straws. In muddying the waters of the self, he seems to have muddled the working of the mind.

Perhaps there is a further parallel between this curious essay and *The Picture of Dorian Gray*. The conclusion of the novel, in both senses of the word, is that Dorian Gray destroys himself when he tries to destroy his conscience. There is no conclusion to the essay, in either sense of the word, but the reader may conclude that Wilde has defeated himself critically when he attempts to explain away the conscience aesthetically. Certainly, he fails to do it convincingly.

The burning question, of course, is whether Wilde was convinced himself by his arguments. Was he in earnest, or simply playing with morality? Could he have written at the end of 'The Critic as Artist', as he had written at the end of 'The Truth of Masks', that he did not agree with everything he had said and, indeed, that 'there is much with which I entirely disagree'? Was Wilde aesthetically schizophrenic, hearing voices which contradicted those of his deeper self? If so, did he believe these voices as being as true as their contradictions? Did he believe that black was white, and that white was black? Was he, to coin his own enigmatic phrase, splendidly insane? If not, there is the suspicion that he was being ingenious without being ingenuous. Was he simply playing with fire for the mere hell of it while his heart was set on heaven? Was he playing at criticism while his heart was in his art? Was the true Oscar Wilde revealed in *The Picture of Dorian Gray* and concealed in 'The Critic as Artist'?

The suspicion that Wilde was being disingenuous was widespread among many of his contemporaries. The poet Francis Thompson wrote in August 1890, shortly after the first part of 'The Critic as Artist' was published, that Wilde was a 'witty paradoxical writer, who, nevertheless, *meo judicio*, will do nothing permanent because he is in earnest about nothing'.[1] Thompson must also have had Wilde in mind when he referred to the decadent writers as men whose brains had exhausted themselves in the 'parturition of an epigram'.[2] Similarly, it is likely that Thompson was thinking of Wilde when he wrote these lines in a poem called 'Fool by Nature and by Art':

Nay, this alone were prodigal Nature's plan;
Behold the Artist supplement the Man!
In the small line, with dainty exquisiteness
Of feeble polish, polished feebleness,
Wrought and perfected till each vein concealed
Of native weakness shines with skill revealed.
Scan thou the truth it can so well impart:–
A fool by nature, is twice fool by art.[3]

Thompson's criticism gains both potency and poignancy from the fact that he was himself of the decadent school, and most certainly not of the puritanical school that criticized Wilde on purely knee-jerk reactionary grounds. Throughout the 1880s Thompson was dependent on opium at various times and to various degrees. His drug addiction led to a life of penury and squalor in post-Dickensian London. He was often hungry, homeless, reduced to street dereliction and befriended by prostitutes. His experiences inspired his most famous poem, 'The Hound of Heaven', written in 1889, which prefigured Wilde's own approach to repentance and remorse in *De Profundis* and *The Ballad of Reading Gaol*. Yet the most striking links of affinity between Wilde and Thompson are the remarkable similarities between *The Picture of Dorian Gray* and Thompson's short story 'Finis Coronat Opus'. Thompson's hero, Florentian, could almost pass for Dorian Gray. He is young, noble, popular, influential, rich, 'and possessed the natural gifts which gain the love of women'.

But the seductions which Florentian followed were darker and more baleful than the seductions of women; for they were the seductions of knowledge and intellectual pride. In very early years he had passed from the pursuit of natural to the pursuit of unlawful science; he had conquered power where conquest is disaster, and power servitude.[4]

Like Dorian Gray, Florentian makes a pact with the devil in order to achieve his heart's desire. Whereas Dorian had desired physical beauty and eternal youth, Florentian desired poetic genius and supremacy in the arts. In return for this, the devil demands the blood-sacrifice of Florentian's wife. Florentian removes the crucifix from the altar, treads the prostrate cross underfoot and places a bust of Virgil in its place. He then murders his wife on the altar of Art. As with Dorian Gray his wish is granted but brings nothing but misery and despair. Before his final destruction he is granted one last glimpse of lost innocence:

> If this fame was not worth the sinning for – this fame with the multitude's clapping hands half-drowned by the growl of winds that comes in gusts through the unbarred gate of hell? If I am miserable with it, and might have been happy without it? With her, without ambition – yes, it might have been. Wife and child! I have more in my heart than I have hitherto written. I have an intermittent pang of loss. Yes, I, murderer, worse than murderer, have still passions that are not deadly, but tender.
>
> I met a child today; a child with great candour of eyes. They who talk of children's instincts are at fault: she knew not that hell was in my soul, she knew only that softness was in my gaze. She had been gathering wild flowers, and offered them to me. To me, to *me!*'[5]

In the desolation of life and the love of art, Thompson and Wilde were kindred spirits. Thompson's censure of Wilde's lack of earnestness can only have referred to Wilde's criticism, not to his art. It is difficult to conceive that the creator of 'Finis Coronat Opus' would have felt anything but respect for the creator of *The Picture of Dorian Gray*. It is, however, intriguing that Thompson's hero falls because he elevates Art above morality. This, of course, is what Wilde does in his criticism, though never in his art. In Wilde's criticism art is not an ideal but an idol. Did Thompson have Wilde in mind when he created Florentian, the doomed hero of his story? It is at least possible because Thompson's early verse resonates with Wilde's influence. It is surely not coincidental that Thompson's favourite 'sandalled' – 'Thy naked feet unsandalled', 'In sandalled shadow of the Triune feet' – and lines like 'The silver-stoled damsels of the sea' should reverberate as distant echoes of the last verse of Wilde's 'The Harlot's House':

And down the long and silent street,
The dawn, with silver-sandalled feet,
Crept like a frightened girl ...

By the summer of 1890 Thompson had outgrown Wilde's influence to such a degree that Wilde would soon be paying homage to his former disciple. Between August and October 1890 Thompson was writing his verse sequence, 'Sister Songs'. When Wilde heard some of 'Sister Songs' read aloud, he exclaimed, 'Why can't I write poetry like that? That is what I've wanted to do all my life.'[6]

Painfully aware of his own limitations as a poet, Wilde sought other modes of expression for his art. At around this time he wrote 'The Fisherman and His Soul', a parable in the same mould as 'The Nightingale and the Rose', 'The Young King' and 'The Selfish Giant'. It centred on a young fisherman's love for a mermaid and his desire to be rid of his soul so that he could marry her and live in the depths of the sea. He goes to the priest to seek advice: 'Father, I am in love with one of the Sea-folk, and my Soul hindereth me from having my desire. Tell me how I can send my Soul away from me, for in truth I have no need of it. Of what value is my soul to me? I cannot see it. I may not touch it. I do not know it.' The priest is horrified and reminds the fisherman that 'the Soul is the noblest part of man, and was given to us by God that we should nobly use it. There is no thing more precious than a human soul, nor any earthly thing that can be weighed with it.'

Determined nonetheless to send his soul away so that he may marry the mermaid, he consults a witch for the secret he desires. She invites him to a witches' Sabbath at midnight where she promises that the secret will be revealed. At midnight, as he dances with the witch, he notices 'a man dressed in black velvet': 'The young Fisherman watched him, as one snared in a spell. At last their eyes met, and wherever he danced it seemed to him that the eyes of the man were upon him.' The dancers stop and, two by two, the witches kneel before the man and kiss his hands.

As they did so, a little smile touched his proud lips ... But there was disdain in it. He kept looking at the young Fisherman.

'Come! let us worship,' whispered the Witch, and she led him up, and a great desire to do as she besought him seized on him, and he followed her. But when he came close, and without knowing why he did it, he made on his breast the sign of the Cross, and called upon the holy name.

No sooner had he done so than the witches screamed like hawks and flew away, and the pallid face that had been watching him twitched with a spasm of pain.

Before the man departs he turns round and looks at the young fisherman sadly. At the very last moment, through an unwitting prayer, Satan has been denied the boy's soul.

Still determined to marry the mermaid, the fisherman discovers from the witch a way in which he can send his soul into exile, loosing it from his body so that he can fulfil his desire. 'What men call the shadow of the body is not the shadow of the body, but is the body of the Soul,' the witch explains. 'Stand on the sea-shore with thy back to the moon, and cut away from around thy feet thy shadow, which is thy Soul's body, and bid thy soul leave thee, and it will do so.' Throughout the rest of the tale, the fisherman learns from his exiled soul, who returns once a year to tell him of its adventures, that love is stronger than either wisdom or riches. Eventually he is lured on to dry land in pursuit of transient pleasure, betraying his love. Finding her dead on the beach when he returns he is filled with remorse and confesses his sins in her unhearing ears. Willingly he allows the sea to exact its revenge, clinging to the dead mermaid on the beach until the incoming tide consumes him.

The priest, going to bless the sea the following morning in the wake of the previous night's storm, is horrified to find the young fisherman drowned in the surf, and clasped in his arms the little mermaid.

And he drew back frowning, and having made the sign of the Cross, he cried aloud and said, 'I will not bless the sea nor anything that is in it. Accursed be the Sea-folk, and accursed be all they who traffic with them.'

The priest orders the people to bury the fisherman and the mermaid in unconsecrated ground with no stone to mark the grave. In a corner of a field, 'where no sweet herbs grow, they dug a deep pit, and laid the dead things within it'.

Three years later, the priest enters the chapel intent on preaching on the wrath of God. Bowing before the altar, he notices that it is decorated with strange flowers that he has never seen before, 'and their odour was sweet in his nostrils, and he felt glad, and understood not why he was glad'.

And after that he had opened the tabernacle, and incensed the monstrance that was in it, and shown the fair wafer to the people, and hid it again behind the veil of veils, he began to speak to the people, desiring to speak to them of the wrath of God. But the beauty of the white flowers troubled him, and their odour was sweet in his nostrils, and there came another word into his lips, and he spake not of the wrath of God, but of the God whose name is Love. And why he so spake, he knew not.

And when he had finished his word the people wept, and the Priest went back to his sacristy, and his eyes were full of tears.

The priest asks the deacons where the flowers have come from and is told that they grew above the unmarked grave where the fisherman and mermaid were buried. 'And the Priest trembled, and returned to his own house and prayed.'

'The Fisherman and His Soul' was published in 1891 in a collection of short stories under the collective title *A House of Pomegranates*. It shared with the other stories a deep sense of morality. In each of the stories there is a constant tension between good and evil, pride and humility, sin and penitence, love and cruelty, greed and selflessness. Once again, Wilde's art had confounded his criticism. The mask of the critic had been peeled away to reveal the artist beneath.

1 John Evangelist Walsh (ed.), *The Letters of Francis Thompson*, New York: Hawthorn Books Inc., 1969, p. 44.
2 Paul van Kuykendall Thomson, *Francis Thompson: A Critical Biography*, New York: Thomas Nelson & Sons, 1961, p. 64.
3 Ibid.
4 Wilfred Meynell (ed.), *The Works of Francis Thompson Vol. III*, London: Burns & Oates, 1913, p. 116.
5 Ibid., p. 133.
6 Everard Meynell, *The Life of Francis Thompson*, London: Burns & Oates, 1913, p. 252.

SEVENTEEN

Friends and Relations

I don't think now that people can be divided into the good and the bad as though they were two separate races or creations. What are called good women may have terrible things in them, mad moods of reckless-ness, assertion, jealousy, sin. Bad women, as they are termed, may have in them sorrow, repentance, pity, sacrifice ...

Rumours of Wilde's homosexuality began to spread in the months following publication of *The Picture of Dorian Gray*. Suspicions had been aroused by the thinly veiled allusions to 'Socratic' love in the novel and were further exacerbated by Wilde's indiscreet conver-sations on the delights of male beauty. It was noted that he now pre-ferred to surround himself with beautiful young men, such as John Gray, in haunts like the Café Royal. On one occasion, his friend Frank Harris was astounded to overhear Wilde describing the physical charms of Olympic athletes in ancient Greece to 'a pair of extremely suspect youths'.[1]

The consequences of Wilde's increasingly overt attitude were felt on 4 July 1891 when he was invited to join the exclusive Crabbet Club. Wilfrid Scawen Blunt, the club's founder and president, sat beside Wilde when his membership was discussed and recorded the embar-rassment when accusations of homosexuality were levelled against him. George Curzon, appointed as devil's advocate, opposed Wilde's membership on the grounds of his 'little weaknesses'. Blunt recalled that Curzon, who had been at Oxford with Wilde, showed no mercy in his attacks, 'playing with astonishing audacity and skill upon his reputation for sodomy and his treatment of the subject in *Dorian Gray*. Poor Oscar sat helplessly smiling, a fat mass, in his chair ... I felt sorry for him – it seemed hardly fair.' When Wilde rose to reply he was at first shaken by the unexpected nature of Curzon's attacks, but 'he pulled himself together as he went on and gradually warmed into an amusing and excellent speech'.[2] In fact, if Wilde's account of the proceedings is to be believed, he simply decided to exchange abusive blows. Wilde told Frank Harris that he had derided Curzon's mediocrity, his desperately hard work in pursuing a second-class degree and then a second-class career.[3] Wilde never returned to the Crabbet Club but his hostile reception was a frosty foretaste of what the future held in store.

The increasing hostility was evident in two novels published in 1890 in which characters based on Wilde are treated far from sympathetically. In Henry James's *The Tragic Muse*, the aesthete Gabriel Nash seems loosely based on Wilde. In a remarkable but presumably coincidental similarity with Wilde's *Dorian Gray*, Nash sits for a portrait but disappears before it is finished. No one knows where he has gone, and the unfinished image on the canvas fades away as mysteriously as the original. Clearly James was implying that Wilde's aesthetic theories were divorced from reality and ultimately insubstantial. A more vindictive and less subtle caricature of Wilde appeared in André Raffalovich's *A Willing Exile*. In the novel Oscar and Constance are represented as Cyprian and Daisy Brome:

Cyprian was, or seemed to be, intimate with countless young or youngish men; they were all curiously alike. Their voices, the cut of their clothes, the curl of their hair, the brims of their hats, the parties they went to: Daisy could not see much difference between them ... Affectation characterized all these men, and the same sort of affectation. They were all gushers, professional gushers ... Married (some were married) or unmarried, they gushed alike, only some were ruder than others, and some were duller than others ...

Cyprian's cult for his own looks ... increased instead of diminished. He lived with people who talked much about beauty ... He had acquired the habit of comparing himself to every one he met and of debating who was better looking, he or the other ... He had two flowers (or rather, bunches of flowers) sent him every day, one before lunch, and the other before dinner. His clothes much occupied him; he was never tired of discussing male fashions, and sometimes Daisy, after having been away an hour, would find him and a chum still pursuing the analysis of another man's garments.[4]

André Raffalovich, destined to be one of Wilde's most outspoken critics, was for a while one of his intimate friends. Descended from a Russian Jewish international banking dynasty, Raffalovich enjoyed enormous inherited wealth which he lavished on favoured members of the literati. Originally from Paris, Raffalovich had heard Wilde lecture in the United States in 1882 and, following his emigration to London two years later, integrated himself into the city's fashionable literary life. It was inevitable, therefore, that he and Wilde should eventually meet. Wilde attended various gatherings at Raffalovich's house, including lunch with Walter Pater and evening parties at which Henry James, George Moore and a host of others were present. At first, Wilde and Raffalovich appeared to be kindred spirits. 'You could give me a new thrill,' Wilde remarked to him. 'You have the right measure of romance and cynicism.'[5] They went to the theatre together and dined at the Alexandra Hotel, Hyde Park Corner. At this stage Wilde was circumspect about his sexuality, in public at least. 'Whatever his temptations or his eagerness,' Raffalovich remembered, 'he wished to be prudent, ultra-prudent.' He cautioned Raffalovich that 'we must be most careful of the people we are seen with. I am so conspicuous, and you are not *le premier venu*. We can't be too careful.' Referring to others who had gained an element of notoriety, Wilde continued his cautionary discourse: 'At first they enjoyed the romance of being conspicuous and disapproved of, but after a time they would give much to be as unnoticed as they were before they had *a bad reputation*.'[6] He was soon to forget the wisdom of his own words, falling into reckless indiscretion.

Wilde was more forthcoming in private. He sent Raffalovich an invitation which left the recipient in little doubt as to its seductive intent: 'come for me on Sunday at nine o'clock. Constance will be away.' He was also candid in private conversations with Raffalovich, talking for several hours on aspects of homosexuality. At the time Wilde had just read Rachilde's *Monsieur Vénus* in which a lesbian dresses her lover as a man. He was clearly excited by the sexual ambivalence displayed in the controversial novel. Recalling the nature of their conversations, Raffalovich noted that Wilde's words 'must at times have resembled Dante's *Purgatorio*, Canto xxvi' in which the lustful, both heterosexual and homosexual, lament a life spent like brute beasts, the slaves of appetite.

The estrangement between Wilde and Raffalovich began as the result of a passing remark by Constance. 'Oscar says he likes you so much,' Constance told Raffalovich, 'that you have such nice improper talks together.' Raffalovich, who was very fond of Constance, wondered whether this was a kindly warning or merely a mechanical repetition of her husband's words. Either way, he was embarrassed and enraged at Wilde's suggestion that he was guilty of any impropriety. 'I had listened eagerly to his wit and wisdom and experience, to his store of unusual stories ... but I had added nothing but what he called my blend of romance and cynicism, my boyish queries ... I was furious: never again did I speak with him without witnesses.'⁷

Their relationship continued falteringly but Raffalovich found himself increasingly alienated by Wilde's decadence. On one occasion he reproved Wilde for defending certain disreputable characters. 'But surely, Oscar, you don't want Cyril to grow up like one of those men?' Wilde replied dismissively: 'you appeal to the Father, not to the Thinker'. Aware of the cooling of their friendship, Wilde adopted a malicious attitude and Raffalovich became the victim of one of Wilde's better, and more bitter, epigrams: 'Dear André! He came to London to found a *salon* and only succeeded in opening a *saloon*.'⁸ Continuing the joke, Wilde remarked on arriving at Raffalovich's house in the company of five others that he wanted a table for six. Raffalovich was not amused. It was the last time that Wilde received an invitation from him. The animosity was heightened by Raffalovich's friendship with John Gray, which Wilde must have resented.

John Gray remained Wilde's most intimate friend until well into 1892 when Wilde's friendship with Lord Alfred Douglas and Gray's with Raffalovich severed and then soured their relationship. Wilde and Gray were assumed to be lovers and their intimacy provided a rich source of gossip. At a meeting of the Rhymers' Club at the beginning of February 1891, Wilde turned up to listen to Gray reading his own verse. Lionel Johnson and Ernest Dowson, two of the club's most prominent members, alluded to the meeting. Johnson wrote in a letter of 5 February that 'I have made great friends with the original of Dorian: one John Gray, a youth in the Temple, aged thirty, with the face of fifteen.' Actually, Gray was still not twenty-five. On 2 February, Dowson wrote that 'Dorian' Gray had read 'some very beautiful and obscure versicles in the latest manner of French Symbolism'.[9] A month later Wilde declared his intention of writing an article entitled 'A New Poet' for the *Fortnightly Review*, and was only waiting for Gray to produce enough poems to warrant such a fanfare.

A year later, in February 1892, Wilde took the chair at a meeting of the Playgoers' Club when Gray delivered a talk on 'The Modern Actor'. The *Daily Telegraph* quoted some of Gray's remarks in illustration of what it felt was the perverse attitude of modern critics, describing Gray as a *'protégé'* of Wilde's. Perhaps Gray was sensitive about such a description because Wilde wrote to the *Telegraph* on 19 February denying any undue influence. 'Your writer describes the author of the brilliant fantastic lecture on "The Modern Actor" as "a *protégé*" of mine. Allow me to state that my acquaintance with Mr John Gray is, I regret to say, extremely recent, and that I sought it because he had already a perfected mode of expression both in prose and verse.'[10] Wilde concluded his letter by stating that Gray needed no protection, 'nor, indeed, would he accept it'. Within four months, however, Gray was accepting Wilde's patronage, if not necessarily his protection. On 17 June Wilde agreed to defray all the publishing costs of Gray's first book of verse, *Silverpoints*.

Gray's sensitivity, and the perplexity and complexity of his relationship with Wilde, was brought to the fore when Gray sued the *Star* newspaper for suggesting that he was the original of Dorian Gray in Wilde's novel. The libel action elicited a humorous response from many friends of Wilde and Gray. Ernest Dowson informed a friend of 'the latest news – that Gray, of whom I am seeing a good deal just at present, pursues the *Star* for a libel asserting him to be "the original Dorian of that name".' Dowson added, with scarcely concealed amusement, that 'this will be droll'.[11] The case was settled in Gray's favour. There was, however, a curious postscript to this episode. In January 1961 there was offered for sale in New York a first edition of *The Picture of Dorian Gray* containing an autograph letter from Gray to Wilde signed 'Yours ever, Dorian'. Although it is clear that Dorian Gray was not intended as a portrait of John Gray in anything but the purely physical sense, the existence of the letter would have been a cause of considerable embarrassment to Gray had it been known to the *Star*'s lawyers.

John Gray's determination to distance himself from the destructive character of Dorian Gray is, of course, understandable. Yet perhaps he was also trying to distance himself from the decadent influence of Wilde. Throughout 1892, despite his acceptance of Wilde's offer to finance publication of his verse, Gray sought to assert his own independence. Through his friendship with the young French poet Pierre Louÿs, he had been introduced to the literary life of Paris, meeting Verlaine, Mallarmé, Marcel Schwob and other Symbolist writers. He began to contribute to *Le Revue Blanche*, *L'Hermitage* and other reviews, and pioneered the introduction of contemporary French literature to the British public throughout the 1890s.

Towards the end of the year, Ernest Dowson wrote that Gray was 'incurably given over to social things', adding that 'this is sad'.[12] In fact, Gray's addiction to 'social things' was a mask concealing a deep anxiety. The endless round of social events was merely a dust-storm of diversions in a wasteland of desolation and despair. Towards the end of 1892 he informed Pierre Louÿs that he was contemplating suicide and Richard Ellmann suggests that this may have been due to the fact that Gray felt jilted in the wake of Wilde's infatuation with Lord Alfred Douglas. It is true that, as late as October 1892, Gray had inscribed his translation of Paul Bourget's *A Saint and Others* with a tribute to Wilde, 'To My Beloved Master, My dear Friend, Homage.' Yet perhaps the real key to Gray's despair was the conflict within himself between love and lust, faith and the flesh. The battle for his own soul is best discerned in the poems in *Silverpoints* in which Wilde believed that Gray had achieved 'a perfected mode of expression'.

In *Silverpoints* the poetry palpitates with the passionate claims of love and lust. In 'Le Chevalier Malheur' it is the penetrative imagery of homosexual eroticism which triumphs and in 'Summer Past', which is dedicated to Wilde, there are memories of 'Warm hours of leaf-lipped song, And dripping amber sweat'. This contrasts with the Christian imagery in other poems, such as 'Parsifal Imitated from the French of Paul Verlaine' in which the imagery of the Catholic Mass is dominant in the 'great gift, the living Blood' and in the worshipping of the 'mysterious Wine'. The most powerful imagery to emerge from *Silverpoints* relates not to the fleshly passion of man but to the Passion of Christ. In 'A Crucifix', dedicated to Ernest Dowson, the 'loving pallor' of Christ looks down from the Cross 'on human blindness ... to overturn Despair's repose, And urge to Hope and Love, as Faith demands'. This is paralleled in 'Mon Dieu M'A Dit' in which Christ speaks to the sinner from the Cross. His 'insulted, stabbed' feet, 'the nails, the sponge, the gall' and the bitter tears of His mother,

> Must teach thee love, amidst a world
>   where flesh doth reign,
> My flesh alone, my blood,
> my voice, the voice of God.

Most significant of all are the very last lines of the last verse in *Silverpoints* where the erotic imagery of lust, the fleshly passion of man, is subsumed within, and subject to, the Love and Passion of Christ.

> All thine isle showed me, Venus! was upthrust,
> A symbol calvary where my image hung.
> Give me, Lord God, to look upon that dung,
> My body and my heart, without disgust.

In these four lines, Gray's final words in *Silverpoints*, is the key to his despair. If he had committed suicide at the end of 1892 as his desperate letter to Pierre Louÿs had indicated, these words would have been his last will and testament. The fact that he did not do so suggests that the poem had been answered as a prayer.

In the event, the publication costs of *Silverpoints* were not paid by Wilde. By the time the volume was published, at the beginning of March 1893, Gray had informed Louÿs that he had broken with Wilde. His decision, rooted in his own determination to reform his life, was no doubt influenced by his growing friendship with André Raffalovich whose hostility to Wilde was well known. Gray's friendship with Raffalovich, which apparently remained purely platonic, alienated Gray from both Wilde and his circle. One result was a bitchiness in the response to *Silverpoints*. Richard Le Gallienne reproved Gray for his modish decadence and Theodore Wratislaw, writing in the *Artist and Journal of Home Culture*, was even more severe, dismissing Gray as 'an artist with a promising future behind him'.[13] Wilde's recently acquired friend, Ada Leverson, whom he called the Sphinx, surveyed in *Silverpoints* 'the tiniest rivulet of text meandering through the very largest meadow of margin'. Wilde, she wrote, should take the idea one step further, publishing a book *all* margins, full of beautiful unwritten thoughts. Wilde approved. 'It shall be dedicated to you and the unwritten text illustrated by Aubrey Beardsley. There must be five hundred signed copies for particular friends, six for the general public, and one for America.'[14]

Wilde's reference to Aubrey Beardsley illustrated the young artist's recent rise to prominence. He would soon be considered as important to the 'Decadent Nineties' as was Wilde himself. Yet Wilde claimed later, with at least a degree of justification, that he had created Beardsley. It is likely that Beardsley's style became more satirical and sinister because of Wilde's influence. They had first met on 12 July 1891 at the house of Edward Burne-Jones when the eighteen-year-old Beardsley arrived unannounced. Wilde and Constance took Beardsley and his sister Mabel home in their carriage and they became friends. The friendship would come to memorable and immortal fruition in their collaboration on *Salomé*, Wilde's play which Beardsley illustrated.

Wilde had written most of *Salomé* before the end of 1891, a year which has been rightly called his *annus mirabilis*. In this year he published four books – two volumes of stories, one of critical essays and a novel. He also wrote his first successful play, *Lady Windermere's Fan*, which would première at the St James's Theatre on 20 February 1892.

As with Wilde's other art *Lady Windermere's Fan* is intrinsically moral in tone and intention. Stylistically, Wilde was perfecting the drawing room dialogue which would secure him a place among the great modern dramatists. Embedded within it, like gems in a crown, are the epigrammatic wit and wisdom for which Wilde is deservedly celebrated. Thus, Lady Windermere dismisses the materialism and scientism of late Victorian England with succinct brilliance. 'Nowadays people seem to look on life as a speculation. It is not a speculation. It is a sacrament. Its ideal is Love. Its purification is Sacrifice.' Lord Darlington, when told by another character that all people are good, replies, 'No, we are all in the gutter, but some of us are looking at the stars.' Perhaps most memorable of all is Lord Darlington's definition of a cynic as 'a man who knows the price of everything and the value of nothing'.

A recurring theme in Wilde's art which resurfaces in *Lady Windermere's Fan* is the redemption of ostensibly evil or 'bad' people through acts of love, and the confounding of ostensibly 'good' people when they succumb to the 'holier-than-thou' judgements of the pharisee or the puritan. When Mrs Erlynne endeavours to persuade Lady Windermere to return to her husband, Lady Windermere scoffs at her advice on the grounds that Mrs Erlynne is a woman of ill repute: 'You, whose whole life is a lie, how could you speak the truth about anything?' When Mrs Erlynne persists, Lady Windermere's hardheartedness is reiterated: 'You talk as if you had a heart. Women like you have no hearts. Heart is not in you. You are bought and sold.' Mrs Erlynne is hurt by the words but her selflessness remains:

Believe what you choose about me. I am not worth a moment's sorrow. But don't spoil your beautiful young life on my account! ... You don't know what it is to fall into the pit, to be despised, mocked, abandoned, sneered at – to be an outcast! to find the door shut against one, to have to creep in by hideous byways, afraid every moment lest the mask should be stripped from one's face, and all the while to hear the laughter, the horrible laughter of the world, a thing more tragic than all the tears the world has shed. You don't know what it is. One pays for one's sin, and then one pays again, and all one's life one pays. You must never know that. – As for me, if suffering be an expiation, then at this moment I have expiated all my faults, whatever they have been; for tonight you have made a heart in one who had it not, made it and broken it. – But let that pass. I may have wrecked my own life, but I will not let you wreck yours ... You couldn't stand dishonour! No! Go back, Lady Windermere, to the husband who loves you, whom you love. You have a child, Lady Windermere ... God gave you that child. He will require from you that you make his life fine, that you watch over him. What answer will you make to God if his life is ruined through you?

Lady Windermere returns to her husband and child and soon finds herself defending Mrs Erlynne from Lord Windermere's assertion that she is bad, 'as bad as a woman can be'.

Arthur, Arthur, don't talk so bitterly about any woman. I don't think now that people can be divided into the good and the bad as though they were two separate races or creations. What are called good women may have terrible things in them, mad moods of recklessness, assertion, jealousy, sin. Bad women, as they are termed, may have in them sorrow, repentance, pity, sacrifice. And I don't think Mrs Erlynne a bad woman – I know she's not.

Considering the paradox and theme at the heart of *Lady Windermere's Fan* it comes as little surprise that Wilde originally planned to call the play *A Good Woman*. The theme and the paradox preoccupied Wilde in 1891 to such an extent that he planned an altogether more risqué and audacious play on the same theme. The subject would be Salomé, the ultimate 'bad' woman and sex symbol of the New Testament whose dancing for Herod secured the beheading of St John the Baptist. Wilde's *Salomé* would be driven by the same potent and explosive compound of love and lust, faith and the flesh which had inspired the conflicting passions in John Gray's *Silverpoints*. Gray's poems had pitted homosexual passion against the Passion of Christ; Wilde's play would pit heterosexual passion against the martyrdom of John the Baptist. In both cases, love and lust were locked in mortal conflict.

1 Brian Roberts, *The Mad Bad Line: The Family of Lord Alfred Douglas*, London: Hamish Hamilton, 1981, p. 156.
2 Elizabeth Longford, *A Pilgrimage of Passion: The Life of Wilfrid Scawen Blunt*, London, 1979, pp. 290–1; quoted in Ellmann, *Oscar Wilde*, p. 302.
3 Ellmann, *Oscar Wilde*, p. 302.
4 Ibid., pp. 266–7.
5 *Blackfriars*, vol. viii, no. 92, 1927.
6 Ibid.
7 Ibid.
8 Rupert Croft-Cooke, *The Unrecorded Life of Oscar Wilde*, London: W.H. Allen, 1972, p. 10.
9 Ellmann, *Oscar Wilde*, p. 291.
10 *Daily Telegraph*, 20 February 1892.
11 Plarr, *Ernest Dowson*, p. 60.
12 Ibid., p. 72.
13 Ellmann, *Oscar Wilde*, p. 369.
14 Ibid., p. 370.

EIGHTEEN

Saints and Sinners

Love can canonize people. The saints are those who have been most loved.

... we are all in the gutter, but some of us are looking at the stars.

The lustful image of Salomé had been brought luridly alive for Wilde when he had read Huysmans' *A Rebours* on his honeymoon in Paris in 1884. Des Esseintes, the decadent hero of Huysmans' novel, had been fascinated by Gustav Moreau's paintings of the legendary Biblical seductress, believing that they had brought to life the 'weird and superhuman' Salomé of Des Esseintes' dreams.

> No longer was she merely the dancing girl who extorts a cry of lust and concupiscence from an old man by the lascivious contortions of her body; who breaks the will, masters the mind of a King by the spectacle of her quivering bosoms, heaving belly and tossing thighs; she was now revealed in a sense as the symbolic incarnation of world-old Vice, the goddess of immortal Hysteria, the curse of Beauty supreme above all other beauties by the cataleptic spasm that stirs her flesh and steels her muscles, – a monstrous Beast of the Apocalypse, indifferent, irresponsible, poisoning, like Helen of Troy of the old Classic fables, all who come near her, all who see her, all who touch her.[1]

Wilde first announced his intention to write about Salomé to Edgar Saltus, the American novelist. Saltus voiced his approval, declaring his own plans to write about Mary Magdalene. 'We will pursue the wantons together,' he remarked. Saltus's *Mary Magdalen* was published in 1891 and Wilde wrote with evident approval that it was a 'strange book, so pessimistic, so poisonous and so perfect'.[2]

Wilde's obsession with Salomé was at its height during an extended visit to Paris in 1891. The extent of her hold over him was evident in conversations he had with Enriqué Gomez Carrillo, a young diplomat and writer. Learning that Gomez came from Madrid, Wilde talked enthusiastically of the Prado Museum which was 'filled with Salomés'. He spoke of Titian's portrait of her, before which Tintoretto exclaimed, 'Here is the man who paints with living flesh!' 'No doubt you have seen that Salomé,' Wilde continued, 'she is standing up after her triumph, holding up on a silver tray the head of the Precursor.' He also discussed with Gomez the other Salomés exhibited at the Prado by Stanzioni and Alessandro Veronese. Ultimately, however, Wilde's fascination was only aroused but not satisfied by these depictions of his fantasy. He believed that the greatest artists had been captivated by Salomé but had never captured her. She had always slipped through their fingers. Rubens' painting had made her look sluttish, Leonardo's was too reserved and other-worldly. Her charms had also eluded the best efforts of Albrecht Dürer, Ghirlandajo, Piazza, Van Thulden and Leclerc. Worst of all, Wilde believed, were the portraits by Regnault and Paul de Saint Victor which made her look like a gypsy with the skin of an Englishwoman. Wilde agreed with Huysmans that only Moreau's paintings had captured a sense of the true Salomé and he often quoted Huysmans' famous words from *A Rebours*:

> She is almost naked! In the heat of the dance her veils have become loosened, the brocaded robes have fallen away, and only the jewels protect her naked body. A slender belt binds her waist, a superb jewel shines like a star between her breasts; below a band of garnets covers her thighs and two shining emeralds hide her sex.

From the very first day they met, Gomez recalled, Wilde never ceased to speak of Salomé. Women passing in the street would remind him of her and he would wander through the Parisian streets, looking in jewellers' windows and imagining the perfect jewellery for the adornment of her body.

> One evening after a long empty silence, he suddenly said to me right in the middle of the street:

– Don't you think she would be better completely naked?

At once I understood we were talking about Her.

– Yes, he continued, utterly naked. But with jewels, many jewels, interlacing strands of jewels; all the gems flashing, tinkling and jingling at her ankles, her wrists, her arms, about her neck, around her waist; their reflections making the utter shamelessness of that warm flesh even more shocking ... Her lips in Leonardo's painting reveal the limitless cruelty of her soul. Her lust must be an abyss, her corruptness, an ocean. The very pearls must die of love upon her bosom. The fragrance of her maidenhood must make the emeralds dim, and inflame the rubies' fire. On that burning flesh even the sapphire must lose the unstained purity of its azure blue.[3]

On another occasion, at the home of the poet Jean Lorrain, Wilde turned pale at the sight of a sculpture of a woman's decapitated head. 'But it's Salomé!' he exclaimed, already perceiving the climax to his own version in which Salomé shares the fate of her victim. With this ending in mind he began a short story entitled 'The Double Beheading'. Feeling that Salomé had slipped through his fingers as stealthily and seductively as she had slipped through the fingers of many of his predecessors, he tore up his efforts and considered writing a poem. Eventually, he settled on writing a play. Significantly, he chose to write it in French. This, perhaps, was an act of homage to the influences that were feeding his creativity as he commenced writing. Gustave Moreau's sensuous symbolism described so erotically by Huysmans was never far from his mind, and he must have felt the images of Mallarmé's poem 'Hérodiade' playing on his imagination. There was, according to Gomez, another earthier reason for Wilde's choice of the French language for his *Salomé*. 'He was once more obsessed by the desire of seeing Sarah Bernhardt, by some miracle a young woman again, dancing naked before Herod.'[4]

The power of Wilde's Salomé is beyond doubt. She is Lust Incarnate. She stands in relation to the Blessed Virgin as Satan stands in relation to Christ. If Satan is the Anti-Christ, Wilde's Salomé is the Anti-Virgin. She desires the body of John the Baptist precisely because it is the forbidden fruit. When she first sets eyes on him it is his chastity which arouses her. 'I am sure he is chaste as the moon is. He is like a moonbeam, like a shaft of silver. His flesh must be cool like ivory. I would look closer at him.'

There are parallels between Salomé's temptation of John the Baptist and Satan's temptation of Christ. As with Christ in the wilderness, John is tempted three times. At first, Salomé desires his body which is 'white like the lilies of a field ... white like the snows that lie on the mountains ... There is nothing in the world so white as thy body. Let me touch thy body.' The temptation is resisted and John tells her, 'I will not listen to thee. I listen but to the voice of the Lord God.' Next she desires his hair. 'There is nothing in the world so black as thy hair ... Let me touch thy hair.' Again she is rejected. 'Back, daughter of Sodom! Touch me not. Profane not the temple of the Lord God.' Finally, she desires his mouth which 'is redder than the feet of those who tread the wine-press ... There is nothing in the world so red as thy mouth ... Let me kiss thy mouth.' For the third and final time, the temptation is resisted. 'Never, daughter of Babylon! Daughter of Sodom! Never.'

When Salomé is presented with John's decapitated head she looks on it in triumph. 'Ah! thou wouldst not suffer me to kiss thy mouth, Jokanaan. Well! I will kiss it now. I will bite it with my teeth as one bites a ripe fruit.' Yet the fruit of her lust, so sweet in its tempting expectation, is bitter to taste. She wonders whether the bitterness on John's lips is the taste of blood or the taste of love. Worst of all is the realization that the fruit of her lust is also a fruit of frustration. Although he is now apparently within her power she can't make his eyes look at her, or his mouth speak to her or reciprocate her kiss. The kiss, though taken, is not given. It is barren. Sterile. Unrequited.

Wilde's forceful depiction of evil in *Salomé* has led many critics to the wrong conclusion. Christopher S. Nassaar wrote that Wilde's play was overtly Satanist. 'In *Salomé*,' Nassaar writes, 'Satanism ... shatters all moulds and restrictions and is elevated to the status of a religion'.[5] Nothing could be further from the truth. At the climax to Wilde's play, Salomé's sin has left her unfulfilled, frustrated and without hope: 'Well, thou hast seen thy God, Jokanaan, but me, me, thou didst never see ... I saw thee, Jokanaan, and I loved thee ... I am athirst for thy beauty; I am hungry for thy body; and neither wine nor fruits can appease my desire. What shall I do now, Jokanaan? Neither the floods nor the great waters can quench my passion.' Having slain the object of her desire even the hope of its fulfilment has been removed, leaving nothing but desolation and despair. By the play's conclusion, Salomé is reduced to dementia, repeatedly uttering the refrain, 'I have kissed thy mouth'.

Wilde then adds a symbolic *coup de grâce* in the form of a masterful stage direction: *A moonbeam falls on Salomé, covering her with light.* On a psychological level the moonbeam serves as a symbol of lunacy, spotlighting the madness of her sin. Salomé has become a lunatic of lust. On the deeper spiritual level the moonbeam is the mystical light of St John the Baptist shining on Salomé from beyond the grave. When Salomé had first seen him she had remarked that he was 'chaste as the moon. He is like a moonbeam, like a shaft of silver.' On a mystical level Wilde is hinting that redemption is possible even for a woman as 'bad' as Salomé through the prayers and forgiveness of her saintly victim.

Yet even this ingenious twist is not the end. One final masterstroke remains. As the moonbeam falls on Salomé, Herod turns and utters the play's last three doom-laden words: 'Kill that woman!' As the soldiers slay Salomé, the drama's remaining loose ends are neatly tied up. Her death fulfils John's prophecy that he had heard in the palace 'the beating of the wings of the angel of death', but the prophecy is itself only a reflection of a deeper symmetry. Herod kills the object of his lust as surely as Salomé had killed the object of hers. Thus all-consuming lust lives up to its name. It consumes all.

Once again, Wilde emerges in *Salomé* as a Christian moralist *par excellence*. Far from Satanism shattering all moulds and restrictions and being elevated to the status of a religion, evil is seen in Wilde's play to be shattering itself, imposing its own restrictions and relegating itself to the status of madness. To accuse Wilde of Satanism because of his stark depiction of evil is akin to accusing Dante of the same for his descriptions of the Inferno.

If some critics could not see the play's moral depths beneath the immoral surface, others only perceived the amorality amidst the morality. Richard Ellmann makes much of Salomé's agnosticism, insisting that 'faith does not concern her'.[6] This, of course, is true. Yet Ellmann deduces from this that it doesn't concern Wilde either. This is to miss the point of the play. It is precisely *because* Salomé is without faith that she falls into the errors which ultimately destroy her. With no clear understanding of the true nature of love, its source and its sustaining power, she fails to perceive life's highest common factors and turns to its lowest common denominators. Incapable of love she is left with lust.

When Edgar Saltus read *Salomé* he was quick to return the compliment which Wilde had paid him for his book on Mary Magdalene. He told Wilde that the last line had made him shudder. 'It is only the shudder that counts,' Wilde answered.[7]

Wilde's intentions in writing *Salomé* were evident, paradoxically, in the story about her which he failed to write. In its earlier form, which was possibly what he had in mind when he began writing the short story which he subsequently scrapped, Wilde thought about calling his story or play 'The Decapitation of Salomé'. It would continue beyond where the finished play concluded. Herod, incensed at Salomé's kissing the decollated head of St John, wants to kill her, but at the pleas of Herodias he agrees to banish her instead. She wanders into the desert where she lives a solitary, maligned existence, clothed in animal skins, and subsisting on locusts and wild honey like the Prophet himself. When Jesus passes by, she recognizes Him as the One whom the voice of St John had heralded. She believes in Him but, feeling unworthy of living in His shadow, wanders off again, intent on carrying the Word to far-flung corners of the world. She passes over rivers and seas until, leaving the fiery deserts behind, she arrives at the deserts of snow. Crossing a frozen lake, the ice breaks under her feet. She falls into the water and the jagged ice cuts into her flesh. She is decapitated but not before she can call out the names of Jesus and John. Thereafter, whoever passes the site of her death can see, on a silver plate of re-formed ice, a beautiful severed head on which gleams the crown of golden nimbus.[8] In this way, even the greatest of Biblical sinners has been redeemed. Thus, in both the play and its unfinished form, *Salomé* served as a reiteration of the motif which runs through so much of Wilde's art: redemption and the triumph of love. All saints were sinners and all sinners could be saints.

1 J.K. Huysmans, *Against the Grain*, New York: Illustrated Edition Company, 1931, p. 141.

2 Hart-Davis, *Letters of Oscar Wilde*, p. 275.

3 Gomez Carrillo, 'Comment Oscar Wilde rêva Salomé', *La Plume*, Paris, 1902; reprinted in Mikhail, *Interviews and Recollections*, vol. 1, pp. 192–5.

4 Ibid.

5 Christopher S. Nassaar, *Into the Demon Universe: A Literary Exploration of Oscar Wilde*, New Haven and London: Yale University Press, 1974, p. 93.
6 Ellmann, *Oscar Wilde*, p. 325.
7 Ibid., p. 322.
8 Ibid., p. 325.

NINETEEN

Fatal Attraction

(*Enter* Lord Alfred)
Dear Lord Alfred, do join us.

'I flee from what is moral as from what is impoverished,' Wilde told Gomez Carrillo in 1891, 'I have the same sickness as Des Esseintes.'[1] In these words of anguish and resignation Wilde was encapsulating his inner confusion. Increasingly addicted to life's lusts he sought liberation from his conscience and from the constraints of Christian morality. Even as he was writing of the dangers and evils of lust in *Salomé* he was struggling to free himself from the strictures implicit in its dramatic climax.

As a means of self-justification, he began to yearn for a new religion which would be made in the image of his own desires. 'We are not yet released from the Syrian embrace and its cadaverous divinities,' Wilde told the poet Ernest Raynaud during his stay in Paris in 1891. 'We are always plunged into the kingdom of shadows. While we wait for a new religion of light, let Olympus serve as a shelter and refuge. We must let our instincts laugh and frolic in the sun like a troop of laughing children.'[2] In some respects, Wilde was like the Fisherman in his story, trying desperately to cut his soul away from himself so that he could fulfil his desires without self-reproach. The efforts to do so produced some intriguing results. There was the rejection of the natural for the unnatural. His own theories, he told Raynaud, were more beautiful than 'the languishing beauty of the countryside', adding that 'the solitude of the country stifles and crushes me'.

I am not really myself except in the midst of elegant crowds, in the exploits of capitals, at the heart of rich districts or amid the sumptuous ornamentation of palace-hotels, seated by all the desirable objects and with an army of servants, the warm caress of a plush carpet under my feet ... I detest nature where man has not intervened with his artifice.

The social snobbery found philosophical expression in Nietzschean elitism. The artist, he asserted, was like a diamond while the mass of humanity was merely charcoal. In Nietzschean terms, the artist was the Superman, or *Ubermensch*, while the masses were the *Untermenschen*, who were worthy only of contempt. Such a line of reasoning led Wilde to conclusions which prefigured the warped logic of later pseudo-Nietzscheans such as Josef Mengele. Whereas Mengele sanctioned the torture of human beings in the name of science, Wilde sanctioned it in the name of art: 'When Benvenuto Cellini crucified a living man to study the play of muscles in his death agony, a pope was right to grant him absolution. What is the death of a vague individual if it enables an immortal word to blossom and to create, in Keats's words, an eternal source of ecstasy?'[3]

Of course, as Wilde knew, no pope could grant absolution for such a crime unless the culprit felt and confessed true contrition. Certainly no pope had the right to sanction such an abomination. The key question is whether Wilde, in sincerity, could sanction the abomination himself. One suspects that he could not, in which case his words lack any substance beyond the desire to shock.

The suspicion that everything he had said was little more than disingenuous posturing was reinforced some moments later when Wilde discussed the importance of paradox. Wilde insisted that paradox was the best way of getting at truths which were otherwise inexpressible. He pointed out that the New Testament was full of paradoxes which had become less startling through familiarity. 'What greater enormity could there be than "Blessed are the poor"?' he asked. Wilde's selection of this particular paradox is remarkable considering that it is a succinct refutation of the Nietzschean elitism he had just been preaching.

The conflict between the Wilde who expressed himself in his art and the Wilde trying to escape from himself in his criticism was evident earlier in the conversation with Ernest Raynaud. Before Wilde embarked on his Nietzschean discourse he had refused impatiently to discuss his art. Raynaud had endeavoured to speak of Wilde's writings but was stopped with a gesture: 'Oh let's drop that! I consider those things to be so unimportant.' Clearly Wilde was all too painfully aware of the contradictions inherent in his dualistic approach to life and art. Any honest discussion of his art would inevitably be a rebuttal of his critical pretensions.

On a purely social level Wilde's elliptical eloquence had its advantages. It was used with dramatic effect to attract and beguile a swelling group of young admirers. During his stay in France the young André Gide fell under his spell. At this stage Gide was still a virgin and his homosexuality latent and unpractised. Wilde's witty insinuations and debauched charm infatuated the sexually frustrated Gide so that he felt 'devirginated' psychologically even though no physical relationship developed between them. On 1 January 1892, two weeks after his last encounter with Wilde, Gide wrote in his diary of Wilde's negative influence. 'Wilde, I believe, did me nothing but harm. In his company I lost the habit of thinking. I had more varied emotions, but had forgotten how to bring order into them.'[4] Wilde, for his part, disliked the sordid side of Gide's character, complaining that 'he has a dirty mind, and whatever my views may be about sin, I dislike dirt'.[5] Meanwhile, the sordid side of Wilde's character was captured by the wit of Gide's friend Paul Valéry who joked that Wilde took any subject and 'mechanically transforms it at once into a satanic aphorism'.[6]

Wilde returned to London on or around 22 December 1891, in time to spend Christmas with his wife and sons. His family, however, were being exiled to the margins of his life. At the centre were the impressionable young admirers who clung to his every word. One letter, inviting 'My Dear Delightful Viking' to lunch at the Lyric, was illustrative of the flirtatious tone he adopted with his disciples.[7] One of Wilde's most prominent and devoted admirers at this time was the young Max Beerbohm. The precocious nineteen-year-old was a total convert to Wildeanism, emulating his master with an almost religious zeal. Beerbohm, who had first met Wilde in 1888, while still at school at Charterhouse, referred to Wilde as 'the Divinity'. He donned his master's mask so self-consciously through an excess of youthful enthusiasm that he would have been guilty of parody if not proved innocent through naïveté. The disciple's disguise prompted a witty response from his master. 'When you are alone with him,' Wilde asked Ada Leverson, 'does he take off his face and reveal his mask?'[8]

As Beerbohm matured he distanced himself from Wilde, particularly after the latter's downfall. Unlike many of Wilde's other disciples he did not share his master's homosexual inclinations and caricatured him savagely in later years. Yet his admiration remained. In 1954, when Compton Mackenzie unveiled a plaque to commemorate Wilde's centenary at the house in Tite Street where Wilde and Constance lived for eleven years, Beerbohm made a memorable and generous tribute. Beerbohm was eighty-two years old and too frail to travel to London for the unveiling ceremony, but his words were read by Mackenzie:

I have had the privilege of listening to many masters of table talk – Meredith and Swinburne, Edmund Gosse and Henry James, Augustine Birrell and Arthur Balfour, Gilbert Chesterton and Desmond MacCarthy and Hilaire Belloc – all of them splendid in their own way. But Oscar was the greatest of them all – the most spontaneous and yet the most polished, the most soothing and yet the most surprising ... Nobody was willing to interrupt the music of so magnificent a virtuoso. To have heard him consoled me for not having heard Dr Johnson or Edmund Burke, Lord Brougham or Sidney Smith.[9]

Beerbohm was but one of several young men who orbited Wilde's circle in the early 1890s. Lionel Johnson and Ernest Dowson, the two leading lights in the Rhymers' Club, 'hovered reverently' round Wilde, according to Victor Plarr. It appears that Plarr, another prominent member of the Rhymers' Club, remained immune to Wilde's charms, marvelling at 'the fascination which poor Wilde exercised over the otherwise rational'. Wilde sat 'enthroned and surrounded by a deferential circle'.[10] The novelist Morley Roberts described a gathering at which Wilde 'wore a black shirt front and that Dowson and Johnson, small fairy creatures in white, climbed about upon it'.[11] In spite of the effeminate imagery adopted by Roberts, it seems that Dowson was not physically attracted to Wilde. His tastes were strictly heterosexual though he became as enslaved as Wilde to licentious liaisons. Lionel Johnson, however, shared Wilde's sexual preferences and was, apparently, seduced by Wilde at their first meeting. Wilde had travelled to Oxford in February 1890 and was told, possibly by Walter Pater, about a new young poet at New College. His curiosity aroused, Wilde called on Johnson. Wilde spoke with 'infinite flippancy' of everyone, was 'delightful' and left the young poet besotted. 'I am in love with him,' Johnson informed a friend afterwards.

Johnson was utterly entranced by *The Picture of Dorian Gray*, as was Max Beerbohm who wrote his 'Ballade de la Vie Joyeuse' about it. Like Beerbohm, Johnson expressed his admiration for Wilde's novel in verse, choosing Latin as the mode which best expressed his mood. Entitled 'In Honorem Doriani Creatorisque Eius', 'In Honour of Dorian and His Creator', Johnson's poem speaks of 'strange loves', the plucking of strange flowers, 'apples of Sodom' and 'tender sins'. Johnson lent his copy of *Dorian Gray* to a young cousin from Winchester College who was now up at Magdalen. The cousin, Lord Alfred Douglas, was soon 'passionately absorbed' in it, informing A.J.A. Symons that he read it 'fourteen times running'. In late June 1891, Douglas persuaded Johnson to take him to meet Wilde in Tite Street. It was the first fateful meeting in their ultimately fatal relationship. Six years later Henry Davray, one of Wilde's translators, helped a drunken Lionel Johnson home. Johnson looked at the framed portraits of Wilde and Douglas on his wall, and moaned, 'Mon Dieu! Mon Dieu!'[12]

Wilde's eye for classical beauty found in the faultless features of the youngest son of the Marquess of Queensberry an object of idolatry. Douglas's alabaster complexion, his prominent .ips, flowing blond hair and sunken surly eyes immortalized themselves in Wilde's mind as a Grecian bust. Since, in Wilde's mind, life followed art, Douglas appeared as a vision of a statuesque Greek god, a reincarnation of ancient perfection. He was word made flesh. Wilde had felt the same about John Gray but Gray's image was fading with the remnants of their friendship. Time was ripe for a new apparition, a new idol, a new object for his devotion.

Soon after their first meeting Wilde formally introduced Douglas to Constance who seems to have liked him. Presumably she was oblivious to her husband's feelings towards this latest admirer. Her innocence appears to have shielded her from the seamier side of Wilde'~ life which became seamier still following his association with

Douglas. In the spring of 1892 Wilde came to Douglas's rescue when an indiscreet letter had led to his being blackmailed. Wilde went up to Oxford and stayed the weekend in Douglas's rooms in the high street, resolving the crisis by instructing his solicitor to pay the blackmailer a hundred pounds for the incriminating document. It would not be the last time that blackmail would play a part in their relationship. By early summer, Wilde was sufficiently under Douglas's spell to write of him to Robert Ross that he was 'quite like a narcissus – so white and gold'. Douglas was now known to Wilde as 'Bosie' and Wilde wrote to Ross that 'Bosie is so tired: he lies like a hyacinth on the sofa, and I worship him'.[13]

During August and September Wilde took a farmhouse in Felbrigg, a village near Cromer in Norfolk, to write a play for Herbert Beerbohm Tree, Max Beerbohm's half-brother, who was manager of the Haymarket Theatre. At the same time Constance went with the children to stay at a relative's house at Babbacombe Cliff, near Torquay in Devon. Wilde invited Douglas to stay with him in Norfolk while he wrote the play, *A Woman of No Importance*. Writing to Constance, Wilde informed her that Douglas had fallen ill. Richard Ellmann suggests that the illness, real or contrived, may have been used by Wilde as the pretext for not joining his wife and children in Devon. In spite of her husband's increasing neglect, Constance remained as loyal and devoted as ever, writing to Wilde on 18 September of her concerns for Douglas and her willingness to help.

> Dearest Oscar, I am so sorry about Lord Alfred Douglas, and wish I was at Cromer to look after him. If you think I could do any good, do telegraph for me, because I can easily get over to you.[14]

She was not wanted and not sent for. Slowly Constance was beginning to realize that she was surplus to her husband's needs, a woman of no importance. One wonders whether Wilde had his wife in mind during the writing of *Lady Windermere's Fan* the previous year. In the original draft of the play Lady Windermere complains of her treatment at the hands of her husband: 'How perfectly horrible! Why do men marry us? Why do they lie to us? Do they want us to be as bad as they are themselves? How hideous life is.'[15] Wilde crossed through this passage during his final revision of the play and it does not appear in the finished version.

The relationship between Wilde and Douglas, though intense, was not constrained by any commitment to sexual fidelity. Douglas was promiscuous and introduced Wilde to the world of homosexual prostitution. From the autumn of 1892 onwards he encouraged Wilde to form casual relationships with young men who would prostitute themselves for a few pounds and a good dinner. Wilde also became friends with others who shared his and Douglas's taste in teenage male prostitutes. Douglas introduced him to Maurice Schwabe, a nephew of the Solicitor-General, and through him Wilde met Alfred Taylor, a former public schoolboy at Marlborough who was the son of a cocoa manufacturer. Taylor, in turn, introduced Wilde to a wider circle of boys, most notably Sidney Mavor whom Wilde would continue to see for a period of eighteen months. In October 1892 Schwabe introduced Wilde to Freddy Atkins, a wretched seventeen-year-old who supplemented his income as a prostitute by blackmailing his clients. For a man in Wilde's position this was dangerous company. Yet he seemed as reckless as they were wretched and heedless of the peril he was putting himself in.

During the following year Wilde began to stay in hotels on a regular basis, informing Constance that it was necessary so that he could work without interruption. At the Albemarle Hotel from 1 to 17 January he was interrupted regularly by several young men, arousing the suspicions of the proprietor who welcomed his departure. In February Wilde met up with a seventeen-year-old named Alfred Wood, who had been passed on to him by Douglas. As arranged they met at the Café Royal before proceeding to the Florence in Rupert Street where they dined in a private room. Having wined and dined they returned to Tite Street. (When Constance was away there was no need to stay in hotels.) They continued to meet and Wilde lavished money, cigarette cases and other gifts upon him, as he did with the other boys, cultivating a reputation for generosity of which they took full advantage.

Douglas also took full advantage of Wilde's generosity. Between the autumn of 1892 and spring 1895 Wilde estimated that he spent more than £5,000 on Douglas. On an ordinary day with Douglas in London, Wilde would spend between £12 and £20 on luncheon, dinner, supper, amusements and hansom cabs. Wilde later complained that he had paid for Douglas's insistence on a life of 'reckless profusion'.

Douglas and Wilde continued to share the services of Alfred Wood. Douglas gave Wood some cast-off clothes, carelessly forgetting that there were some compromising letters from Wilde in the pockets. Seizing the opportunity, Wood sought to blackmail Wilde, seeking £60 so that he could go to America. In the event Wilde paid him £30.

At this period Wilde and Douglas also met, through Taylor, a boy named Charles Parker whose liaisons with them would seal their fate a couple of years later. For the time being, however, their promiscuity, and the various sexual partners they shared, remained hidden from all but a select crowd of secretive *illuminati*. To the uninitiated and naïve, Douglas's and Wilde's friendship was presumed to be platonic. Max Beerbohm probably guessed the truth beneath the respectable surface and considered Douglas 'a very pretty reflection of Oscar'. Beerbohm approved of Douglas, describing him as 'very charming' and 'nearly brilliant' but added, with reference to Douglas's fiery temper and reckless personality, that he was 'obviously mad (like all his family, I believe)'.[16] The reference to madness as a family trait was not a unique observation. Brian Roberts in his study of Lord Alfred Douglas's family entitled his book *The Mad Bad Line*, an allusion to a phrase Wilde had used to describe Douglas's heritage in *De Profundis*. The eccentric streak which appears to be an inherent characteristic of the Queensberrys dated back to James (1672–1711), son of the second Duke of Queensberry, who was reputedly 'an idiot from birth'. The reputation for madness, or at least for eccentricity, was heightened by the controversial figure of Douglas's father, John Sholto Douglas, ninth Marquess of Queensberry. According to Roberts, Lord Alfred Douglas and his father were 'the last true representatives of their "mad bad line".'[17]

The Marquess of Queensberry's belligerence and his mercurial unpredictability were traits that his son had inherited. Best known to posterity as the founder of modern boxing which is still governed by the Queensberry rules, the Marquess was most notorious in his own day for his fulminations against Christianity. A little over a decade earlier the Scottish lords had voted not to re-elect him as one of their representatives to the House of Lords on the grounds that he had publicly denied the existence of God. In 1880 he published in pamphlet form his poem *The Spirit of the Matterhorn* in which he advanced the theory that the body predetermined the soul. Consequently one must choose one's mate carefully, or eugenically, because future generations inherit not just their bodies but their souls from their parents. 'Go, tell mankind, see that thy blood be pure.'

In December 1885 he attempted to break up a performance of Tennyson's *The May Queen* as a protest against the negative characterization of an atheist in it. The stunt brought him added notoriety. 'The more the Marquess of Queensberry orates to his own class,' the editor of a weekly, the *Bat*, commented, 'the less effect he seems to create. His celebrated speech on his brother peer's play only succeeded in obtaining for him ejection from the theatre.'[18] Queensberry's reply was published in the following issue:

> Sir, – I thank you for your advertisement in your scurrilous journal –
> Conservative, I presume. You say I was ejected from a certain theatre.
> So I was. Also another advertisement. I believe the play was taken off
> three weeks afterwards ... Thanking you for further advertisement,
> yours faithfully,
>
> QUEENSBERRY

A little over a year later, on 22 January 1887, Queensberry's wife gained a divorce from him on the grounds of his adultery. Yet if he had proved a poor husband, he was a better father – taking an intense interest in his children's lives, watching over their welfare and assisting them financially when required. Wilde's friendship with his son was bound to come under his scrutiny sooner or later. It was only a matter of time. When at last his considerable rage was aroused he would prove a formidable opponent. Wilde's wit would find its match in Queensberry's pugilistic pugnacity. In playing with Douglas, Wilde was playing with fire.

At first, however, neither Queensberry nor his former wife suspected anything sinister in their son's relationship with Wilde. Lady Queensberry even invited Oscar and Constance to her house in Bracknell where she confided in Wilde her concerns over her son's academic difficulties at Oxford, his vanity and his financial extravagance. According to Desmond MacCarthy, Lady Queensberry always looked 'as though she had been struck, and was still quivering from the blow',[19] and one can imagine Wilde's suppressed amusement as he watched her admonishing her son's weaknesses. Prone to vanity and financial extravagance himself, Wilde was hardly likely to condemn it in others. Furthermore, he was secretly besotted with her son and probably found his alleged defects part of the attraction.

Wilde's amusement at Lady Queensberry's proprietary approach to motherhood found comic expression in the character of Lady Bracknell in *The Importance of Being Earnest*. One can imagine the hilarity that Wilde's caricature caused when 'Lady Bracknell' was created, Wilde and Douglas both chuckling at Lady Queensberry's expense. She had become the model for the most brilliant of Wilde's comic creations. Perhaps, however, the choice of name was unnecessarily tactless, if not cruel. Lady Queensberry could not fail to recognize herself in Wilde's ridiculous creation, rueing the time she had invited him to Bracknell. In true Victorian, or Bracknellian, fashion she would not have been amused.

Eventually, in the sobering light of his prison cell, Wilde would regret that he had not listened to Lady Queensberry more seriously. In his long letter to Douglas, written in Reading gaol and later to be published as *De Profundis*, Wilde wrote that he blamed himself for allowing Douglas to bring him to 'utter and discreditable financial ruin'. He referred back to the meeting with Lady Queensberry at Bracknell in October 1892 and reiterated her belief that her son's chief faults were his vanity and the fact that he was 'all wrong about money'. Wilde had a distinct recollection of how he had laughed at her warnings. 'I had no idea that the first would bring me to prison, and the second to bankruptcy.'

1 Ellmann, *Oscar Wilde*, p. 325.
2 Ibid., p. 329.
3 Ibid.
4 Ibid., p. 335.
5 Douglas, *Without Apology*, p. 274.
6 Ellmann, *Oscar Wilde*, pp. 335–6.
7 Unpublished and undated letter to an unidentified correspondent, British Library, Department of Modern Manuscripts.
8 Ellmann, *Oscar Wilde*, p. 292.
9 Quoted by Wilde's son, Vyvyan Holland, in Introduction to *Complete Works of Oscar Wilde*, *op. cit.*, p. 11.
10 Plarr, *Ernest Dowson*, p. 64.
11 Ibid.
12 Ellmann, *Oscar Wilde*, p. 306.
13 Hart-Davis, *Letters of Oscar Wilde*, p. 314.

14 Ellmann, *Oscar Wilde*, p. 356.
15 Original typescript of Acts I and II of *A Good Woman* (later *Lady Windermere's Fan*), Magdalen College Archives.
16 Ellmann, *Oscar Wilde*, p. 364.
17 Roberts, *The Mad Bad Line*, p. 294.
18 *Bat*, 15 December 1885.
19 Ellmann, *Oscar Wilde*, p. 363.

TWENTY

Courting Conviction

> Hate blinded you ... You thought simply of how to get your father into
> prison. To see him 'in the dock', as you used to say ... Well, you had your
> desire gratified. Hate granted you every single thing you wished for. It
> was an indulgent Master to you. It is so, indeed, to all who serve it.

In February 1892, *Lady Windermere's Fan* went into rehearsal at the
St James's Theatre. The first performance, on 20 February, was a
sell-out. His old flames Florence Balcombe, now Stoker, and Lillie
Langtry were present at the opening night, as was his wife. However,
Wilde only had eyes for Edward Shelley, a clerk at the Bodley Head.
That night he did not return home to Tite Street with Constance but
stayed at the Albemarle Hotel with Shelley. The play was an instant
success, running until the end of July before touring the provinces.
On 31 October it was again being staged in the West End. 'You have
had a brilliant success!' Lady Wilde wrote to him on 24 February, 'and
I am so happy.'[1] After the performances, basking in his triumph,
Wilde sometimes went to the Crown, off Charing Cross Road, where
he held court among his disciples. There, with Symons, Dowson,
Beardsley, Beerbohm and Johnson in attendance, he would take centre stage and drink hot port until after midnight.

Even in triumph Wilde was never far from controversy. In the
second week of June, as *Lady Windermere's Fan* was packing in the
audiences at the St James's Theatre, his *Salomé* was being rehearsed at
the Palace Theatre. Everything looked perfect for its successful production. Sarah Bernhardt had even agreed to play the part of Salomé,
fulfilling Wilde's fantasy. Two weeks into rehearsals it became apparent that E.F.S. Pigott, the licenser of plays, was considering whether it

should be banned. His right to do so was based on an old Puritan law that forbade the depiction on the stage of Biblical characters. Ironically, the law had been enacted to prevent 'papist idolatry' but was being used by later generations of puritans to prevent 'obscenity'. Displaying his own disdain for the law, Wilde pointed out that Saint-Saëns' *Samson and Delilah*, Massenet's *Hérodias* and Rubinstein's *Judas Maccabaeus* had all fallen foul of the censor. In an interview with Robert Ross for the *Pall Mall Budget*, Wilde threatened to leave England and settle in France if *Salomé* was banned. 'I will not consent to call myself a citizen of a country that shows such narrowness in artistic judgement. I am not English. I am Irish which is quite another thing.'[2] Wilde's threat was treated with ridicule by the press. Much merriment was had at Wilde's expense over the fact that he would be subject to military service if he became a French citizen. *Punch* published a caricature of Wilde in the uniform of a French conscript and the *New York Times* declared on 3 July that 'all London is laughing at Oscar Wilde's threat to become a Frenchman'. Whistler, savouring every moment of Wilde's embarrassment, added his own vitriolic contribution: 'Oscar has scored another brilliant – exposure.'[3] Wilde was hopelessly isolated. Only William Archer and Bernard Shaw took his side in his battle against the censor. The rest of the critics, along with many leading actors such as Henry Irving, publicly endorsed the censorship in testimony before a commission of inquiry.

While controversy raged over *Salomé* Wilde was in the midst of writing his next play. *A Woman of No Importance* was an altogether safer prospect, steering clear of the Biblical and keeping to the drawing room domesticity that had characterized *Lady Windermere's Fan*.

Wilde's characters in *A Woman of No Importance* mimic the *bons mots* which were such a feature of his own table talk. 'How clever you are, my dear!' Lady Hunstanton says to Mrs Allonby. 'You never mean a single word you say.' In between, Wilde squeezes moments of social insight which bestow on the drama a depth beyond the witty frivolity. Hester's discourse against hypocrisy suggests Wilde's anger at the way *Salomé* had been misunderstood and condemned in ignorance:

You love the beauty that you can see and touch and handle, the beauty that you can destroy, and do destroy, but of the unseen beauty of life, of the unseen beauty of a higher life, you know nothing. You have lost life's secret. Oh, your English society seems to me shallow, selfish, foolish. It has blinded its eyes, and stopped its ears. It lies like a leper in purple. It sits like a dead thing smeared with gold. It is all wrong, all wrong.

Beneath the prim, proper and respectable surface there is always the hint of scandal, the scent of decay and the unseen debauchery. Outside the cosy Victorian drawing room lurks the seamy world of Dorian Gray. The character of Lord Henry Weston is a thinly disguised reincarnation of Lord Henry Wotton in Wilde's novel. He has 'a hideous smile and a hideous past'. He is asked everywhere, no dinner party is complete without him, but he has left a trail of ruined reputations behind him. Those he has ruined are 'outcasts', 'nameless'.

Lord Henry Weston remains only a sinister shadow who never makes an appearance in the play. He is mentioned but not seen, the spectre of the unmentionable, unseen world. The protagonist in the play who most resembles him is Lord Illingworth, an arch-cynic whose past sins set the dramatic events in motion. He and his fellow cynic Mrs Allonby have some of the best lines, much as the devil is reputed to have the best tunes, but as the plot unfolds it enfolds him in its snare. Mrs Arbuthnot is the woman of no importance of the play's title, so named by Lord Illingworth at the conclusion of Act I. She has had his illegitimate child and has borne the shame of doing so, living a lie and lying to her son so that he should not know the truth. When Lord Illingworth discovers that Gerald Arbuthnot is his son, he endeavours to poison his mind against her.

LORD ILLINGWORTH: I suppose your mother is very religious, and that sort of thing.

GERALD: Oh, yes, she's always going to church.

LORD ILLINGWORTH: Ah! she is not modern, and to be modern is the only thing worth being nowadays. You want to be modern, don't you, Gerald? You want to know life as it really is. Not to be put off with any old-fashioned theories about life. Well, what you have to do at present is simply to fit yourself for the best society. A man who can dominate a London dinner-table can dominate the world. The future belongs to the dandy. It is the exquisites who are going to rule.

Lord Illingworth continues by bestowing some sartorial wisdom, informing Gerald that he must learn how to tie his tie better. 'Sentiment is all very well for the buttonhole. But the essential thing for a necktie is style. A well-tied tie is the first serious step in life.'

Lord Illingworth's 'philosophy of the superficial' is contrasted with Mrs Arbuthnot's religious philosophy. When Gerald discovers that Lord Illingworth is his father he tries to persuade his mother to marry him. She refuses adamantly, vowing that she will never 'stand before God's altar and ask God's blessing on so hideous a mockery' as a marriage between her and her son's father.

> I will not say the words the Church bids us to say. I will not say them. I dare not. How could I swear to love the man I loathe, to honour him who wrought you dishonour, to obey him who, in his mastery, made me to sin? No; marriage is a sacrament for those who love each other. It is not for such as him, or such as me. Gerald, to save you from the world's sneers and taunts I have lied to the world. For twenty years I have lied to the world. I could not tell the world the truth ... But not for my own sake will I lie to God, and in God's presence.

She explains to her son that she had turned to the Church as an outcast from the world: 'where else could I turn? God's house is the only house where sinners are made welcome ...'

In the widely contrasting characters of Mrs Arbuthnot and Lord Illingworth, and in their equally contrasting philosophies, Wilde appears to be pitting the two aspects of his own personality against each other. Lord Illingworth is the worldly Critic, whose philosophy of the superficial is both cynical and humorously entertaining; Mrs Arbuthnot the Artist who expresses herself with a religious sensibility that values life in terms of morality. It is intriguing, therefore, to see who will be triumphant at the conclusion of Wilde's play, the Artist or the Critic.

As the play approaches its climax, the three characters Lord Illingworth had sought to corrupt – Mrs Arbuthnot, Gerald and Hester, the honourable girl whom he had tried to force his attentions upon – are reconciled in love. Gerald and Hester are to be married and they accept Mrs Arbuthnot's secret shame with compassion. In contrast,

Lord Illingworth makes his final exit, having failed in his efforts to manipulate Mrs Arbuthnot for his own ends. Shortly after he leaves, Gerald returns and notices a glove on the floor which Lord Illingworth has left. 'Whose glove is this?' he asks. Turning round, his mother replies: 'Oh! No one. No one in particular. A man of no importance.'

Wilde's message is unmistakable. Even Lord Illingworth's name is a coded symbol, a combination suggestive of ill-worth.

With unerring consistency Wilde's art had emerged yet again as a towering contradiction of his criticism. Wilde the Artist had produced in *A Woman of No Importance* another gem to be set within the crown of his literary reputation. Beside this edifying achievement, Wilde's cynical alter ego stoops like a critic of no importance who is only worthy of Lady Hunstanton's words: 'How clever you are, my dear! You never mean a single word you say.' This, however, was the judgement of art. The Critic saw it differently. Wilde's double life, the secret affair with Douglas, the clandestine liaisons with male prostitutes and the double-crossing of his wife on an almost daily basis, had enshrined the *double entendre* at the very core of his psyche. His higher self, emerging triumphant in his art, still clung, almost unwillingly, to the religious sensibility which had accompanied him throughout his life. His lower self, pouring forth epigrams at the dinner table or in his criticism, sought licentious liberation from the moral constraints that his higher self, the voice of conscience, sought to impose. He told Herbert Beerbohm Tree, who played Lord Illingworth, that the character he was portraying was 'certainly not natural. He is a figure of art. Indeed, if you can bear the truth, he is Myself.'[4] If Wilde was in earnest and not merely speaking for effect, the judgement of his play would suggest that he thought very little of himself. If so, the cynical pose and the quicksilver wit were only masks to conceal his self-loathing.

A Woman of No Importance opened at the Haymarket Theatre on 19 April 1893. It was as successful as its predecessor. At the curtain call on the opening night, with dignitaries such as Balfour and Chamberlain in attendance, the actors were heartily applauded. Wilde, however, was greeted with jeers of derision. Such was his public reputation, so assiduously cultivated by himself, that the audience saw him as the real-life Lord Illingworth. Wilde was shaken by the hostile reception. Standing before the curtain, he only said, 'Ladies and gentlemen, I regret to inform you that Mr Oscar Wilde is not in the house.' He then made his exit from the stage, as disappointed and confounded by his reception as Lord Illingworth had been when he made his final exit a few moments earlier. It was living proof of one of Wilde's favourite maxims. Life was following art.

If another story is to be believed, Wilde was to have a further disconcerting experience the following night. After attending the second night of his play, at which the Prince of Wales was present, he dined at Blanche Roosevelt's house. Before dinner the guests put their hands through a curtain so that the palmist Cheiro could read their palms without knowing their identities. When Wilde held out his hands, Cheiro found the markings on each so different from the other that he explained that in palmistry the left hand denoted hereditary tendencies and the right hand individual developments. He said that the left hand in front of him promised a brilliant success but the right hand indicated impending ruin. 'The left hand is the hand of a king, but the right that of a king who will send himself into exile.' Wilde was superstitious and found himself deeply shaken for the second time in twenty-four hours. At what date would his ruin come about, he enquired. Cheiro replied that it would happen in his fortieth year. Wilde was thirty-eight at the time and his downfall was almost exactly two years away. Without another word Wilde left the party.[5] Richard Ellmann recounts this episode without comment but its source is somewhat suspect. The story was told by Cheiro himself in his memoirs, published twenty years later, and smacks of self-justification after the event. Nonetheless, Ellmann's discussion of Wilde's sense of doom illustrates that Wilde would have taken the palmist seriously if the incident had occurred as alleged. In *De Profundis* the word 'doom' is used repeatedly, and Wilde pointed to 'the note of Doom that like a purple thread runs through the gold cloth of *Dorian Gray*'. Perhaps, even at this early stage in his relationship with Douglas, Wilde sensed that he was a man condemned.

A month earlier, after Douglas had thrown one of the temper tantrums which became a recurring feature of their relationship, Wilde had determined never to speak to him again. He had been revolted by the scene Douglas had made and was resolved to end the affair. Faced with Douglas's pleas for forgiveness he relented and allowed the friendship to resume. It would be the pattern that punctuated their life together. In *De Profundis* Wilde complained that his fault was not that he did not part from Douglas but that he did it too often, every three months according to Wilde's own estimation. Each time the acrimonious parting was followed by a reconciliation. In June 1893, after another violent display of Douglas's temper, Wilde told him that they were spoiling each other's lives and that it would be wisest to part. Again, the separation lasted only a matter of days before Wilde relented.

Wilde's friends began to discern Douglas's destructive influence. 'Poor Oscar!' Max Beerbohm wrote to Robert Ross in 1893. 'I saw him the other day, from a cab walking with Bosie and some other members of the Extreme Left. He looked like one whose soul had swooned in sin and revived vulgar. How fearful it is for a poet to go to bed and find himself infamous.'[6] In August, Beerbohm observed Wilde, Douglas and Robbie Ross cavorting ostentatiously with vine leaves in their hair. 'Nor have I ever seen Oscar so fatuous,' Beerbohm remarked, adding that Wilde was describing those he met as 'Juno-like' and 'Olympian quite' while waving his cigarette round and round his head. 'Of course I would rather see Oscar free than sober, but still, suddenly meeting him ... I felt quite repelled.'[7]

One morning in April 1893 Pierre Louÿs arrived at the room in the Savoy Hotel which Wilde and Douglas were sharing. While he was there Constance arrived, because she saw so little of her husband, to bring him his post. She besought him to come home but Wilde replied heartlessly that he had been away so long that he had forgotten the number of their house. Constance smiled miserably through her tears and left. This was a moment of revelation for Louÿs who returned to Paris disgusted at what he had seen, informing the poet Henri de Regnier that Wilde was now a self-confessed pederast who had abandoned his wife and children for Douglas. A month later he wrote to John Gray, notifying him that he had broken with Wilde.[8]

A confession that Wilde made to Nellie Melba, the celebrated prima donna, illustrated the suffering he was causing both his wife and children at this time. He told her that he had been telling his sons stories the night before about little boys who were naughty and made their mothers cry, and what dreadful things would happen to them unless they became better. 'Do you know what one of them answered? He asked me what punishment would be reserved for naughty papas, who did not come home till the early morning, and made mother cry far more.'[9] This was the year that Wilde's poem 'To My Wife' was published, evoking a love he was tarnishing with neglect.

> And when wind and winter harden
> > All the loveless land,
> It will whisper of the garden,
> > You will understand.

Possibly it was an empty gesture, but perhaps it also conveyed a genuinely wistful regret, a sad-eyed backward glance at the world, the woman and the love he was casting away.

The new world Wilde inhabited revolved around Douglas whose disastrous influence extended to Wilde's work as well as to his life. In September Wilde rented some private rooms purely in order to work on his new play, *An Ideal Husband*. He had sought solitude not only from his wife and children but from Douglas also. They had quarrelled for months over Douglas's inept translation of *Salomé* from the French and Wilde, unable to work in Douglas's presence, had not even started writing the play for which he was under contract. For the first week Douglas stayed away and Wilde wrote the whole of the first act. Following Douglas's arrival, uninvited, during the second week, Wilde's work on the play practically ceased. Each day Douglas would sit idly chatting until 1.30 at which point he expected Wilde to take him for luncheon at the Café Royal or the Berkeley. Luncheon with its liqueurs lasted until 3.30, after which Douglas retired to White's for an hour. At tea-time, before Wilde had barely had time to pick up the threads of his work, Douglas returned, staying until it was time to dress for dinner. Clearly work was impossible. Wilde lamented later that his life was 'entirely sterile and uncreative' when he was with Douglas, adding that for one of his creative temperament 'it was a position both grotesque and tragic'.

In desperation, Wilde wrote to Lady Queensberry on 8 November about Douglas's state of health. He was, Wilde wrote, 'sleepless, nervous, and rather hysterical. He seems to me quite altered.' Douglas was 'quite astray in life' and would, unless Lady Queensberry acted promptly, come to grief. His life was 'aimless, unhappy and absurd'. Wilde suggested that Lady Queensberry send her son to Egypt for a time, fearing that if he remained in London he would 'spoil his young life irretrievably, quite irretrievably' and that it would be 'quite ruined'.[10] Wilde was anxious that Lady Queensberry should not mention to Douglas that he had written to her, no doubt fearing Douglas's violent temper. His advice was heeded and Lady Queensberry persuaded Douglas to go to Egypt.

During his absence Wilde 'collected again the torn and ravelled web of my imagination' and completed the three remaining acts of *An Ideal Husband*. He also conceived and began work on two other plays, *A Florentine Tragedy* and *La Sainte Courtisane*.

Wilde's allusions in his letter to Lady Queensberry about Douglas's life being spoiled or ruined were not merely abstract fears but were rooted in a real scandal in which Douglas had been recently implicated. Max Beerbohm divulged mysteriously in a letter to a friend that the scandal also involved Robert Ross, 'a schoolboy', 'a furious father', 'a headmaster' and, on the fringes, Wilde himself.[11] It had begun when Ross visited the Reverend Biscale Hale Wortham, who kept a boys' school in Bruges. A sixteen-year-old boy named Philip Danney, son of an officer in the Guards, was staying there, and Ross invited him to London. The boy accepted. On hearing from Ross that he had the sixteen-year-old staying with him, Douglas rushed to London and whisked the boy off to Goring in Sussex where he was staying with Wilde. According to Oscar Browning, the boy slept with Douglas on Saturday and Wilde on Sunday. On Monday he returned to London and slept with a woman prostitute at Douglas's or Wilde's expense. On Tuesday he returned to Bruges three days late. Interrogated by his master, the boy confessed everything. When his father, Colonel Danney, was informed he consulted the police solicitors. Ross and Douglas rushed to Bruges in an attempt to smooth things over. Ross insisted that the whole affair was 'an absolute fabrication'. Wilde's name was kept out of the matter. Colonel Danney wished to prosecute but was informed by the lawyer that although Ross and Douglas would probably get two years, his own son would be likely to receive six months himself. Reluctantly, Colonel Danney let the matter drop. Ross's relations heard of the affair, and considered him 'the disgrace of the family, a social outcast, a son and brother unfit for society of any kind'.[12]

It is not clear how much Douglas's family were aware of their son's role in the whole episode. Lady Queensberry may have taken Wilde's letter at face value or she may have known more than she cared to admit. Either way, her decision to send her son to Egypt allowed Douglas to slip quietly away from his indiscretion until the dust had settled. Meanwhile the Marquess of Queensberry was beginning to suspect a sinister side to his son's friendship with Wilde. Throughout 1893, his suspicions aroused, he began to insist that Douglas stop seeing Wilde. Lady Queensberry also believed that Wilde's influence was detrimental to her son's health. On the eve of Douglas's departure for Cairo she was explicit in her insistence that he terminate his relationship with Wilde. She told him she would almost like to murder Wilde for what he had done to him, suggesting that she knew a good deal more than Wilde or Douglas suspected. Wilde was a bad influence and nobody could consider him a good man.

Incensed by his mother's use of the word 'good', Douglas wrote to her from Egypt on 10 December stating that he did not believe that anybody could be called 'good'. It was not a word which was applicable to individuals. This in itself sounded suspiciously like Wilde's influence and Lady Queensberry's suspicions must have been confirmed when her son illustrated his point by quoting Wilde's stricture in the Preface to *Dorian Gray* that there was no such thing as a moral or an immoral book. Lady Queensberry's riposte was direct and to the point: 'If Mr Wilde·has acted as I am convinced he has the part of a Lord Henry Wotton to you I could never feel differently towards him than I do, as the murderer of your soul.' Clearly she had read *Dorian Gray* and her words suggest that she may also have read the poem by Douglas's cousin, Lionel Johnson, entitled 'To the Destroyer of a Soul', which had been addressed secretly to Wilde. Johnson, like Gray, Louÿs and Beerbohm, had distanced himself from Wilde in the wake of his anarchic affair with Douglas. It was from Wilde, Lady Queensberry insisted, that her son had learned his 'eccentricities and peculiar views of morality'.

During his stay in Egypt, Douglas received a series of letters from his father which were similar to those from his mother in their objections to Wilde's influence. The wayward son, who had grown to despise his father, answered him with increasing impertinence. Father and son were squaring up for the mother of all battles and Wilde would be both the cause and the excuse.

Wilde had tried to make a final break during Douglas's absence in

Egypt, severing all communications and failing to answer Douglas's letters, but once again he relented. After Douglas's return to England their relations resumed much as before. On 1 April 1894, Queensberry wrote his son an ultimatum concerning 'your intimacy with this man Wilde'.

It must either cease or I will disown you and stop all money supplies. I am not going to try and analyse this intimacy, and I make no charge; but to my mind to pose as a thing is as bad as to be it. With my own eyes I saw you both in the most loathsome and disgusting relationship as expressed by your manner and expression. Never in my experience have I ever seen such a sight as that in your horrible features. No wonder people are talking as they are. Also I now hear on good authority, but this may be false, that his wife is petitioning to divorce him for sodomy and other crimes. Is this true, or do you not know of it? If I thought the actual thing was true, and it became public property, I should be quite justified in shooting him at sight. These christian English cowards and men, as they call themselves, want waking up.
Your disgusted so-called father,

QUEENSBERRY[13]

'What a funny little man you are,' Douglas replied by telegram the following day. His words were deliberately designed to cause maximum offence, lacking in tact what they gained in impact. Wilde was horrified, writing later that 'it was a telegram of which the commonest street-boy would have been ashamed'.[14] Queensberry was furious, describing his son as an 'impertinent young jackanapes' and threatening to give him 'the thrashing you deserve' if he sent any further telegrams of a similar nature. He accused Douglas of being 'crazy', adding that he was considered crazy at Oxford, 'and that accounts for a good deal that has happened'. Then came the threat which prophesied Wilde's doom. 'If I catch you again with that man I will make a public scandal in a way you little dream of; it is already a suppressed one. I prefer an open one, and at any rate I shall not be blamed for allowing such a state of things to go on.'[15]

Father and son were now locked in mortal conflict. Wilde, as the catalyst for their mutual antagonism, was in a singularly dangerous position and seemingly unable to extricate himself. From the desolation of his prison cell he would complain that he had been used by Douglas to get at his father. 'In your hideous game of hate together, you had both thrown dice for my soul.' It was only partially true. Wilde could have ended the relationship himself, especially as he saw the spectre of his own downfall looming ever closer. He chose not to. In making the choice he was also dicing with disaster. In his obsession with Lord Alfred Douglas, Wilde must have known that he was courting conviction.

1 Ellmann, *Oscar Wilde*, p. 347.
2 Ibid., pp. 351–2.
3 Ibid., p. 352.
4 Ibid., p. 359.
5 Cheiro [Count Louis Hamon], *Cheiro's Memoirs: The Reminiscences of a Society Palmist*, Philadelphia, 1913; quoted in Ellmann, *Oscar Wilde*, p. 360.
6 Ellmann, *Oscar Wilde*, p. 371.
7 Ibid., p. 372.
8 Ibid., pp. 371–2.
9 Ibid., p. 371.
10 Hart-Davis, *Letters of Oscar Wilde*, pp. 346–7.
11 Ellmann, *Oscar Wilde*, p. 382.
12 Ibid., p. 383.
13 Ibid., p. 394.
14 Hart-Davis, *Letters of Oscar Wilde*, p. 446.
15 Ellmann, *Oscar Wilde*, p. 395.

TWENTY ONE

Descent

> LADY CHILTERN: I know that there are men with horrible secrets in
> their lives – men who have done some shameful thing, and who in
> some critical moment have to pay for it, by doing some other act of
> shame – oh! don't tell me you are such as they are!

The controversy surrounding Wilde's *Salomé* was resurrected in
1894 when the English translation of the play was published. This
time, however, it was not so much the play itself which was the cause
of scandal but Aubrey Beardsley's illustrations. The verdict of most
critics was exemplified by the judgement of *The Times* that the volume
was 'morbid, bizarre, repulsive and very offensive'. According to
Lewis Broad, in *The Friendships and Follies of Oscar Wilde*, 'the diablerie
of the illustrator has been blamed for intensifying the distaste and
disgust of the critics'. Broad agreed with their verdict, asserting that
Beardsley's illustrations were not merely decadent but degenerate.
'There was an evil about them, but it was the evil of Beardsley's conception not of Wilde's *Salomé*, an evil of sophistication. Wilde's characters are lustful in their evil; Beardsley's figures are degenerate.'[1]
This is a little harsh. If Beardsley's illustrations exuded degeneracy it
was through the masterful visualization of the degeneracy exuded by
Salomé herself. The evil about them was the evil of Salomé, or the evil
of her mother Herodias. The sinister, sensual overtones of Beardsley's
illustrations conveyed sexual undertones that were as scantily disguised as Salomé's nakedness. Quite simply, Beardsley had sought to
convey the nakedness of Salomé's lust as starkly in his illustrations as
Wilde had sought to do in the unravelling of his play. The artists had
complemented each other with sublime aptness.

As with Wilde's play, Beardsley's illustrations were subject to censorship. One of the drawings, of Herodias, had to be withdrawn as indecent prior to publication. The artist's reaction and humour were exhibited in a quatrain:

Because one figure was undressed
This little drawing was suppressed.
It was unkind. But never mind,
Perhaps it was all for the best.[2]

Wilde recognized that Beardsley's drawings were 'quite wonderful' but was concerned that their sensuality had smothered the spirituality of his play. He was worried that Beardsley's emphasis on the physical was eclipsing the metaphysical message which he had sought to convey. 'My Herod is like the Herod of Gustave Moreau, wrapped in his jewels and his sorrows. My Salomé is a mystic, the sister of Salammbô, a Saint Thérèse who worships the moon.' Ironically, considering the similar criticisms which his play had provoked, Wilde deprecated Beardsley's naughtiness. He complained that, in his play, Salomé's dance had been more metaphysical than physical but that, in the illustrations, the opposite was conveyed. There was also an element of artistic jealousy in Wilde's dismissal of the air of French sophistication in Beardsley's work. 'Yes, dear Aubrey is almost too Parisian, he cannot forget that he has been to Dieppe – once.'[3]

The inner turmoil between the physical and metaphysical urges in Wilde's psyche was epitomized by the conflicting impulses at work in his life. Increasingly convinced that Douglas had exerted a disastrous influence on his life and a destructive influence on his art, Wilde sought to make the final break with him during the three months that Douglas was in Egypt. Wilde's belief appears to be vindicated by the relative happiness of his life during Douglas's absence. At Christmas 1893 he was, in the words of Gertrude Pearce, his son's tutor who spent the festivities with Wilde and his family, 'as happy as a boy', doling out the Christmas pudding and pulling crackers.[4] During this period he also wrote the last three acts of An Ideal Husband, complaining to a friend that 'the critics will say, "Ah, here is Oscar unlike himself!" – though in reality I became engrossed in writing it, and it contains a great deal of the real Oscar'. It is interesting that Wilde should be so worried about being misinterpreted by the critics and so candid about revealing 'the real Oscar', especially as he had been at such pains in the past to be misunderstood and to conceal himself. Was this new spirit of confession linked to a genuine contrition? Either way, considering Wilde's admission that the play contained much of his true self, it warrants particular attention.

The pivotal force in *An Ideal Husband* is an attempt by the unscrupulous Mrs Cheveley to blackmail Sir Robert Chiltern. Matters are complicated by Lady Chiltern's adoration of her husband and her belief in his incorruptibility, as well as by her puritanism. When Sir Robert states that people should not be entirely judged by their past, Lady Chiltern disagrees: 'One's past is what one is. It is the only way by which people should be judged.'

The character in the play who most resembles Wilde, and to whom Wilde may have been referring when he spoke of revealing the real Oscar, is Lord Goring. In some respects Lord Goring resembles Lord Illingworth in *A Woman of No Importance*. He is a dandy, he is a wit, he is an anti-puritan. Yet in other, key respects he is the antipathy of Lord Illingworth, his antidote. Whereas Lord Illingworth's decadent malevolence has a poisoning influence in the earlier play, Lord Goring's influence is benign. When Lady Chiltern insists that her husband is 'as incapable of doing a foolish thing as he is of doing a wrong thing', Lord Goring replies with uncharacteristic earnestness: 'Nobody is incapable of doing a foolish thing. Nobody is incapable of doing a wrong thing.' Surprised by the nature of his reply, Lady Chiltern asks whether he is a pessimist.

No, Lady Chiltern, I am not a Pessimist. Indeed I am not sure that I quite know what pessimism really means. All I do know is that life cannot be understood without much charity, cannot be lived without much charity. It is love, and not German philosophy, that is the true explanation of this world, whatever may be the explanation of the next. And if you are ever in trouble, Lady Chiltern, trust me absolutely, and I will help you in every way I can. If you ever want me, come to me for my assistance, and you shall have it. Come at once to me.

Lady Chiltern looks at him in surprise: 'Lord Goring, you are talking quite seriously. I don't think I ever heard you talk seriously before.'

Lord Goring laughs and makes his apologies: 'You must excuse me, Lady Chiltern. It won't occur again, if I can help it.'

This dialogue discloses both the play's moral and Wilde's motive for writing it. Victorian puritanism imposes an unrealistic ideal of human behaviour, a perfunctory perfection. Against such idealism Wilde sets up the reality of imperfect, or fallen, humanity and establishes love as the ground for the forgiveness of failings. This is encapsulated at the play's climax when Mabel Chiltern, Sir Robert's sister, is engaged to be married to Lord Goring. She declares that she doesn't expect Lord Goring to be 'an ideal husband'. She wants only to be 'a real wife to him'. *An Ideal Husband* concludes with Lady Chiltern's forgiveness of her husband's fall. She no longer idolizes the untrue ideal husband, but loves the imperfect real husband. Sir Robert asks her whether it is love she feels for him, or merely pity. Kissing him, she replies with the final words of the drama: 'It is love, Robert. Love, and only love. For both of us a new life is beginning.'

The last words of *An Ideal Husband* were written at a time when Wilde was resolved to begin a new life himself. He believed that he had put the sordid degradation of the previous year behind him and was seeking a fresh stability, a fresh start. He had not been an ideal husband but perhaps there was an inkling in the subject matter of his play that he sought to salvage his marriage. In spite of his neglect, he loved his children and was still fond of Constance. It is significant that his poem 'To My Wife' was published at around this time and perhaps this was a further indication that he was seeking a reconciliation.

The sober and sombre side of Wilde's character was evident in a letter to the poet W.E. Henley in February 1894. Learning that Henley's daughter, his only child, had died aged six on 11 February, Wilde offered his condolences. 'I am very sorry indeed to hear of your great loss. I hope you will let me come down quietly to you one evening and ... we will talk of the bitter ways of fortune, and the hard ways of life.' More significantly, Wilde's words about the importance of art as a consolation amid the harshness of life could be seen as a personal credo and *confiteor*. 'But, my dear Henley, to work, to work; that is your duty; that is what remains for natures like ours. Work never seems to me a reality, but a way of getting rid of reality.' Yet if work was an escape from the problems of daily life, its product, the art itself, was higher than daily life. Art was not an escape from truth, but its liberation. The facts of life were inferior to the truth of life conveyed in art. This was evident in the same letter to Henley in a discussion of Degas. Wilde dismissed the biographical details of Degas's life as largely irrelevant. 'You asked me about Degas ... Why say anything about his person? His pastels are himself.'[5] One can assume that Wilde used the same criteria about himself. His true self, his deepest self, was to be found in his art. In fact, Wilde was to confess as much in his letter to Douglas from prison. 'You knew what my Art was to me, the great primal note by which I had revealed, first myself to myself, and then myself to the world; the real passion of my life; the love to which all other loves were as marsh-water to red wine ...'

In the same prison letter to Douglas, Wilde discussed the period of relative tranquillity which preceded Douglas's return from Egypt. He was gaining peace with himself, harmony in his art and had 'got my life into my own hands ... when suddenly, unbidden, unwelcome, and under circumstances fatal to my happiness you returned'.

Wilde had resolutely refused to reply to the letters sent by Douglas from Egypt. In March 1894, informing Wilde that he was en route to Paris, Douglas beseeched him to rendezvous with him there. Wilde replied by telegram that he would neither write to him nor see him. Undaunted, Douglas continued to shower Wilde with telegrams from various places on his way from Egypt to France, begging at least one meeting in Paris. When Douglas arrived at his Paris hotel he found a letter from Wilde waiting for him. It reiterated Wilde's determination to avoid meeting him. In desperation, Douglas sent a telegram to Tite Street which contained a threat to commit suicide if Wilde would not meet him. Wilde took the threat seriously. Douglas had told Wilde morbid stories of how members of his family 'had stained their hands in their own blood'. As recently as 1891 his uncle, Lord James Edward Sholto Douglas, had cut his own throat in the Euston Hotel. His grandfather, the eighth Marquess of Queensberry, had died in mysterious circumstances, reputedly in a shooting accident. Douglas implied that this was also suicide. Faced with the threat of Douglas's own suicide, Wilde reluctantly agreed to one last interview. He travelled to Paris and was won over by Douglas's charm, his remorse, his tears and his affection. Once more Wilde had succumbed to the fatal attraction, its deadly delights luring him towards destruction.

Within two days of their return to England, the Marquess of Queensberry was issuing ominous threats to his son, promising to make 'a public scandal' if he did not desist from meeting Wilde. By June, Wilde was taking the threats seriously enough to consult a solicitor.

On 30 June Queensberry made an unannounced visit to Wilde in Tite Street. The ensuing confrontation was described twice by Wilde and once by Queensberry, each embellishing the truth to his own advantage. Queensberry claimed that Wilde had behaved in a cowardly fashion whereas Wilde insisted that he had denied all charges and made Queensberry leave the house. The version Wilde offered in *De Profundis* described Queensberry waving his fists in the air 'in epileptic fury', uttering expletives and 'screaming the loathsome threats he afterwards with such cunning carried out'. Wilde also mentioned that Queensberry had brought a minder with him, presumably a pugilist, which makes it unlikely that Wilde 'drove him out' as he later claimed.

Meanwhile, Douglas's personal vendetta against his father was inflaming the already volatile situation. He sent a postcard to Queensberry declaring that he treated his 'absurd threats with absolute indifference'. In an obvious effort to goad his father into further acts of fury, he added that, since the confrontation at Wilde's house, he had deliberately made a point of being seen in public with Wilde as much as possible. As if daring his father to further public displays of anger he even listed the restaurants which he and Wilde frequented. Douglas then raised the ante by suggesting that Wilde could prosecute Queensberry for libel:

If O.W. was to prosecute you in the Central Criminal Court for libel you would get seven years' penal servitude for your outrageous libels. Much as I detest you, I am anxious to avoid this for the sake of the family; but if you try to assault me, I shall defend myself with a loaded revolver, which I always carry; and if I shoot you or he shoots you, we shall be completely justified, as we shall be acting in self-defence against a violent and dangerous rough, and I think if you were dead not many people would miss you.[6]

Douglas's ploy appears to have worked because his father was roused to new levels of fury. Queensberry went from restaurant to restaurant looking for Wilde, intent on confronting him in public about his relationship with his son. Fortunately their paths never crossed. Increasingly concerned, Wilde again contemplated legal action to bind Queensberry over to keep the peace. His solicitor wrote to Queensberry asking him to retract his libels or risk litigation. The Marquess replied that he had nothing to retract, having made no direct accusation against Wilde, but he reiterated his demand that Wilde's relationship with his son should cease. At this point both antagonists let the matter rest. Queensberry's anger continued to simmer beneath the surface, threatening to boil over, but for the moment there was an uneasy stalemate.

Wilde turned his attention to his art. From August to October he retired to Worthing with his wife and children, determined to write *The Importance of Being Earnest*. In the triviality, charm and wit of the most popular of Wilde's plays is to be found the incarnation of his belief that work was 'a way of getting rid of reality'. It was, as the transparent irony of the title suggested, the least earnest of his plays. *The Importance of Being Earnest* was a light-hearted escape from the sordid aspects of his life, an escapist fantasy. In its lack of earnestness, Wilde had omitted the serious characterization of his earlier plays, preferring a two-dimensional approach where the shallowness of the characters prevents either ascent to morality or descent to immorality. The fullness of reality is sacrificed to something lighter, something funnier. Complexity is surrendered to comedy, ethical force forsaken for ethereal farce.

Douglas paid one visit to Worthing while Wilde was there. The letter he wrote to Robert Ross afterwards illustrated that Constance's attitude to him had cooled considerably. 'I had great fun, though the last few days the strain of being a bone of contention between Oscar and Mrs Oscar began to make itself felt.'[7] As Wilde wrote to Douglas in *De Profundis*, 'Our friendship had always been a source of distress to her ... because she saw how your continued friendship altered me, and not for the better.' When Wilde had first arrived at Worthing he wrote to Douglas to deter him from visiting, presumably suspecting the tension it would cause. Yet he also exhibited both displeasure at being confined in the same house as his wife and children and a clear preference for Douglas's company. He complained of the 'horrid ugly Swiss governess' who was looking after Cyril and Vyvyan and declared with distaste that 'children at meals are tedious'.[8] Admittedly, the purpose of Wilde's letter had been to convince Douglas that he would be bored if he came to Worthing. His words may have been intended merely as a deterrent and were not necessarily an expression of his true feelings. Either way, Wilde's tone of disgust in his letter to Douglas would seem to confirm Constance's belief that Douglas's influence was poisonous.

Most people did not agree with Constance's judgement, believing that it was Wilde who was poisoning Douglas, not the contrary. This was a reasonable enough assumption. Wilde was sixteen years older than Douglas. He was approaching his fortieth birthday whereas Douglas was still in his early twenties. Wilde was heralded as a wit without equal, a genius who could hold his own in any company. He had a reputation as a debauchee and a corrupter of disciples. To most observers it was inconceivable that the boy could corrupt the man, the lesser talent influence the far greater, the disciple beguile the master. It was hardly surprising, therefore, that most people sympathized with Queensberry in his efforts to save his son from what they perceived as Wilde's malevolent clutches.

The image of Wilde as predator and Douglas as prey was reinforced in September with the publication of Robert Hichens's novel *The Green Carnation*. It was intended as a parody but was so close to the perceived reality that Ellmann considers it more like a documentary. There was little doubt that the two principal characters, Lord Reggie and Mr Amarinth, were intended to represent Douglas and Wilde. In the novel, Lord Reggie is completely under the influence of Mr Amarinth. He imitates his master to such an extent that he ceases to have any personality of his own. In Hichens's novel the thinly disguised Wilde totally dominates his disciple, moulding him into an image of himself. It was hardly surprising that Queensberry was incensed when he read the book, seeing it as confirmation of his own fears. He must have been further incensed at the depiction in the novel of the character of Lord Reggie chasing a boy.

At first Wilde and Douglas were both amused by *The Green Carnation*. Wilde wrote to Ada Leverson that he didn't believe Hichens capable of anything so clever.[9] A week later he was forced to write to the *Pall Mall Gazette* distancing himself from the novel. The *Gazette* had suggested that Wilde was the true author of the book, a suggestion which other newspapers were quick to take up. Wilde now declared that the novel was 'middle-class and mediocre' and could not be declared a work of art.[10] In spite of his protestations the damage had been done. Few doubted that Wilde was the subject of the novel even if he wasn't its author. The controversy surrounding its publication only served to heighten the hostility towards Wilde which many people felt.

With Queensberry still baying for his blood *The Green Carnation* had been published at a dangerous time for Wilde and Douglas. Max Beerbohm sensed the danger, sketching an imaginary scenario in a letter to a friend which would be uncannily and prophetically close to the truth: 'Oscar has at length been arrested for certain kinds of crime. He was taken in the Café Royal (lower room). Bosie escaped, being an excellent runner, but Oscar was less nimble.'[11]

Wilde's relationship with Douglas continued to arouse hostile reactions from his friends. Beerbohm, Louÿs, Johnson, Gray and Raffalovich had already distanced themselves and there were signs that another close friend, Robert Ross, was seeking to break away from the decadent lifestyle in which Wilde and Douglas were ever more inextricably embroiled. Ross was received into the Catholic Church in 1894, influenced no doubt by his friend More Adey but inspired also by a sincere desire to find a sense of order and peace in his previously hedonistic life. Unlike many of Wilde's other erstwhile friends Ross remained loyal to his mentor, especially during those times when his friendship was most needed. Yet Ross's conscience was troubled by the nature of Wilde's association with Douglas, a fact which would lead to Ross and Douglas becoming bitter enemies. Ross must also have been disconcerted by Wilde's increasingly antagonistic stance towards orthodox Christianity which coincided with his relationship with Douglas.

Wilde's wilful perversion of traditional Christian teaching was expressed in a series of prose poems, the first of which had been published the previous year in the *Spirit Lamp*, an Oxford magazine which Douglas was editing. This was 'The House of Judgement' in which a man who has lived a life of sin is confronted at his death with the consequences of his actions. As the Book of Life is read, it emerges that he has been cruel, has spilt innocent blood, has idolized lust and has betrayed his friends. He answers defiantly when God decrees that he is to be sent to Hell that God cannot send him there, 'Because in Hell have I always lived'. The man's wisdom outwits God who has no answer. Eventually God answers that as he cannot send the man to Hell he will send him to Heaven. The man tells God that he cannot send him to Heaven either, 'Because never, and in no place, have I been able to imagine it'. Again, the mind of God is no match for the man's wit. The prose poem ends with God being dumbfounded: 'And there was silence in the House of Judgement.'

In 'The Master' a man weeps following Christ's crucifixion. Yet he does not weep for Christ but for himself because 'they have not crucified me'. In 'The Artist' the image of *The Sorrow that endureth for Ever*, which the Artist had fashioned as 'a sign of the love of man that dieth not', is destroyed and cast into the furnace so that the Artist can fashion an image of *The Pleasure that abideth for a Moment*. In 'The Doer of Good' Christ is confronted by those he has healed, each of whom is ungrateful and has turned to a life of sin. The leper lives a life of debauched luxury. The blind man uses his restored sight to lust after a woman, possibly Mary Magdalene, who laughs when she recognizes Christ, mocking Him: 'But you forgave me my sins, and the way is a pleasant way.' Finally He meets a young man who is weeping by the roadside. Looking up, the man recognizes Christ: 'But I was dead once and you raised me from the dead. What else should I do but weep?'

These *Poems in Prose*, published in the *Fortnightly Review* in July 1894, were the products of Wilde's dark alter ego. With the re-establishment of Douglas as the dominant force in his life the darker side prevailed to an ever greater degree. It was symbolized by Wilde's attitude on Christmas Day 1894. A year earlier, with Douglas safely away in Egypt, Wilde had been 'happy as a boy' in the role of paterfamilias, dishing out the Christmas pudding and pulling crackers. A year later he had metamorphosed from Bob Cratchit to Scrooge, insisting that the cast of *An Ideal Husband* rehearse on Christmas Day. The actors felt aggrieved and one of them, Charles Brookfield, confronted Wilde on the subject. 'Don't you keep Christmas, Oscar?' he asked. 'No, Brookfield,' replied Wilde, 'the only festival of the Church I keep is Septuagesima. Do you keep Septuagesima, Brookfield?' 'Not since I was a boy.' 'Ah, be a boy again,' said Wilde.[12] The 'boy' who uttered these words was very different from the 'boy' of the previous Christmas.

As Douglas gained the ascendancy in Wilde's life, its descent into the abyss seemed ever more likely.

1 Lewis Broad, *The Friendships and Follies of Oscar Wilde*, London: Hutchinson, 1954, pp. 108–9.
2 Ellmann, *Oscar Wilde*, p. 355.
3 Ibid.
4 Ibid., p. 390.
5 Hart-Davis, *Letters of Oscar Wilde*, p. 352.
6 Ellmann, *Oscar Wilde*, p. 396.
7 Quoted in *Daily Telegraph*, 19 April 1913.
8 Hart-Davis, *Letters of Oscar Wilde*, p. 360.
9 Ellmann, *Oscar Wilde*, p. 400.
10 *Pall Mall Gazette*, 2 October 1894.
11 Ellmann, *Oscar Wilde*, p. 400.
12 Ibid., p. 404.

TWENTY TWO

Abyss

For two days you ... feasted your eyes with the spectacle of your father standing in the dock of the Central Criminal Court. And on the third day I took his place ... In your hideous game of hate together, you had both thrown dice for my soul ...

In the months preceding the final debacle Wilde and Douglas continued much as ever. On 16 October 1894, Wilde's fortieth birthday, he received a vindictive letter from Douglas in the wake of Douglas's latest tantrum. A few days earlier Douglas had become irritated when Wilde fell ill, subjecting him to a stream of vitriolic abuse which became so violent that Wilde believed Douglas was about to physically attack him. This was confirmed in the letter, Douglas warning Wilde that 'it was an ugly moment for you, uglier than you imagine'. Douglas gloated that when he had left on the evening of his rage he had booked into the Grand Hotel in Brighton and charged all his hotel expenses to Wilde. The letter concluded in similar heartless fashion: 'When you are not on your pedestal you are not interesting. The next time you are ill I will go away at once.' In *De Profundis*, Wilde recalled how these words had returned to haunt him when he lay alone in his prison cell.[1] Not for the first time following a violent display of Douglas's temper, Wilde sought to sever relations. Once again he relented within days and the tempestuous affair continued.

A few weeks later, Wilde agreed to write for the first issue of a new Oxford magazine started by an undergraduate named Jack Bloxam. The magazine was to be called the *Chameleon* and its purpose, surreptitiously at least, was to gain acceptance for homosexuality at Oxford. Bloxam was following the example set eighteen months earlier by

Douglas who had edited the *Spirit Lamp* with the same intention. Wilde wrote 'Phrases and Philosophies for the Use of the Young' for Bloxam's magazine. This consisted of a string of aphoristic affectations, summed up in the first: 'The first duty in life is to be as artificial as possible. What the second duty is no one has as yet discovered.' The epigrams are funny and pithily quotable but most were written purely in jest. They were not intended to be taken seriously, at least not if another of the epigrams is to be believed: 'Dullness is the coming of age of seriousness.' Neither were they to be taken as true: 'A truth ceases to be true when more than one person believes in it.' Their style, however, conveyed an air of subversive decadence which undermined conventional values. Having no intrinsic truth in themselves they nonetheless attacked truth *per se*.

'Phrases and Philosophies for the Use of the Young' may have irritated those who already disliked Wilde's decadent posturing but they would not have elicited any stronger reaction. The sentiments expressed in the epigrams were typical of the wit that his friends and enemies had come to expect. There were no great surprises. The real harm to Wilde's already suspect reputation was caused not by his own words but by those of the *Chameleon*'s editor. In the issue in which Wilde's 'Phrases and Philosophies' appeared, Bloxam published his own short story, 'The Priest and the Acolyte'. In the story the priest is caught with a boy. In his shame he poisons the wine in the chalice before administering the sacrament to his young communicant and himself. Wilde had mixed views about the story. It was too direct and lacked nuance, whereas 'God and other artists are always a little obscure'. Its main redeeming feature was that it was 'at moments poisonous'.[2] The other damaging item in the *Chameleon* was Douglas's poem 'Two Loves' with its now famous line about 'the Love that dare not speak its name'.

The fury which greeted the publication of the *Chameleon* in December 1894 ensured that the first issue would also be the last. Jerome K. Jerome, whose novel *Three Men in a Boat* had once been praised by Wilde as 'funny without being vulgar', attacked the *Chameleon* in *To-day*. The latter journal also recommended that the police should take action against the *Chameleon*'s editor. More ominously, a copy of the *Chameleon* found its way into the hands of the Marquess of Queensberry who assumed that 'The Priest and the Acolyte', which

was unsigned, had been written by Wilde. In the trial which beckoned, Queensberry's lawyers were to make much of the story, as well
as Douglas's poem and Wilde's 'Phrases and Philosophies'.

Wilde was now walking precariously on a tightrope, proceeding
proudly before the fall. For the time being, he remained perched in a
position of fame which reached new heights with the opening of *An
Ideal Husband* at the Theatre Royal, Haymarket on 3 January 1895. The
Prince of Wales, Balfour, Chamberlain and a host of other government
ministers were at the première. At the final curtain there was rapturous applause and calls for the author. Wilde, however, had already
left the theatre. He had arranged to dine with Douglas.

Wilde's triumph at the Theatre Royal was soon to be surpassed by
the opening of *The Importance of Being Earnest* at the St James's Theatre
on 14 February. Before then, on 17 January, he and Douglas departed
for Algeria in pursuit of boys. A letter Wilde wrote to Robert Ross
from his hotel in Algiers is awash with references to 'quite lovely'
boys, villages peopled by 'fauns' and thinly veiled allusions to the
procurement of cheap male prostitutes.[3] He also informed Ross that
he and Douglas had taken to hashish: 'it is quite exquisite: three puffs
of smoke and then peace and love'.[4]

An intriguing record of Wilde's and Douglas's sojourn in Algeria is
provided by André Gide in his autobiography. When Gide arrived in
Blidah, a town thirty miles from Algiers which was a favourite haunt
of Europeans in search of boys, he was surprised to find himself staying in the same hotel as Wilde and Douglas. The three men spent the
evening together and Douglas confessed to Gide that he had 'a horror
of women' and only liked boys. As if to prove the point, Douglas,
apparently after another fierce quarrel with Wilde, 'eloped' with an
Arab boy to Biskra. So besotted was Douglas with his 'marvellous'
young Arab that he disappeared for several weeks. He was still in
Algeria on 14 February, preferring the attentions of his new adolescent
acquisition to being with Wilde on the opening night of his new play.

In Douglas's absence, Wilde and Gide returned to Algiers in pursuit of some pleasure of their own. At a café in the town, Gide was
captivated by an Arab boy playing the flute or, as Wilde put it erotically in his letter to Ross, fluting on reeds. 'Dear,' Wilde asked him,
'vous voulez le petit musicien?' Gide, 'in the most choked of voices', said
yes. Wilde burst into what Gide described as 'satanic laughter' and

made the necessary arrangements. In heavier mood, Wilde confided to Gide that Queensberry was causing him problems. 'My friends advise me to be careful,' he said. 'Careful! How could I be that? It would mean going backward. I must go as far as possible. I cannot go any further. Something must happen ... something else ...'[5]

Wilde left Algeria on 31 January and stopped off in Paris en route. He visited Degas and informed him cheerily, 'You know how well known you are in England?' 'Fortunately less so than you,' Degas replied.[6] It was an ominous riposte.

Soon after his return to England, Wilde discovered through a mutual acquaintance that Queensberry was planning to disrupt the opening night of The Importance of Being Earnest. He alerted George Alexander, the play's producer, who cancelled Queensberry's ticket and made arrangements for the police to be present. Although Wilde had thwarted his adversary on this occasion it was evident that their personal feud was entering a new and dangerous phase.

Wilde had now completely neglected his wife and children, preferring to live entirely away from home. He did his utmost to avoid meeting Constance. On 28 January, while Wilde was in Algeria, Constance was forced to approach Robert Ross to request that he ask Wilde to send her some money. Six weeks later she thanked Ross for sending it, confessing that she didn't even know her husband's address. In fact, Wilde had taken rooms at the Avondale Hotel in Piccadilly. For a while Douglas stayed there with him, running up an extravagant bill on Wilde's account. Wilde tolerated Douglas's financial excesses until Douglas proposed to keep a young man in the hotel at Wilde's expense. Wilde refused. Douglas stormed out and took up residence in another hotel with the friend.

The end game in Queensberry's battle with Wilde began at 4.30 on 18 February 1895 when the Marquess left his card for Wilde at the Albemarle Club. This was handed to Wilde by the hall porter when he next visited the club. On the card, in Queensberry's handwriting, was written what Wilde deciphered as 'To Oscar Wilde, ponce and Somdomite'. Wilde was too infuriated to find any amusement in his adversary's misspelling. In fact, Queensberry claimed in court that his barely legible scrawl had in fact said 'To Oscar Wilde, posing as a Somdomite', an easier accusation to defend. Following so shortly after the thwarted effort to disrupt the opening night of The Importance of

Being Earnest, Queensberry's unwelcome appearance at Wilde's club indicated that a public scandal was inevitable. There was no escaping the Marquess's rage in London. He returned to his hotel with thoughts of fleeing to Paris, hoping to escape from the son as much as from the father. Unfortunately, the hotel manager refused to allow him to check out until he had settled his bill, threatening to impound his luggage if he failed to do so. Wilde did not have the money. He was trapped.

In desperation Wilde turned to Robert Ross, ever his help in times of need or crisis, informing him that Queensberry had left a card at his club 'with hideous words on it'. There was little option but a criminal prosecution. 'My whole life seems ruined by this man ... On the sand is my life spilt.'[7] Ross advised Wilde to take no action. Douglas, however, urged Wilde to prosecute his father for libel. Prompted by Douglas's malevolent attitude, Wilde and Douglas had several meetings with the solicitor C.O. Humphreys, during which, in Wilde's words, they sat 'with serious faces telling serious lies'. On 1 March Wilde obtained a warrant for the arrest of Queensberry, who was arrested on the following day and charged with criminal libel.

In the weeks before the full trial commenced Wilde was urged by several friends to drop proceedings. Frank Harris and Bernard Shaw both predicted disaster. Against such advice, only the obstinate insistence of Douglas kept Wilde from withdrawing the charge. On 25 March some ill-fated optimism had been injected by the fashionable fortune-teller Mrs Robinson, who had 'prophesied complete triumph'.[8] The full horror of what Wilde had unleashed upon himself became clear five days later when Queensberry entered his Plea of Justification. It listed fifteen separate counts in which Wilde was alleged to have solicited boys to commit sodomy.

The trial opened on 3 April 1895 at the Old Bailey. Edward Carson, Wilde's childhood friend and colleague at Trinity College, was representing Queensberry. His opening speech hammered home the weight of evidence against Wilde. Queensberry had been animated from beginning to end 'by one hope alone – of saving his son'. Wilde, on the other hand, was consorting with 'some of the most immoral characters in London', such as Alfred Taylor, 'a most notorious character – as the police will tell the court'. Carson vividly contrasted Wilde's artistic elitism and his contempt for the public with his democratic taste for common boys. He mentioned Wilde's payment of blackmail to Alfred Wood who would testify in court. Carson did not allege any misconduct between Wilde and Douglas. 'God forbid! But everything shows that the young man was in a dangerous position in that he acquiesced in the domination of Mr Wilde, a man of great ability and attainments.' He was now going to bring forward several young men who would testify to 'shocking acts' with Wilde. Alfonso Harold Conway, for example, would testify to Wilde's having dressed him up in good clothes, so as to make him appear a fit companion.

At this point, hopelessly outgunned, Wilde's counsel, Sir Edward Clarke, plucked Carson by the gown and with the judge's permission went aside to confer with him. Clarke had decided to abandon the prosecution and hoped that Carson would accept a verdict of not guilty. Such a verdict would imply that Wilde was '*posing* as a sodomite', but would not concede that he had committed sodomy as indicated in the Plea of Justification. Carson, seeing no advantage in accepting half a loaf when the whole loaf was already in his grasp, refused to compromise. The Plea of Justification must stand. The judge agreed and instructed the jury to that effect. After the jury returned their verdict, Queensberry was applauded loudly by those who had packed the public gallery. The judge made no attempt to stop the cheering, but simply folded up his papers and left. The verdict meant that Queensberry had been justified in calling Wilde a sodomite in the public interest. Queensberry's triumph was Wilde's downfall.

Wilde was arrested on 6 April and was charged at Bow Street Police Court with offences under Section Eleven of the Criminal Law Amendment Act, 1885. Bail was refused and he was detained on remand at Holloway until his first trial began at the Old Bailey on 26 April. The seriousness of Wilde's predicament was illustrated by Douglas's cousin, George Wyndham, a Member of Parliament who was to become Chief Secretary for Ireland in Arthur Balfour's government. On the day after Wilde's arrest, Wyndham had spoken to Balfour about the implications of the failed libel case. Balfour had discussed the case with lawyers who had seen the incriminating evidence against Wilde. In his opinion Wilde was 'certain to be condemned'. The case was 'in every way a very serious one, involving the systematic ruin of a number of young men'. According to Wyndham there was very little sympathy for Wilde. 'Public feeling in

London is fiercely hostile to him, among all classes.'[9] When Wyndham attacked Ross for allowing Wilde and Douglas to be together, Ross had replied that, on the contrary, he and all Wilde's friends had been trying to separate them for years.

On 19 April Constance wrote a heartbroken plea to the fortune-teller, Mrs Robinson, only a few weeks after the latter had prematurely predicted Wilde's triumph.

> My dear Mrs Robinson, What is to become of my husband who has so betrayed and deceived me and ruined the lives of my darling boys? Can you tell me anything? You told me that after this terrible shock my life was to become easier, but will there be any happiness in it, or is that dead for me? And I have had so little. My life has all been cut to pieces ...[10]

Constance added that she would have to seek a judicial separation or a divorce in order to secure legal guardianship of her sons. It says much for her compassion that she should still find words of sympathy for her husband, even in circumstances of such strain: 'What a tragedy for him who is so gifted.'

On 24 April Queensberry forced a bankruptcy sale of Wilde's effects by demanding payment of his £600 costs. Constance suffered the humiliation of having her home ransacked as the receivers took possession of Wilde's property. Among the items sold were presentation volumes from Hugo, Whitman, Swinburne, Mallarmé, Morris and Verlaine; drawings by Burne-Jones and Whistler; paintings by Monticelli and Simeon Solomon; Wilde's own manuscripts and books; expensive china; and Thomas Carlyle's writing desk. There was still not enough to pay off the debts and Wilde's estate remained in receivership until long after his death.

At Wilde's trial the prosecution produced a string of witnesses, each testifying to the sordid details of the accused's life. Several young men claimed to have been recruited by Alfred Taylor, Wilde's co-defendant, to minister to Wilde's wishes. Alfred Wood testified that Wilde had paid him £35 for the return of incriminating letters which Wilde had written to Douglas. Various members of staff at the Savoy Hotel testified that they had seen boys in Wilde's bed while he was dressing or, more graphically, that there had been fecal stains on the bed sheets. Wilde admitted that he knew the boys who had testi-fied but denied that he had indecent relations with them. As for the evidence of the hotel employees, Wilde replied that it was 'entirely untrue' and that he couldn't answer for what hotel servants said years after he had left the hotel. Wilde's counsel based its defence on the corrupt nature of many of the witnesses. They were professional blackmailers, petty criminals and liars. Their evidence could not be trusted. After nearly four hours of deliberation the jury failed to reach a verdict. It seems that ten or eleven jurors had sought conviction and only one or two had voted for acquittal. Wilde had escaped by the skin of his teeth. It was only a temporary respite.

A retrial was ordered and Wilde was granted bail in the interim. His friends tried to persuade him to leave the country before the com-mencement of the second trial but he refused. During a conversation with Frank Harris about the nature of the evidence against him, Wilde commented that Harris was speaking 'with passion and conviction' as if he thought that he was innocent. 'But you are innocent,' said Harris, 'aren't you?' 'No,' Wilde replied. 'I thought you knew that all along.' Looking at his friend, Wilde asked whether the knowledge of his guilt would make a difference to their friendship. Harris assured him it would not.

The second trial began on 22 May and was, to all intents and pur-poses, a rerun of the first. The prosecution dredged through the weight of sordid evidence and the defence once again questioned the credibility of the witnesses. This time there were no dissenting voices on the jury and Wilde was found guilty. If Wilde had hoped for leniency, even at this late stage, his hopes must have been shattered on the hard edges of the judge's summing up. Turning to the prison-ers, Mr Justice Wills expressed his disgust at the nature of their crime in unequivocal terms.

Oscar Wilde and Alfred Taylor, the crime of which you have been con-victed is so bad that one has to put stern restraint upon one's self to prevent one's self from describing, in language which I would rather not use, the sentiments which must rise in the breast of every man of honour who has heard the details of these two terrible trials ...

It is no use for me to address you. People who can do these things must be dead to all sense of shame, and one cannot hope to produce any effect upon them. It is the worst case I have ever tried. That you, Taylor, kept a kind of male brothel it is impossible to doubt. And that you, Wilde, have been the centre of a circle of extensive corruption of the most hideous kind among young men, it is equally impossible to doubt.

I shall, under such circumstances, be expected to pass the severest sentence that the law allows. In my judgement it is totally inadequate for such a case as this. The sentence of the Court is that each of you be imprisoned and kept to hard labour for two years.

'My God, my God!' Wilde exclaimed, his face white with anguish and incomprehension at the severity of the sentence. He seemed to sway for a moment before the warders took hold of him and conducted him to the cells.

Led into the shadows of a twilight world by Douglas and by his own desires, Wilde had wandered to the very edge. Then, as he hesitated on the brink, one disastrous error of judgement had sent his lofty reputation tumbling into the abyss of his worst fears.

1 Hart-Davis, *Letters of Oscar Wilde*, pp. 438–9.
2 Ibid., p. 379.
3 Hart-Davis, *More Letters of Oscar Wilde*, pp. 128–9.
4 Ibid., p. 128.
5 Ellmann, *Oscar Wilde*, pp. 405–6.
6 Ibid., p. 406.
7 Hart-Davis, *Letters of Oscar Wilde*, p. 384.
8 Ibid., p. 385.
9 Douglas, *Without Apology*, p. 310.
10 Hart-Davis, *Letters of Oscar Wilde*, p. 389.

TWENTY THREE

Purgatory

How else but through a broken heart
May Lord Christ enter in?

Almost without exception the press was united in its praise for the verdict. One by one, the country's leading journals queued up to gloat over Wilde's downfall. The *Daily Telegraph* struck a note of jubilation: 'Open the windows! Let in the fresh air.' The *News of the World* on 26 May rejoiced that 'The aesthetic cult, in the nasty form, is over.' The editorial of the *St James's Gazette* on 27 May proclaimed that 'a dash of wholesome bigotry' was preferable to over-toleration. There was certainly more bigotry than toleration in the press coverage, and precious little sympathy for the condemned man. An exception was *Reynold's News* on 20 May which refused 'to gloat over the ruin of the unhappy man'.

Even those who had no desire to gloat were unprepared to sympathize publicly with Wilde's plight. He had become a pariah, a social leper, who was best kept at arm's length. Prominent figures with whom Wilde had wined and dined kept a discreet distance. The Prince of Wales, a great admirer of Wilde's plays, had figured in minor scandals himself and was in no position to defend his favourite dramatist. There was a conspiracy of silence in the social world. Those who once hung on his every word at dinner parties, shunned any mention of him except in furtive whispers. Gleeson White, an art critic, observed both wryly and shrewdly that Wilde 'will never lift his head again, for he has against him all men of infamous life'.[1] He also had against him all women of infamous life as Wilde's disciple Ernest Dowson discovered. Dowson, always kind-hearted, had refused to disappear discreetly like so many of Wilde's other friends. He had called on Wilde during Wilde's brief period of bail between the two trials and he was present at the Old Bailey on the day that the verdict and sentence were pronounced. Yet he was to suffer for his unembarrassed sympathy for his fallen friend. One evening a prostitute, overhearing his views on Wilde, called after him, "'Ere's another of the dirty buggers.'[2]

In private, if not in public, some of Wilde's literary peers expressed disquiet at the 'wholesome bigotry' and puritanical prurience of the public's reaction to Wilde's downfall. In the midst of Wilde's trials, Henry James wrote in a letter to Edmund Gosse of his feelings of disgust, not so much for the nature of Wilde's crime as for the 'ghoulish' nature of the public's gloating at Wilde's expense:

> it has been, it is, hideously, atrociously dramatic and really interesting – so far as one can say of a thing of which the interest is qualified by such sickening horribility. It is the squalid gratuitousness of it all – of the mere exposure – that blurs the spectacle. But the *fall* from nearly twenty years of a really unique kind of 'brilliant' conspicuity (wit, 'art', conversation – one of our two or three dramatists etc.) to that sordid prison cell and this gulf of obscenity over which the ghoulish public hangs and gloats – it is beyond any utterance of irony or any pang of compassion! He was never in the smallest degree interesting to me – but this hideous human history has made him so – in a manner.[3]

James's humane response is particularly striking because he was never an admirer of Wilde, in fact the contrary. He had satirized Wilde in his novel *The Tragic Muse* and had criticized Wilde's work on several occasions. Others who sympathized with Wilde at the time did so in secret, and only later would his tragic fall elicit words of charity.

The Bishop of London, Dr Winnington Ingram, spoke out belatedly in Wilde's defence. 'I knew Wilde, and, in spite of his one great vice – which was surely pathological – I never met a man who united in himself so many lovable Christian virtues.'[4]

A former friend turned adversary who had more to say than anyone about Wilde's conviction was André Raffalovich. Within weeks of Wilde's imprisonment Raffalovich began writing a small book which would be published as *L'Affaire Oscar Wilde* in Paris in the autumn of

1895. Raffalovich agreed with Dr Ingram's verdict that Wilde's vice was pathological but failed to appreciate the 'lovable Christian virtues' that the Bishop found so attractive. Instead, Raffalovich concentrated on Wilde's corrupting influence:

> Quand je l'accuse de criminalité, je ne m'occupe plus des actes sexuels qu'on lui a reprochés, mais du rôle qu'il a joué, de l'influence qu'il a prise et si mal employée, des jeunes vanités qu'il a faussées, des vices qu'il a tant encouragés.[5]
>
> *[When I accuse him of being a criminal, I am no longer concerned with the sexual acts for which he has been criticized, but with the role that he has played, with the influence he has had and so badly used, with the vain youths that he has perverted and with the vices he has so encouraged.]*

Raffalovich's interest in the 'Oscar Wilde Affair' was coloured by his friendship with John Gray, one of the vain youths who had fallen under Wilde's influence. Gray now regretted his youthful liaisons with Wilde and was worried that his name would crop up in the trial. In fact, he had genuine cause for concern. *The Picture of Dorian Gray* was cited specifically in Queensberry's Plea of Justification as an 'immoral work' and Gray must have dreaded his name being linked with the novel's infamous hero. Fearing that one of his skeletons would be found in Wilde's cupboard, Gray instructed the well-known barrister Francis Mathew to attend the Wilde trials with a watching brief. The decision to do so was probably at Raffalovich's prompting and expense. In the event, cross-examination on *The Picture of Dorian Gray* elicited the influence of Huysmans' *A Rebours* on Wilde's novel but Gray's name was not mentioned.

Raffalovich has been criticized for writing *L'Affaire Oscar Wilde*, which is certainly very bitter in places, but his motives for doing so were not as negative as some have suggested. Many years later he sought to justify his position. 'If you had lived through that time and seen at least one tortured victim as I did, and sinister shadows cast on tracts of human relationships, you would have understood my feelings.'[6] One can assume that the 'tortured victim' to whom Raffalovich is referring was John Gray.

Gray's own reaction to Wilde's fall has gone unrecorded but a story Gray related to a friend many years later may throw some light on the anguish he felt when Wilde was arrested. Gray was walking up Coventry Street 'when a stranger approached him and imparted to him some information that was, for him, utterly devastating'. Stunned by the revelation, he made his way to the nearby church of Notre Dame de France. Kneeling before the image of the Blessed Virgin, he sought consolation in prayer. After a few minutes, or so it seemed, he was disturbed by an old woman bearing keys who told him that she was waiting to lock up. He suddenly realized that it was getting dark and that he had been on his knees for hours. Gray's biographer, Brocard Sewell, suggests that the information which was so utterly devastating may have been news of Wilde's arrest and that the intensity of Gray's reaction to it may have influenced his decision to enter the priesthood.[7]

It was partly under Gray's influence that Raffalovich was received into the Catholic Church at the Jesuit church in Farm Street on 3 February 1896. Many years later, playing down his own role, Gray wrote that the quiet example of Raffalovich's housekeeper, Florence Gribbell, was an important factor in his friend's decision. Raffalovich had thoroughly disapproved of Gribbell's own conversion a year or so previously and had raised a 'ghastly row', but he had observed the positive change it had wrought on her life.[8] Following his reception, Raffalovich went on pilgrimage to Loreto and arranged for Masses to be said in the Santa Casa for the conversion of Oscar Wilde and Alfred Douglas.

If the only assistance that Raffalovich could offer Wilde and Douglas was spiritual, his financial assistance at this time extended beyond his patronage of Gray to his support for the impoverished Aubrey Beardsley. The young artist had suffered more than most from Wilde's arrest and imprisonment. In the eyes of the press, and consequently the public, he was inextricably linked with Wilde. His decadent style was seen as akin to Wilde's, and his illustrations for Wilde's *Salomé* merely reinforced their perceived unity of purpose. Beardsley's link with Wilde was strengthened by a report in the press that Wilde was led away with a copy of *The Yellow Book* under his arm when he was arrested. *The Yellow Book* was a controversial quarterly produced by the Bodley Head which was famous (or infamous) for its air of decadence in general but for Beardsley's illustrations in particular. Ironically, the 'yellow book' which Wilde was carrying when he was arrested was not the Bodley Head quarterly but a French novel, *Aphrodite*, by Wilde's estranged friend Pierre Louÿs. The damage, however, was done. Beardsley was condemned by association with Wilde and suffered the severest consequences as a result.

In the wake of Wilde's arrest, an angry mob hurled stones through the window of the Bodley Head shop. All Wilde's books were withdrawn from the shop and pressure mounted for Beardsley's drawings to be removed from the next issue of *The Yellow Book*. Several prominent Bodley Head authors added their voices to the demands. Wilfrid Meynell and William Watson joined forces to put pressure on *The Yellow Book*'s editor, and Mrs Humphry Ward regarded it as her duty, in view of her 'position before the British public', to support their call for Beardsley's dismissal. Edmund Gosse was a lone dissident voice. Regardless of whether 'the British public considered Beardsley's art immoral', Gosse argued, it 'was not sufficient reason for an act that would connect him in the public mind with a form of vice with which he had no connection whatsoever'.[9] Gosse's pleas left his literary peers unmoved. In the public mind Beardsley's name was already bound up with Wilde's and most writers were determined to distance themselves from both.

Yielding to pressure, John Lane dismissed Beardsley from his post as art editor of *The Yellow Book* and withdrew all his drawings from the forthcoming issue. Beardsley's livelihood depended on his work for *The Yellow Book* and on the quick publication of his new work. He found himself abandoned at the very moment when Wilde's trial had made him unemployable. He was also shaken by the persistent innuendoes of the newspapers which implied that he was, like Wilde, a homosexual and that his work was 'unclean'. In fact, Beardsley was not homosexual. Like Ernest Dowson, another heterosexual in Wilde's circle, he was branded by association as 'another of the dirty buggers'. In the general *crise de moralité* which followed Wilde's downfall anyone remotely associated with him faced ostracism.

It was at this time that Beardsley was saved from destitution by the friendship of André Raffalovich, whose patronage enabled him to continue his work without financial anxiety. Surely Raffalovich's beneficence, in circumstances which flew in the face of puritanical public opinion, frees him from the allegations of some of Wilde's more blinkered admirers that his attacks on Wilde were the results of prudishness, prurience or hypocrisy.

Of course, the person facing the brunt of the fall-out following Wilde's conviction was Lord Alfred Douglas. His mother, in a desperate bid to instil some order into her son's unruly life, consulted Father Sebastian Bowden at the London Oratory, who was an old friend. This was the same Father Bowden whom Wilde had approached in 1878 when he was contemplating reception into the Church. At Lady Queensberry's request, Father Bowden wrote to Douglas offering spiritual advice. He also asked More Adey, a friend of Wilde and Douglas, to exert what influence he had to prevent Douglas doing anything rash or regrettable. Adey informed Bowden that Douglas was planning a trip to Florence to see Lord Henry Somerset, a figure whose reputation was almost as scandalous as Wilde's. With an air of resignation, Father Bowden wrote to Adey of his fears that Douglas 'is at present so self-willed and blinded as to be humanly speaking beyond Redemption'.[10] Many years later, when Douglas wrote his memoirs, he recalled a conversation with Wilde shortly before the commencement of the ill-fated libel case. It illustrated his own opposition to Catholicism at the time but also a renewed yearning by Wilde for conversion. Wilde told Douglas that if he won the libel case he and Douglas 'must both be received into the dear Catholic Church'. Douglas responded angrily that if Wilde didn't win the case 'we certainly won't be received anywhere else'.[11]

While his friends and enemies reacted to his fate, Wilde was finding himself subject to the harsh realities of prison life. On the day of his conviction he was driven in a prison van to Holloway where his personal belongings were removed from him. He was ordered to strip to his shirt and a detailed description of his appearance was taken. After the obligatory bath he emerged to find a full suit of regulation prison clothes, drab in colour and covered with broad arrows. Marched to his cell, he received his first prison meal, an allowance of thin porridge known as skilly, and a small brown loaf.

During the week of 9 June Wilde was moved to Pentonville where he received a full medical examination. If pronounced fit he would commence the rigours of the 'hard labour' to which he had been sentenced. During the first month he would spend six hours a day on the treadmill, twenty minutes on and five minutes' rest, making an ascent of 6,000 feet. At night he would sleep on a bare board raised a few inches above the floor. After the first month he would be put to some monotonous industrial employment, such as postbag-making, tailoring, or picking oakum. Wilde's body, unaccustomed to physical exertion, was not equal to these demands. Within two weeks of his conviction his health had been affected. 'Already Wilde has grown much thinner,' *Reynold's News* reported, 'and since his conviction he has preserved, it is said, a settled melancholy and reticence. He has had great difficulty in getting sleep, and from time to time he loudly bemoans the bitterness of his fate.'[12]

Wilde's desolation was relieved, at least temporarily, by a visit from R.B. Haldane on 12 June. Haldane, who had known Wilde earlier, was a member of a Home Office committee investigating prisons. As such, he had access to any prison at any time. When Haldane entered Wilde's cell he found the prisoner reticent and unwilling to speak. Then, Haldane recalled, he put his hand on Wilde's shoulder and told him that he had not fully used his literary gift because he had lived a life of pleasure and had not made any subject his own. His misfortune had given him the great subject he needed and could be a great blessing to his literary vocation. Haldane told Wilde he would use his influence to obtain books for him, and pen and ink so he could write. Wilde burst into tears. Haldane had expressed in words Wilde's own thoughts since his conviction. Haldane's analysis was essentially the view Wilde would express in *De Profundis*. He confessed his guilt to Haldane, adding that the temptation of such a life had been too great for him. He would try to do what Haldane proposed and beseeched him eagerly to obtain books. He had only been allowed the Bible and *Pilgrim's Progress* and greatly desired more reading matter. Among the books he requested was Flaubert's *La Tentation de Saint Antoine* but Haldane reminded him half jokingly that Flaubert had dedicated his works to the lawyer who had defended him against a charge of indecent publication. This made the granting of such a request unlikely. Wilde laughed for the first time, and cheered up a little. The two men then decided on fifteen volumes, including works by St Augustine, Pascal and Newman. The governor of Pentonville objected that the supply of such books was contrary to the Prison Act of 1865. Haldane, however, had the backing of the Secretary of State. The governor's objections were ignored and the books duly delivered. They would accompany Wilde for the rest of his sentence. For the moment, pen and ink were still not permitted but, three years later, when Haldane received anonymously in the post a copy of *The Ballad of Reading Gaol*, he considered it the fulfilment of Wilde's promise to write of his experiences.

On 4 July Wilde was transferred from Pentonville to Wandsworth. Here he received his second visitor, Otho Holland, Constance's brother. He was told that Constance had fled to Switzerland to protect Cyril and Vyvyan from the scandal in England and that she was being urged by her solicitor, J.S. Hargrove, to take divorce proceedings. Wilde told his brother-in-law that he wished at all costs to avoid this, fearing the prospect of a permanent parting from his wife and children. He promised to write to Constance as soon as prison regulations allowed, which would be in September when the first three months of his sentence had been served. Holland informed his sister of Wilde's intentions. At around the same time she also received a letter from one of Wilde's friends, Robert Sherard, pleading on Wilde's behalf for a reconciliation. After all that she had been through, Constance was still able to forgive her husband and, on 9 September, wrote that she was willing to take him back. On the same day, she wrote to the governor of Wandsworth prison, requesting permission to visit her husband as soon as possible.

Having decided, against the advice of her solicitor, not to proceed with the divorce, Constance was filled with trepidation when Hargrove arrived in Switzerland. She asked her brother to be present when she met him, seeking moral support as she braced to tell him that she had contradicted his advice. To her surprise, Hargrove pulled out of his pocket a letter from Wilde. It was addressed to Constance. He had read it and said that it was one of 'the most touching and pathetic letters that had ever come under his eye'. In view of such 'a humble, penitent letter' he admitted the possibility that Constance might wish to forgive her husband, which was not a view he would have countenanced beforehand. Greatly relieved, Constance showed him Sherard's letter and informed him that she had already decided not to proceed with the divorce. Hargrove did not discourage her but informed her that any reconciliation would mean starting afresh under a new name on 'the other side of the world'. Constance replied that she was ready for whatever sacrifice was required. Her brother believed that it would be possible for Constance and Oscar to live in France or Spain, sending the boys to school in England. Eventually after ten or fifteen years he hoped that Wilde could cautiously make his way back again into England.[13]

Constance's request for special permission to see her husband was granted. The interview took place on 21 September. Her shocked impressions were conveyed in a letter to Robert Sherard on the following day. 'It was indeed awful, more so than I had any conception it could be. I could not see him and I could not touch him, and I scarcely spoke.'[14] Wilde told her that he had been mad for the last three years and that if he ever saw Douglas again he would kill him. Constance told him that he could rejoin her and her sons when he was released from prison, news which cheered him greatly. On 15 October Constance informed a friend that, while she was changing her name to Holland to protect her children, she was withdrawing from divorce proceedings. 'My poor misguided husband, who is weak rather than wicked, repents most bitterly all his past madness and I cannot refuse him the forgiveness he has asked.'[15]

A week later, when Wilde was visited by Lily, his brother's wife, she found him in the infirmary, very sick with dysentery. He told her that he was hungry but that he could not eat the food. He was living on a diet of beef tea. 'Mentally he is very unhappy ... He is very altered in *every* way.'[16] Wilde's deterioration also worried Robert Ross and Robert Sherard when they visited him. Sherard wrote to More Adey, informing him that Wilde was 'very bad indeed. All elasticity and resistance seem to have gone out of him, and his state, under the circumstances is really alarming. It was very terrible.' Adey wrote urgently to Constance, expressing his serious concern. 'He is evidently much changed for the worse both mentally and bodily. He is looking frightfully emaciated, his hair is falling off and is streaked with white, and his eyes have a vacant expression.' Wilde did not wish to speak at all but when he did it was often without relevance to the conversation. Adey was fearful that something must be done immediately before Wilde became permanently 'silly' or even died from the effects of his imprisonment. 'I entreat you to make a private appeal to the queen for his release.' He suggested that Constance could approach the Bishop of Winchester, who was a personal friend of the queen and 'would present such an appeal if it came from you'.

Evidently, Wilde had also indicated that Constance believed Adey and Ross were seeking to hinder their proposed reconciliation, a belief which Adey was at pains to repudiate. 'I have never had any other hope for Oscar than that you would receive him when he comes out. So wholly untrue is it that I or any of his friends who have been associated with me in this matter have intended to place him in a position to break your marriage or to cause you further unhappiness ...'[17]

On 23 November Wilde was transferred from Wandsworth to Reading. En route he suffered a degree of humiliation surpassing that which he had endured at his trials. For half an hour he stood on a platform at Clapham Junction station, handcuffed and in full prison uniform. A crowd gathered to laugh and jeer, their number being swelled with every arriving train. Such was his distress that the mere memory of it made him weep for months afterwards. Eighteen months later, when petitioning the Home Secretary a few weeks before his scheduled release, he pleaded that he should not be transferred from Reading gaol to any other prison prior to his release. His ordeal at Clapham Junction was 'so utterly distressing, from the mental no less than the emotional point of view', that he felt 'quite unable to undergo any similar exhibition to public gaze'.[18]

Within three months of his arrival at Reading gaol Wilde received a further blow to his already shattered life. On 19 February he was visited by Constance who, in spite of her own failing health, had travelled specially from Genoa to break the news to him of his mother's death. Wilde was devastated. A year later he would write that her death was so terrible that he had no words to express his anguish and his shame. His mother had bequeathed him a name which was both 'noble and honoured' but he had 'disgraced that name eternally'. Nonetheless, he was deeply moved by his wife's sacrifice in travelling all the way from Italy to England so that he would not hear the awful news from 'indifferent or alien lips'. He wrote to Robert Ross that she had been 'gentle and good to me' when she visited. 'I feel that I have brought such unhappiness on her and such ruin on my children that I have no right to go against her wishes in anything ... I have full trust in her.' For her part, Constance wrote of her visit to Wilde in a letter to her brother. 'They say he is quite well, but he is an absolute wreck compared with what he was.'[19]

Wilde's anguish and shame on hearing of his mother's death must have been exacerbated by feelings of guilt that his own downfall had contributed to, or even caused, her death. Lady Wilde's health had gone into terminal decline in the months following her son's conviction. Her final months had been wracked by sorrow for 'dear Oscar'. She had never left her room and had seen almost no one. She was heartbroken that no letters arrived from her son, and had been fearful of writing to him in case they were returned. Her anguished state of mind was illustrated in an entry to a notebook she kept during her final illness. 'Life is agony and hope, illusion and despair all commingled, but despair outlasts all.'[20]

Wilde would doubtless have felt guilty that he had not written to her during the final months of her life, and earlier memories of his filial failings must have returned to haunt him. Two years earlier, Lady Wilde had been distressed by Oscar's failure to turn up at his brother's wedding and she had sought to reconcile her estranged sons. On 29 March 1894 she had written to Wilde:

> I am truly sorry to find that you and Willie meet as enemies. Is this to go on to my death? Not a cheering prospect for me, to have my two sons at enmity, and unable to meet at my deathbed. I think, to please me, you might write the 8 words I asked – 'I forget the enmity. Let us be friends. Signed Oscar.' 8 Words! Can you do it to oblige me? There need be no intimacy between you but at least social civility.[21]

Her pleas were unavailing at the time but must have returned as inquisitorial echoes after her death.

On her deathbed Lady Wilde had asked if Oscar might be brought to see her. She was told it was impossible. 'May the prison help him!' she said and turned to the wall.

In January 1896, the month before Wilde heard from Constance the news of his mother's death, More Adey had arranged with the Home Office, at Wilde's specific request, to send an Italian edition of Dante's *Divine Comedy* to him. Throughout the rest of his sentence it served as a constant companion, more important than any of the other books he received. In the following months the lists of books which Wilde requested are dominated by an intense interest in Christianity in general and Dante in particular. He requested several volumes of Dante criticism, including Father Bowden's new translation of Franz Hettinger. He asked for an English prose translation of the *Divine Comedy*, presumably to read in parallel with the original Italian, and requested Italian and English versions of Dante's *Vita Nuova*.

Fourteen years earlier, during his tour of the United States, Wilde had been pleasantly surprised to find a translation of Dante in one of the whitewashed cells at a prison he visited. 'Strange and beautiful it seemed to me that the sorrow of a single Florentine in exile should, hundreds of years afterwards, lighten the sorrow of some common prisoner in a modern gaol ...'[22] Perhaps Wilde recalled this visit as Dante's profound vision comforted him in similar fashion and in similar circumstances. Throughout 1896 Dante was to Wilde what Virgil was to Dante, his guide through the Inferno. Slowly, with Dante leading him by the hand or heart, he emerged from the depths of despair, from the hell without hope, to the cleansing fires of purgatory.

1 Philippe Jullian, *Oscar Wilde*, London: Paladin, 1971, p. 272.
2 Matthew Sturgis, *Passionate Attitudes: The English Decadence of the Eighteen-Nineties*, London: Macmillan, 1995, pp. 239–40.
3 Ibid.
4 Ibid.
5 Quoted in Croft-Cooke, *Unrecorded Life of Oscar Wilde*, p. 11.
6 Sturgis, *Passionate Attitudes*, p. 239.
7 Sewell, *Footnote to the Nineties*, p. 43.
8 Ibid., p. 88.
9 Sturgis, *Passionate Attitudes*, p. 241.
10 Jonathan Fryer, *André and Oscar: Gide, Wilde and the Gay Art of Living*, London: Constable, 1997, p. 172.
11 Douglas, *Without Apology*, p. 263.
12 *Reynold's News*, 9 June 1895.
13 Hart-Davis, *Letters of Oscar Wilde*, pp. 871–2.
14 Ellmann, *Oscar Wilde*, p. 462.
15 Ibid.
16 Ibid.
17 Rough draft of letter from More Adey to Constance Wilde, undated (November 1895?), Bodleian Library, Oxford.
18 Hart-Davis, *Letters of Oscar Wilde*, p. 529.
19 Ibid., p. 399.
20 Ellmann, *Oscar Wilde*, p. 467.
21 Ibid., p. 385.
22 Hart-Davis, *Letters of Oscar Wilde*, p. 115.

TWENTY FOUR

Out of the Depths

> I have a right to share in Sorrow, and he who can look at the loveliness
> of the world, and share its sorrow, and realize something of the wonder
> of both, is in immediate contact with divine things, and has got as near
> to God's secret as anyone can get.

Wilde's sorrow at his mother's death was tempered by the comfort offered by his wife during the visit at which she had conveyed the news to him. She had kissed him and was at great pains to offer him consolation. They talked of their children and Wilde urged Constance not to spoil Cyril as Lady Queensberry had spoiled Alfred Douglas. He beseeched her to bring him up 'so that if he shed innocent blood he would come and tell her, that she might cleanse his hands for him first, and then teach him how by penance or expiation to cleanse his soul afterwards'.[1]

Constance stayed in London for a few days after her visit to Wilde. On 22 February she visited Edward Burne-Jones and his wife. She told them that Wilde was being given work to do in the garden but that his favourite work was to cover books in brown paper because at least it enabled him to hold books in his hand. When the Burne-Joneses raised the subject of her children, Constance told them that Vyvyan had already forgotten his father but that Cyril continued to ask about him. Cyril had learned from a newspaper that his father was in prison but he thought it was for debt.

On 2 July 1896 Wilde petitioned the Home Secretary in the hope of securing an early release. His words, abject and desperate, confess remorse for his 'terrible offences of which he was rightly found guilty', but point out that such offences were 'forms of sexual madness' to be treated by a physician rather than crimes to be punished by a judge. To illustrate his point he quoted modern research in pathological science, particularly in France, which showed that he had been suffering from 'the most horrible form of erotomania' which had caused him to neglect his wife and children, his position in society and as an artist, the honour of his name and family, and even his 'very humanity itself', leaving him 'the helpless prey of the most revolting passions'.[2] Ironically, Wilde was agreeing with André Raffalovich's *L'Affaire Oscar Wilde* and his more extensive work *Uranisme et unisexualité,* though whether through a genuine belief in their intrinsic worth or through a disingenuous ploy to obtain his freedom is open to question. In language exceeding anything in Raffalovich's critique of his case, Wilde wrote of a 'monstrous sexual perversion' and a 'sexual monomania of a terrible character'. The petition concluded with a request that his imprisonment be ended immediately before insanity claimed his soul as well as his body.

There was never any likelihood that Wilde's petition would succeed in its aim. Two days later he petitioned the Home Secretary again, this time on a matter both practical and pressing. More Adey had written to the governor of Reading gaol requesting a meeting with Wilde on Constance's behalf to discuss an agreement with regard to the guardianship, education and future of their children. Constance, though still ready to forgive her husband, was understandably anxious to settle the legal aspects which arose from Wilde's bankruptcy. Wilde requested that the meeting take place in the Solicitors' Room where there would be a degree of privacy, rather than from behind the customary cage with a warder present, because the meeting would be discussing 'delicate and private matters'.[3] This time the petition was granted.

Adey visited Wilde about three weeks later. His record of the visit provides a valuable insight into Wilde's state of mind in the summer of 1896 when he was a little over half way through his sentence. Wilde informed Adey that he had petitioned the Home Secretary in the hope that he would be treated as an erotomaniac and be sent somewhere to be cured. He was in 'constant fear of breaking down utterly in brain and leaving prison dependent for life on his wife'.

He fully recognizes that his wife must have care of his children, he has no desire that she should not have full controll [*sic*] over them and have her money to do exactly as she likes with. He said, oh, of course, of course. The children could not be with me. People would be always finding out who I was. Whatever my wife wishes should be done.[4]

Later Adey returned to Wilde's preoccupation with his own mental health. 'What he wants is to be saved from madness. His eyes quite different, *wild* ...'

On 30 July Adey wrote to Constance informing her of the outcome of the meeting, telling her of his fears for Wilde's health and requesting that she intervene on her husband's behalf in a written appeal to the Home Secretary:

> I was very much shocked at the state in which I found him. Though he is not looking so ill in body as when I saw him last November, his mental condition is most distressing. He is in terrible apprehension of permanently losing his reason, and lives in great mental agony on that account. I must say, though I shall pain you, that his manner and the expression of his eyes fully justify his fears. The alteration in him is heartrending to see ... He told me to communicate with you and to ask you to write a private letter on his behalf to the Home Secretary to release him in order that he may immediately place himself under competent medical direction out of England, until he is cured. He also begs you to write to Mr Arthur Balfour to ask for his help and influence in his favour ...
>
> Oscar also told me that the constant fear of being rendered a permanent burden upon you and his children in consequence of his mental condition adds greatly to the torture which such a condition occasions him; whereas he hopes that if he were placed under competent medical direction at once, he would be able in about a year's time to provide for himself again ...

Adey confirmed that Wilde agreed not to interfere in any way with the children after his release. He would leave their education entirely to Constance's discretion and the finances would be in her control so that she could bring them up as she thought best.

He also said that he could not ask you to receive him to live with you at present as he was not in a fit mental condition to be with you until he was cured.

He took little interest in anything I told him, but asked eagerly about you and the children. He asked whether I knew where you were staying, how your own health was and your childrens' [sic], and how they were getting on with their lessons ...

The letter concluded with an assurance by Adey that he and his friends would be sorry to see any renewal of the intimacy between Wilde and Douglas. 'On the contrary, we are anxious and wish to forward Oscar's desire to conform to *your* wishes and atone to you in any way he can for the great sorrow he has caused you.'[5]

Wilde's meeting with Adey appears to have been the low water mark in his mental condition. On 27 July he was allowed for the first time to have writing materials in his cell and was to have access to a larger supply of books. Thereafter his health slowly recovered. By the end of September he had improved to such an extent that a letter to Adey exhibited a great deal of sympathy for others as distinct from the earlier obsessive fears for his own sanity. He expressed pleasure at the phenomenal success that Pierre Louÿs's book *Aphrodite* had enjoyed in France, stating that Louÿs was 'most cultivated, refined and gentle'. He remembered how Louÿs had told him three years earlier that he would have to choose between his friendship and that of Douglas. 'I chose at once the meaner nature and the baser mind. In what a mire of madness I walked!' This was a significant change. Wilde now believed that, far from being on the verge of insanity, he was more in his right mind in prison than he had been before his sentence. There were also words of sympathy for Aubrey Beardsley, who was suffering from the consumption which would soon kill him. 'Poor Aubrey ... He brought a strangely new personality to English art, and was a master in his way of fantastic grace, and the charm of the unreal. His muse had moods of terrible laughter. Behind his grotesques there seemed to lurk some curious philosophy ...'[6] It seems that Wilde was purged of the professional jealousy that had slighted Beardsley unjustly after his work on the illustrations for *Salomé*. From the shadows of suffering a warmer Wilde was emerging.

Writing to Robert Ross in November, Wilde acknowledged his calmer, more contented frame of mind. 'I read Dante, and make excerpts and notes for the pleasure of using a pen and ink. And it seems as if I were better in many ways.'[7] It was as though Wilde had been lifted out of the depths of his own despair. He was now ready to take up the pen in a more creative way than merely taking notes on Dante. From January to March 1897 he would write the long letter to Alfred Douglas which would, unwittingly perhaps, become one of his most important works of literature. When it was published posthumously, at first in an expurgated version and then in its entirety, it was entitled appropriately *De Profundis*.

On 18 February 1897, when Wilde was in the midst of writing *De Profundis*, he informed More Adey that it was the most important letter of his life. It would deal with his future mental attitude towards life and the way in which he desired to meet the world again after his release. It was concerned with the development of his character, what he had lost, what he had learned and what he hoped to arrive at. 'At last I see a real goal towards which my soul can go simply, naturally, and rightly.' At all costs, he must finish the letter. 'My whole life depends on it.'[8]

Taken as a whole *De Profundis* is a conundrum of conflicting emotions, a sweet and sour compound of bitter reproachfulness and spiritual serenity. Those parts of the letter which deal specifically with Wilde's life with Douglas are contorted with the pain of the memories as Wilde agonizes over the nature of their relationship. Self-reproach wrestles with self-justification as Wilde both blames himself for many mistakes and Douglas for many more. It is a confession of wrongs, both inflicted and suffered, which was intended in its candour to purge the pain and the guilt from his anguished soul. 'And the end of it all is that I have to forgive you. I must do so. I don't write this letter to put bitterness into your heart, but to pluck it out of mine. For my own sake I must forgive you. One cannot always keep an adder in one's breast to feed on one, nor rise up every night to sow thorns in the garden of one's soul.'

Parallel with the pain is the serenity of a spiritual awakening, a serenity born of sorrow: 'my life, whatever it had seemed to myself and others, had all the while been a real Symphony of Sorrow, passing through its rhythmically-linked movements to its certain resolution, with that inevitableness that in Art characterizes the treatment of every great theme'. Sorrow is a recurring theme throughout *De Profundis*. 'Where there is Sorrow there is holy ground', Wilde affirms, and he quotes Dante's words with approval, 'sorrow remarries us to God'. He had not understood these words before his downfall but he now looked upon them as the key to a fuller life.

> Sorrow, then, and all that it teaches one, is my new world. I used to live entirely for pleasure. I shunned sorrow and suffering of every kind. I hated both. I resolved to ignore them as far as possible, to treat them, that is to say, as modes of imperfection. They were not part of my scheme of life. They had no place in my philosophy. My mother, who knew life as a whole, used often to quote me Goethe's lines – written by Carlyle in a book he had given her years ago – and translated, I fancy, by him also:
>
> Who never ate his bread in sorrow,
> Who never spent the midnight hours
> Weeping and waiting for the morrow,
> He knows you not, ye Heavenly Powers.
>
> ... they were lines my mother often quoted in the troubles of her later life: I absolutely declined to accept or admit the enormous truth hidden in them. I could not understand it ... But ... during the last few months I have, after terrible struggles and difficulties, been able to comprehend some of the lessons hidden in the heart of pain. Clergymen, and people who use phrases without wisdom, sometimes talk of suffering as a mystery. It is really a revelation. One discerns things that one has never discerned before. One approaches the whole of history from a different standpoint. What one had felt dimly through instinct, about Art, is intellectually and emotionally realized with perfect clearness of vision and absolute intensity of apprehension.

Sorrow was 'an intense, an extraordinary reality' behind which was Love, a greater reality still. 'Love of some kind is the only possible explanation of the extraordinary amount of suffering that there is in the world. I cannot conceive any other explanation.' Yet if sorrow was the mask that revealed love, other masks could be deceptive. Elsewhere in

De Profundis Wilde confessed that he and Douglas had been 'deceived and led astray' by the 'mask of joy and pleasure'. 'Behind Joy and Laughter there may be a temperament, coarse, hard and callous. But behind Sorrow there is always Sorrow. Pain, unlike Pleasure, wears no mask.'

Through his own sorrow, his own suffering, Wilde had experienced a spiritual awakening. He now perceived his life, taken in its entirety, as a providential passion play. Even its mistakes were an essential part of the plot, driving the drama towards its logical, and theological, conclusion. His own life, like one of his own plays, turned on a specific moral purpose. Its pivot and its point were one. Life was following art.

> This new life, as through my love of Dante I like sometimes to call it, is, of course, no new life at all, but simply the continuance, by means of development, and evolution, of my former life ... Failure, disgrace, poverty, sorrow, despair, suffering, tears even, the broken words that come from the lips of pain, remorse that makes one walk in thorns, conscience that condemns, self-abasement that punishes, the misery that puts ashes on its head, the anguish that chooses sackcloth for its raiment and into its own drink puts gall – all these were things of which I was afraid. And as I had determined to know nothing of them, I was forced to taste each one of them in turn, to feed on them, to have for a season, indeed, no other food at all.

The discussion of providence led Wilde to the figure of Christ who 'understood the leprosy of the leper, the darkness of the blind, the fierce misery of those who live for pleasure, the strange poverty of the rich'. In the life and passion of Christ, Life and Art were one. All other lives followed the Art and Life of Christ. Each individual passion play of each individual life was but a dim shadow of the Passion Play enacted at Calvary, 'the crucifixion of the Innocent One' whose terrible death 'gave the world its most eternal symbol'. His was the face of Love which gave Sorrow its meaning:

> when one contemplates all this from the point of view of Art alone one cannot but be grateful that the supreme office of the Church should be the playing of the tragedy without the shedding of blood, the mystical

presentation by means of dialogue and costume and gesture even of the Passion of her Lord, and it is always a source of pleasure and awe to me to remember that the ultimate survival of the Greek Chorus, lost elsewhere to art, is to be found in the servitor answering the priest at Mass.

The re-emerging power of the Mass as a source of inspiration was also evident in Wilde's definition of love as 'a sacrament that should be taken kneeling, and *Domine, non sum dignus* should be on the lips and in the hearts of those who receive it'.

In the midst of the discussion of Christ in *De Profundis*, slipped in almost incidentally and as if by accident, is a description of Wilde's own moment of truth, his spiritual awakening alone and desolate in the prison cell. He had come to terms with his loss, he wrote, through a stubbornness of will and a spirit of rebellion. In the end, his pride had been broken by the loss of his very last possession, his son Cyril. Learning that he would not be permitted to see his children upon his release, Wilde was utterly devastated.

I had lost my name, my position, my happiness, my freedom, my wealth. I was a prisoner and a pauper. But I had still one beautiful thing left, my own eldest son. Suddenly he was taken away from me by the law. It was a blow so appalling that I did not know what to do, so I flung myself on my knees, and bowed my head, and wept and said 'The body of a child is as the body of the Lord: I am not worthy of either.' That moment seemed to save me. I saw then that the only thing for me was to accept everything. Since then ... I have been happier. It was of course my soul in its ultimate essence that I had reached. In many ways I had been its enemy, but I found it waiting for me as a friend. When one comes in contact with the soul it makes one simple as a child, as Christ said one should be.

Every morning, after he had cleaned his cell and polished his tins, Wilde began to read the Gospels afresh from a Greek Testament, a dozen or so verses every day. 'It is a delightful way of opening the day ... Endless repetition, in and out of season, has spoiled for us the naïveté, the freshness, the simple romantic charm of the Gospels ... When one returns to the Greek it is like going into a garden of lilies out of some narrow and dark house.'

Wilde's conversion led to a reversion to the Christocentric view of the Renaissance that had characterized his time at Oxford and which had led to his early admiration for Ruskin. In *De Profundis* he writes fervently of 'Christ's own renaissance' which had produced Chartres Cathedral, the Arthurian cycle of legends, the life of St Francis of Assisi, the art of Giotto and Dante's *Divine Comedy*. This had been spoiled by the 'dreary classical Renaissance' of Petrarch, Raphael and Pope which was 'made from without and by dead rules, and does not spring from within through some spirit informing it'. Nonetheless, 'wherever there is a romantic movement in Art, there somehow, and under some form, is Christ, or the soul of Christ'. He was in *Romeo and Juliet*, *The Winter's Tale*, Provençal poetry, Hugo's *Les Misérables*, Baudelaire's *Les Fleurs du Mal* and in the art of Burne-Jones and William Morris.

De Profundis was an effort at expurgation, inspired by Wilde's desire to cleanse himself through confession. The original manuscript, hidden from the eyes of the public for more than half a century, makes interesting reading. Some pages are written in a wild, erratic scrawl, scored through and heavily corrected, whereas others are more ordered, neat and compact with scarcely a correction.[9] It has been suggested that the latter's neatness was the result of Wilde being given the opportunity to make good copies of these particular pages from earlier drafts. If this is so, one has to assume that the governor of Reading gaol was deliberately misleading the prison commissioners when he wrote on 4 April 1897 that each sheet had been carefully numbered before being issued and was withdrawn each evening. The handwriting becomes discernibly smaller, smoother and less erratic, with fewer revisions, on those pages where Christ and not Douglas is the centre of attention. When Wilde is venting his spleen against Douglas the script is wild, tempestuous and flamboyantly large. When he writes of Christ everything on the page appears calmer. Is it not possible that Wilde had partially succeeded in exorcising the bitterness from his heart, his intention when commencing the letter?

His success, however, was only partial. For all its many flashes of brilliance, *De Profundis* remains an enigmatic combination of conflicting forces, sacred and profane. It struggles in its pain, not always successfully, with the bitterness it was intended to overcome. It overstates in its sorrow the place of the Passion, ignoring the Resurrection.

The crucial nature of the Crucifixion is seen by Wilde almost as an end in itself and not as a means to an end. Yet the Passion of Christ, properly understood, points always to the Resurrection. His mysterious Sorrow carries with it the promise of a mysterious Glory. In his suffering Wilde allows the darkness of the sorrow to eclipse the brightness of the glory. The means eclipse the end.

Wilde was very much aware of the letter's inadequacies, as he confessed in its last paragraph. His intention had been to bow his head to everything he had suffered but he was still only able to do this incompletely, imperfectly. 'How far I am away from the true temper of soul, this letter in its changing, uncertain moods, its scorn and bitterness, its aspirations and its failure to realize those aspirations, shows you quite clearly.'

Above all, *De Profundis* showed Wilde at his most honest and candid. Nowhere in its pages is there the barest hint of the disingenuous. He had forsaken all masks to brandish the inadequate, naked truth of his soul. He had sung the *de profundis* of the psalmist in the hope of the *vita nuova* of Dante. From out of the depths he sought the new life:

> for the first year of my imprisonment I did nothing else, and can remember doing nothing else, but wring my hands in impotent despair, and say, 'What an ending! what an appalling ending!' Now I try to say to myself, and sometimes when I am not torturing myself do really and sincerely say, 'What a beginning! what a wonderful beginning!' It may really be so. It may become so.

1 Hart-Davis, *Letters of Oscar Wilde*, p. 499.
2 Ibid., p. 402.
3 Ibid., p. 406.
4 More Adey, scribbled notes of record of visit to Wilde in Reading gaol, July 1896, Bodleian Library Archives.
5 More Adey, letter to Constance Wilde, 30 July 1896, Bodleian Library Archives.
6 Hart-Davis, *Letters of Oscar Wilde*, p. 410.
7 Ibid., p. 413.
8 Ibid., p. 419.
9 *De Profundis*, letter from Reading gaol to Lord Alfred Douglas by Oscar Wilde, autograph, London, British Library, Department of Manuscripts.

TWENTY FIVE

Wilderness

> When I say that I am convinced of these things I speak with too much
> pride. Far off, like a perfect pearl, one can see the city of God. It is so
> wonderful that it seems as if a child could reach it in a summer's day.
> And so a child could. But with me and such as I am it is different. One
> can realize a thing in a single moment, but one loses it in the long hours
> that follow with leaden feet. It is so difficult to keep 'heights that the
> soul is competent to gain'. We think in Eternity, but we move slowly
> through Time: and how slowly time goes ...

Wilde's more settled frame of mind, expressed so eloquently in *De Profundis*, was accompanied by a slow lifting of his spirits as the long-awaited release date approached. They were dampened, however, by two incidents during the last days of his sentence. In the first of these, Wilde heard 'revolting shrieks, or rather howls' as a half-witted inmate, a former soldier named Prince, was flogged for malingering. When Wilde saw him at exercise on the following day he looked more wretched than ever. Two days later, the last time Wilde saw him, he looked close to insanity. The other incident was the imprisonment of three children, convicted for snaring rabbits and unable to pay their fine. Wilde saw them as they were waiting to be assigned to cells, and the look of bemusement and terror on their faces touched him deeply. He beseeched one of the warders, Thomas Martin, to find out the names of the children and the amount of the unpaid fine. 'Can I pay this, and get them out? If so I will get them out tomorrow. Please, dear friend, do this for me. I must get them out.'[1]

Amid the institutional cruelty of the prison system Thomas Martin had been a rare ray of compassion to Wilde. On many occasions he performed acts of kindness. In the days preceding Wilde's release, he asked a wardress, Lizzie Norris, to help him with valeting Wilde's wardrobe. He was determined that Wilde should leave the prison with as much dignity as possible. Norris washed and starched Wilde's shirt and collar, working over a small stove in her quarters, and returned the clothes, properly ironed, for Wilde's release day. If she or Martin had been discovered they would have faced serious disciplinary charges for their acts of kindness. In fact, Martin was dismissed from the prison service within days of Wilde's release. His offence was to give a biscuit to one of the three children, who was crying. As promised, Wilde secured the release of the children and he never forgot the kindness of the two warders who had helped him. He kept in touch with Martin and Norris following his release, sending them Christmas cards with renewed expressions of gratitude seven months later.[2]

In the last few weeks of his imprisonment Wilde contemplated what he would do or, more to the point, where he would go once he was released. A trip to the Spanish Pyrenees was considered, as was voluntary exile to the French coast at Boulogne or Le Havre. His friends Robert Ross and More Adey, both Catholics, suggested that he should go first to a monastery before proceeding to Venice.

Whatever options Wilde had available to him, an immediate return to his wife was not one of them. On 26 March 1897 Constance had written to her brother complaining that she was once more being pressured to return to her husband. She had been told that she would be saving a human soul by taking him back but she believed she had no influence or power to change him. She could not perform miracles. It was more important that she looked after the children and did nothing to risk their future. She was now convinced that her husband's case was hopeless. 'I think his fate is rather like Humpty Dumpty's, quite as tragic and quite as impossible to put right.'[3]

On 18 May Wilde was transferred from Reading gaol to Pentonville where he was due to be released on the following morning. At Wilde's request, arrangements were made to avoid a repeat of the ridicule he had suffered at Clapham Junction station when he had been transferred to Reading eighteen months earlier. In order to travel as incognito as possible, he was permitted to wear his own clothes, freshly laundered by Lizzie Norris, and was not handcuffed. Before he left, he was handed the momentous letter to Alfred Douglas which he had spent the first three months of the year composing. On leaving the prison, after telling the two reporters who had come to observe his departure that he 'coveted neither notoriety nor oblivion',[4] he and two prison officials took a cab to Twyford station. Wilde almost gave the game away when he spread his arms towards a budding bush exclaiming 'Oh beautiful world! Oh beautiful world!' One of the warders implored him to stop. 'Now, Mr Wilde, you mustn't give yourself away like that. You're the only man in England who would talk like that in a railway station.'[5]

Wilde was discharged from Pentonville at 6.15 a.m. on 19 May, the morning after his arrival. He was met by More Adey and the Rev. Stewart Headlam. They avoided the press and drove to Headlam's house. Wilde was in high spirits. He talked of Dante and told Headlam that he looked on all the different religions as colleges in a great university. 'Roman Catholicism is the greatest and most romantic of them.'[6] He then wrote a letter, either to the Jesuits at Farm Street or to Father Sebastian Bowden at the Brompton Oratory,[7] requesting a six-month retreat. Handing the letter to a messenger, he instructed him to wait for an answer. When the messenger returned with the reply, the various friends who had gathered at Headlam's house looked away as Wilde took it and began to read. There was an awkward silence while Wilde digested its contents. Finally, he broke down and sobbed bitterly. He had been refused. He was told that he could not be accepted at his impulse on the spur of the moment. He should ponder the matter and apply again after he had done so.[8]

Within days of his release, Wilde wrote to the *Daily Chronicle* after hearing that his friend Thomas Martin had been dismissed by the prison commissioners for his act of charity to one of the child prisoners. In the past Wilde had criticized both Dickens and Charles Reade for their efforts to draw attention to the cruelties of the prison system. Now, having experienced and witnessed the cruelties himself, he was anxious to add his plaintive voice to theirs. He lambasted a system which treated children so harshly and he took the opportunity to draw attention to the case of Prince, the half-witted soldier who had been flogged during Wilde's final week at Reading.

The following month Wilde began work on *The Ballad of Reading Gaol*, a title suggested by Robert Ross. It was destined to have as much impact on liberalizing attitudes to prison reform as anything written by Dickens or Reade. Sadly, it was also destined to be the last work that Wilde ever brought to fruition. Interspersed with the descriptions of the barbaric aspects of prison life, particularly with regard to the hanging of a convicted murderer, there were hints of Wilde's own spiritual conversion within its walls.

And thus we rust Life's iron chain
  Degraded and alone:
And some men curse, and some men weep,
  And some men make no moan:
But God's eternal Laws are kind
  And break the heart of stone.

And every human heart that breaks,
  In prison-cell or yard,
Is as that broken box that gave
  Its treasure to the Lord,
And filled the unclean leper's house
  With the scent of costliest nard.

Ah! happy they whose hearts can break
  And peace of pardon win!
How else may man make straight his plan
  And cleanse his soul from Sin?
How else but through a broken heart
  May Lord Christ enter in?

Refused the sanctuary of a religious retreat Wilde had little option but to flee into voluntary exile. He settled in Berneval-sur-Mer, a village outside Dieppe, where, for a while at least, he appears to have made real efforts to amend his life. Ernest Dowson, an early visitor, found Wilde in 'splendid health and spirits ... but unlike he was of old in the extreme joy he takes in the country and in simple things'.[9] In an interview with a French journalist he spoke of his 'redemption' in prison and his poetic acceptance of exile. 'It is the sin of pride which has always destroyed men,' he stated. 'I had risen too high, and I fell sprawling in the mire.'[10] During his interview with English journalist

Chris Healy, the conversation drifted on to Aubrey Beardsley who had been received into the Catholic Church a couple of months earlier. Wilde expressed surprise at the news. 'I never guessed, when I invented Aubrey Beardsley, that there was an atom of aught but pagan feeling in him.'[11] Beardsley was received into the Church on 31 March 1897. He had been helped in his final approach to conversion by his friendship with John Gray and André Raffalovich. Writing to Gray on the day of his reception, he described it as 'the most important step in my life'.[12]

When Beardsley visited Wilde shortly after the latter's arrival in Dieppe, Wilde confessed his own yearning for conversion, expressing a heartfelt desire to follow in his former disciple's footsteps.[13] Wilde also expressed approval when he learned that J.K. Huysmans had entered a monastery, declaring that it must be 'delightful to see God through stained-glass windows'.[14] Wilde had read *En Route*, Huysmans' semi-autobiographical novel about religious conversion, in prison. From his initial admiration for *A Rebours* more than a decade earlier he had observed Huysmans' evolution from Satanism and decadence to Catholicism and the cloister with intense interest. Now, more than ever, he seemed to be seeking a similar path. In fact, Wilde must have believed that he and Huysmans were already following similar paths. *A Rebours* had foreshadowed *Dorian Gray* in much the same way that *En Route* had foreshadowed *De Profundis*. Wilde, it seemed, was on the very path that Huysmans had trod. He was merely a few steps behind. If Huysmans had arrived Wilde was en route. Their deep spiritual affinity was illustrated by Huysmans' description of his path from decadence to Christ: 'after having dragged the sickness of my soul around all the clinics of the intellect, I ended up, with God's grace, going to the only hospital where they put you to bed and really look after you – the Church'.[15]

Wilde was, however, further from reaching his goal than he realized, as was perceived by his friend Robert Ross. When Wilde confessed his desire for conversion, Ross, knowing Wilde's erratic temperament, urged caution in the matter, as he told Wilfrid Scawen Blunt:

> When Oscar came out of prison he had the idea of becoming a Catholic, and he consulted me about it, for you know I am a Catholic. I did not believe in his sincerity and told him if he really meant it, to go to a

priest, and I discouraged him from anything hasty in the matter. As a fact, he had forgotten all about it in a week, only from time to time he used to chaff me as one standing in the way of his salvation. I would willingly have helped him if I thought him in earnest, but I did not fancy religion being made ridiculous by him. I used to say that if it came to his dying I would bring a priest to him, not before.[16]

A day or so after his arrival in Dieppe, Wilde wrote a letter to Constance which she described as 'full of penitence'.[17] He yearned once more to return to the stability which she had once offered him, a return to his role of husband and father. Deep down, however, his love for his wife contained an element of ambivalence. It was real enough but was tainted by the inescapable knowledge that there was little common ground between them. The estrangement which had existed before his downfall had been exacerbated by it. There was no such ambivalence in Wilde's love for his children. In *De Profundis* he had complained bitterly that Cyril and Vyvyan had been taken from him by legal procedure. It was, he wrote, a source of infinite pain and distress. The thought of being permanently cut off from them preyed on his mind. His letter to Constance begged for a meeting with her and the children, besieging her with promises to reform and beseeching forgiveness. Constance was touched and tempted by her husband's contrition but was warned by her advisers not to rush into a reconciliation. She replied lovingly but guardedly, neither refusing a meeting nor agreeing to one. She did promise to visit him twice a year and hinted at a possible meeting between him and the two boys. For a while Constance and Oscar wrote to each other every week, he supplicating and she replying kindly that perhaps a meeting would be possible soon.

In her letters Constance made no reference to her ailing health. She had incurred a spinal injury in a fall at Tite Street and an operation had failed to stop a creeping paralysis. A second operation was deemed necessary even though its consequences might be problematic. In late July, probably unaware of the seriousness of his wife's condition, Wilde proposed that Constance should bring the children to Dieppe, after which he would return to live with them. Whether due to her infirmity or to continued reticence about the possible reconciliation, she asked him to wait for a while longer.

Increasingly dejected and lonely in his exile, especially as the initial euphoria of his release from prison diminished, Wilde was finding it difficult to remain patient. Deprived of the company and adulation of all but a few loyal friends, he was missing the inclusive pleasures of the society to which he was accustomed and from which he was now excluded. For someone of his restless temperament the life of an exiled hermit was not likely to be maintained willingly for long. In addition, he had been in his turn besieged by letters from Lord Alfred Douglas who had urged a renewal of their friendship. Wilde had responded with reticence at first but, as ever, had slowly succumbed to Douglas's persistent claims of devotion. More than ever, Wilde was in need of affection. He could not and did not resist Douglas's advances. They agreed to meet up in Naples in September.

Wilde's decision to reunite with Douglas effectively ended any remaining hope of a reconciliation with his wife and children. On 29 September 1897 Constance wrote to Wilde with uncharacteristic anger and bitterness. 'I *forbid* you to see Lord Alfred Douglas. I forbid you to return to your filthy, insane life. I forbid you to live at Naples. I will not allow you to come to Genoa.'[18] Wilde's reply showed no sign of the contrition which had been so evident in his earlier letters. His decision was entirely her fault, he wrote. Her persistent refusals to meet him had left him no choice. In exasperation, Constance wrote to her brother that Wilde had returned to Douglas and had written her 'a horrid letter'. 'If he prefers that life to living here with me – well, I am sorry for him but what can I do?'[19]

In practical terms, Constance responded to Wilde's return to Douglas by cutting off the allowance of £150 a year which she had been paying him. Wilde waxed indignant, refusing to see the justification of her solicitor's claim that he could not expect his wife to subsidize his relationship with Douglas. In similar vein, Lady Queensberry had stopped her son's allowance.

Wilde and Douglas found themselves in financial hardship but it would be an over-simplification to suggest that they were being prised apart by penury. In truth, their reconciliation was a great disappointment to both men. They had changed. The sands of time had shifted. There was no going back to their previous lives. Wilde, seeking in Douglas an oasis in the desert of his life, had found only a mirage. After ten weeks together they agreed to part company.

Douglas left for Rome on 3 December, leaving Wilde alone at the villa in Naples.

Wilde gave the 'bald and brief' facts about his sojourn with Douglas in Naples to Robert Ross. For four months Douglas had showered him with endless letters offering him a home, furnished with affection and care. In reality, Wilde discovered that he had no money and no plans for the future. He lived off Wilde's meagre allowance and, when this was stopped, he left. His brief reunion with Douglas had been 'the most bitter experience of a bitter life ... a blow quite awful and paralysing'. Wilde accepted that it would be better if he never saw Douglas again. 'I don't want to. He fills me with horror.'[20]

For his part, Douglas wrote to Lady Queensberry from Rome on 7 December 1897 to say that he was 'glad, O so glad! to have got away, to have escaped'.

> I wanted to go back to him, I longed for it and for him ... but when I had done it and when I got back, I hated it. I was miserable, I wanted to go away. But I couldn't. I was tied by honour. If he had wanted me to stay I would never have left him, but when I found out that he didn't really want me to stay and that I might leave him without causing him pain and without a breach of loyalty, then I was glad to go.

The ten weeks with Wilde had been 'a sort of prison' but now he had escaped, hopefully for ever, to a better life. 'I am tired of the struggle and tired of being ill treated by the World.' He was ready for a fresh start, having 'lost that supreme desire for his society which I had before, and which made a sort of aching void when he was not with me. That has gone and I think and hope for ever.'[21]

Constance was pleased to learn that Wilde and Douglas had parted but she was no longer under any illusions as regards the fatal flaw at the heart of her husband's personality. She wrote to a friend that Wilde's 'punishment has not done him much good since it has not taught him the lesson he most needed, namely that he is not the only person in the world'.[22] Her affection for him was largely unmarred, however, and her admiration for his genius undiminished. When *The Ballad of Reading Gaol* was published in February 1898, Constance thought it a beautiful work, a jewel wrought from all the horror. She wept because her husband was so gifted while his life was so tragic.[23] Constance's sentiments were echoed by Lily Wilde, Oscar's sister-in-law, who wrote to More Adey on 23 February. 'I was perfectly delighted with the poem and everyone seems to think it wonderful. What a pitiful thing such genius should be wasted and more or less have to wander as an outcast from all society ...'[24] Three weeks later, in another letter to Adey, Lily Wilde extended her sympathy to Constance as well as Oscar: 'I hear very often from Constance ... She seems very sad and lonely and in a shocking state of health ... She has ruined Oscar's life and he hers because they are absolutely unsuited.'[25]

Perhaps the real tragedy of Constance's life was that she continued to love her husband, in spite of all his infidelities and abuses of her trust. On 18 February, a few days after Wilde had left Italy to take up residence in Paris, she wrote of her continued devotion to him, adding that if she ever saw him again she would 'forgive everything'.[26] In March she restored his allowance and prepared a codicil to her will so that payments could continue after her death. She refused, however, to make herself in any way responsible for his debts, complaining to a friend that he had a total inability to grasp financial realities. 'If he had plenty of money he would drink himself to death and do no work, so that would be useless.'[27]

Apart from concerns about her husband's finances, Constance was much concerned at this time about her younger son's desire to become a Roman Catholic. Constance had moved closer to Rome in her sympathies and had anticipated the possibility that Vyvyan might desire conversion when she had decided to send him to a Jesuit school. Having no objections herself, she was nonetheless worried that others would object. Her other son, Cyril, was excelling in his achievements at school, coming top of an examination not only of his own form but of boys in the form above. Her husband, if he had known, would have shared wholeheartedly in her pride.

At the beginning of April Constance wrote a long letter to Vyvyan in which she sought his forgiveness of his father. 'Try not to feel harshly about your father; remember that he is your father and that he loves you. All his troubles arose from the hatred of a son for his father, and whatever he has done he has suffered bitterly for.'[28]

Almost immediately after this typically charitable letter was written she went into a nursing home in Genoa for an operation on her spine. She had been in severe pain for several months and all efforts to alleviate her suffering without resorting to surgery had failed. The operation was unsuccessful. She died on 7 April 1898, at the age of forty.

For Wilde, Constance's death resurrected regrets which could now never be erased from his conscience. 'It is really awful,' he told Carlos Blacker, a friend of both him and his wife. 'I don't know what to do. If we had only met once, and kissed each other. It is too late. How awful life is.'[29] With similar finality, he said to Frank Harris, 'My way back to hope and a new life ends in her grave. Everything that happens to me is symbolic and irrevocable.'[30]

His wife's death, coupled with the loss of his feelings for Douglas, had left Wilde more desolate and alone than ever. He told the Irish-American poet and novelist Vincent O'Sullivan that, for the first time, he had contemplated suicide. The temptation to take his own life had only passed because of the fear of eternal punishment if he succumbed. He felt as though the joy had been sucked from his existence. He was in a wasteland, a wilderness of despair. No longer did he enjoy being recognized but, on the contrary, every time he was pointed out in a crowd he was reminded of the humiliation at Clapham Junction station. O'Sullivan was with Wilde in a restaurant when a crowd of people came in after the theatre. Some of them noisily pointed out Wilde to the rest. O'Sullivan was surprised by the degree to which Wilde was disturbed by the experience. 'He seemed to strangle,' O'Sullivan remembered, 'and then said in a thick voice, "Let us go".'[31] In truly tragic fashion Wilde's life was mirroring that of Dorian Gray ...

As he strolled home ... two young men in evening dress passed him. He heard one of them whisper to the other, 'That is Dorian Gray.' He remembered how pleased he used to be when he was pointed out, or stared at, or talked about. He was tired of hearing his own name now. Half the charm of the little village where he had been so often lately was that no one knew who he was.

1 Hart-Davis, *Letters of Oscar Wilde*, p. 554.
2 *Daily Telegraph*, 2 December 1998.
3 Hart-Davis, *Letters of Oscar Wilde*, p. 515.
4 *New York Times*, 19 May 1897.

5 Shane Leslie, 'Oscariana', *National Review*, 15 January 1963.
6 Ellmann, *Oscar Wilde*, p. 495.
7 Ellmann, *Oscar Wilde*, p. 495, cites a source stating that the letter was addressed to Farm Street; Douglas, *Without Apology*, p. 263, states that Wilde attempted to contact Father Bowden at the Brompton Oratory.
8 Ada Leverson, *Letters to the Sphinx from Oscar Wilde*, London: Duckworth, 1930, pp. 44–7.
9 Sturgis, *Passionate Attitudes*, p. 294.
10 *Gil Blas* (Paris), 22 November 1897; reprinted in Mikhail, *Interviews and Recollections*, vol. 2, p. 355.
11 Healy, *Confessions of a Journalist*, pp. 130–8.
12 Calvert Alexander, SJ, *The Catholic Literary Revival*, Milwaukee: The Bruce Publishing Company, 1935, p. 104.
13 Knox, *A Long and Lovely Suicide*, p. 44.
14 Healy, *Confessions of a Journalist*, pp. 130–8.
15 Beaumont, *The Road from Decadence*, p. 144.
16 Wilfrid Scawen Blunt, *My Diaries: Part Two (1900–1914)*, pp. 146–7; quoted in Maureen Borland, *Wilde's Devoted Friend: A Life of Robert Ross, 1869–1918*, Oxford: Lennard Publishing, 1990, pp. 155–6.
17 Anne Clark Amor, *Mrs Oscar Wilde: A Woman of Some Importance*, London: Sidgwick & Jackson, 1983, p. 210.
18 Hart-Davis, *Letters of Oscar Wilde*, p. 685.
19 Ellmann, *Oscar Wilde*, p. 519.
20 Hart-Davis, *Letters of Oscar Wilde*, pp. 709–10.
21 Douglas, *Without Apology*, pp. 302–5.
22 Ellmann, *Oscar Wilde*, p. 523.
23 Joyce Bentley, *The Importance of Being Constance*, London: Robert Hale, 1983, p. 151.
24 Letter from Lily Wilde to More Adey, postmarked 23 February 1898, Bodleian Library Archives, Oxford.
25 Letter from Lily Wilde to More Adey, postmarked 14 March 1898, Bodleian Library Archives, Oxford.
26 Ellmann, *Oscar Wilde*, p. 523.
27 Amor, *Mrs Oscar Wilde*, p. 223.
28 Ibid., p. 224.
29 Hyde, *Oscar Wilde*, p. 346.
30 Ellmann, *Oscar Wilde*, p. 532.
31 Ibid., pp. 523–4.

TWENTY SIX

Hounded by Heaven

I fled Him, down the nights and down the days;
I fled Him, down the arches of the years;
I fled Him, down the labyrinthine ways
    Of my own mind; and in the mist of tears
I hid from Him ...

Wilde's loneliness and poverty during his wilderness years were exemplified by an incident in a Naples café shortly before he left Italy to take up residence in Paris. In his autobiography, Graham Greene tells how his father and another schoolmaster were sitting in the café when a stranger, hearing them speak English, asked if he might·join them over coffee. He looked vaguely familiar but they failed to recognize him during the hour or so that they were charmed by his conversation. He left them to pay for his drink which was 'certainly not coffee'. 'Think how lonely he must have been to have expended so much wit on a couple of schoolmasters on holiday,' Greene's father remarked. Yet, as Graham Greene commented, Wilde 'was paying for his drink in the only currency he had'.[1]

Wilde's lack of currency often had more to do with his profligate ability to part with it than with any lack of supply. As Constance knew, he merely drank himself to oblivion if finances allowed, showering his wealth on his friends and companions with grandiose abandon. In an effort to control Wilde's insatiable appetite for expensive pleasures, Robert Ross, following Constance's example, took to supplying funds to Wilde in small regular instalments. It was a forlorn effort to restore some order to Wilde's dishevelled decline. It had little effect. Whatever money Wilde received he disposed of with the greatest ease. Demand always outstripped supply. One result was that Wilde became a beggar, pulling impatiently at the purse-strings of any former friends or acquaintances who crossed his path.

Now that Wilde was *persona non grata*, a pariah, there were not many people in Paris who would willingly offer him their companionship. Even old and trusted friends shunned him. André Gide was less than comfortable when he came across Wilde by accident outside a café. At first, after Wilde had called to him, he sat opposite with his back to the passers-by in the hope that he would not be recognized with such a disreputable character. Wilde, however, requested that he sit beside him, adding that 'I'm so alone these days'. After a pleasant conversation, Wilde pleaded poverty. 'You must know – I'm absolutely without resources.' Gide gave him some money but avoided his company in the future. They only met on one subsequent occasion.[2]

Other incidents add to the tale of woe. In May 1898 Henry Davray, Wilde's translator, was passing by a Parisian café when Wilde beckoned to him. Davray was late for an appointment but Wilde insisted that he sit with him for a while. Wilde's appearance looked so 'broken down and harassed' that Davray complied reluctantly with his friend's wishes. Wilde explained that he had fled the boredom of his hotel room and was in need of company. Eventually Davray was forced to telephone to cancel his appointment. Wilde was so afraid of being alone that when Davray rose to leave Wilde went with him. He accompanied Davray through the Luxembourg gardens and made him sit down at another café on the Boulevard Saint-Michel. Finally he confessed his embarrassment. 'I haven't a sou,' he said.[3]

The writer Frédéric Boutet recalled how he and a friend were walking along the Boulevard Saint-Germain in July 1899 when they saw Wilde sitting outside a café in torrential rain. The torrent poured down on him, turning his coat into a sponge. The waiter, anxious to be rid of his last customer, had not only piled up the chairs but had wound up the awning. Wilde could not leave because he could not pay for the three or four drinks he had taken to avoid going back to his squalid lodgings.[4] 'Like dear St Francis of Assisi I am wedded to Poverty,' Wilde had written to a friend a month earlier, 'but in my case the marriage is not a success; I hate the bride that has been given to me.'[5]

Apart from the Dutch liqueur advocaat, and the brandy and absinthe, Wilde began once again to seek solace in the company of young male prostitutes. 'How evil it is to buy love,' he remarked to Robert Ross, 'and how evil to sell it! And yet what purple hours one can snatch from that grey slowly moving thing we call Time.'[6] When Ross sought to persuade Wilde to amend his attitude to life, Wilde responded that his friend could only lecture him about his past and present. He had no future. He was not equal to any serious thought. He had only moods and moments, 'and Love, or Passion with the mask of Love, is my only consolation'.[7]

Wilde was in the same wistfully philosophic mood when he was invited to dine with Maurice Maeterlinck and Georgette Leblanc in May 1898. 'I have lived. Yes, I have lived. I drank the sweet, I drank the bitter, and I found the bitterness in the sweetness and the sweetness in the bitterness.' When Maeterlinck mentioned that Huysmans had entered a monastery, Wilde expressed the same approval, almost word for word, that he had given earlier. 'It must be delightful to see God through stained glass windows.' This time, however, he added an afterthought: 'I may even go to a monastery myself.' Referring to the wretchedness of his existence he complained that 'the cruelty of a prison sentence starts when you come out'. In prison he had been happy, 'because there I found my soul'. In an oblique reference to *De Profundis*, the manuscript of which was safely in the keeping of Robert Ross, Wilde told Maeterlinck and Leblanc that what he had written in prison would one day be read by the world. It was 'the message of my soul to the souls of men'.[8]

Wilde's low opinion of his soul in 1898, and his sense of self-loathing, were clear in a melancholy fable he told to the novelist and critic Wilfred Hugh Chesson:

A man saw a being, which hid its face from him, and he said, 'I will compel it to show its face'. It fled as he pursued, and he lost it, and his life went on. At last his pleasure drew him into a long room, where tables were spread for many, and in a mirror he saw the being whom he had pursued in his youth. 'This time you shall not escape me,' he said, but the being did not try to escape, and hid its face no more. 'Look!' it cried, 'and now you will know that we cannot see each other again, for this is the face of your own soul, and it is horrible.'[9]

Following this flash of rhetoric, Chesson touched on the subject of religion, telling Wilde that he considered it a killjoy and a painmaker. Wilde disagreed. 'There is something very artistic about Christianity,' he said. 'You go into Hyde Park, and a wonderful sentence comes to you on the wind. "What shall it profit a man if he gain the whole world and lose his own soul?"'

Much of the rest of the conversation with Chesson was taken up with a discussion of literature. Wilde spoke with enthusiasm of Dickens, contradicting the hostility he displayed in some of his earlier criticism. He approved of characters such as Micawber, Pecksniff and Mrs Gamp. 'There have been no such grotesques since the Gothic gargoyles,' he said. He quoted the passage in *Martin Chuzzlewit* which compares the rusty gowns and other garments hanging from Sarah Gamp's bed to 'guardian angels' watching her in her sleep. Remarking that he had read the whole of Dante's *Divina Commedia* in prison, he added with potency: 'You can imagine how I tasted every word.' He recommended that Chesson read it with Longfellow's rhymed translation which was superior to Cary's dull blank verse. Speaking of his own work, he told Chesson that it had been a joy to him. 'I wrote *Dorian Gray* in three weeks. When my plays were on, I drew a hundred pounds a week! I delighted in every minute of the day.' At the conclusion of their meeting, Chesson told Wilde that he thought his life was a harmony of two extremes, very rare and very valuable. 'Yes,' Wilde replied, 'artistically it is perfect; socially most inconvenient.'[10]

At around this time Wilde also had lunch with the journalist Chris Healy, at a restaurant on the Boulevard Saint-Michel. According to Healy, Wilde spoke lightly enough about his trial but his eyes lit up with savage indignation when he talked of his treatment in prison. Of one prison official, he said: 'He had the eyes of a ferret, the body of an ape, and the soul of a rat.' Discussing *The Ballad of Reading Gaol* Wilde told Healy that he had 'probed the depths of most of the experiences of life' and that he had come to the conclusion that humanity was meant to suffer. 'There are moments when life takes you, like a tiger, by the throat, and it was when I was in the depths of suffering that I wrote my poem.'[11]

Wilde's comments raise serious questions about his lack of creativity during his final years in Paris. If he had created *The Ballad of Reading Gaol* out of the depths of suffering, why was he unable to create anything of worth during his last years of pain? Perhaps W.H. Auden's assessment comes closest to the truth:

> Other writers – Villon, Cervantes, Verlaine, for example – have suffered imprisonment (Villon even suffered torture), or, like Dante, suffered exile, without their creative powers being affected; indeed, they often wrote their best work after disaster. It was not his experiences in Reading Gaol, dreadful as these were, that put an end to Wilde's literary career, but the loss of social position. Another kind of writer might have found the disreputable bohemian existence to which, as an ex-convict, he was limited a relief – at least there was no need to keep up pretenses – but for Wilde the Bunburying, the double life, at one and the same time a bohemian in secret and in public the lion of respectable drawing rooms, had been the exciting thing, and when the drawing rooms withdrew their invitations he lost the will to live and write.[12]

Further questions are raised if a comparison is made between the parallel lives of Wilde and Verlaine. Ten years Wilde's senior, the events of Paul Verlaine's life prefigured those of Wilde's to a remarkable degree. Verlaine had neglected his wife and son, had deserted them for a fledgling poet ten years his junior, had been sentenced to two years hard labour in consequence of a feud with him, and had unsuccessfully attempted to enter a monastery upon his release. He had died on 8 January 1896, while Wilde was languishing in gaol, after living the last years of his life in Parisian garret poverty. It is almost as though Verlaine was Wilde's precursor and there is little doubt that Wilde was superstitiously or providentially aware of their uncanny bond. 'I am a vagabond,' he told an acquaintance. 'The century will have had two vagabonds, Paul Verlaine and me.'[13] In De Profundis Wilde had described Verlaine as 'the one Christian poet since Dante'. Furthermore, Verlaine's life had been one of the 'most perfect' he had ever come across. Now that Wilde too was living in Parisian garret poverty, did he see himself as re-enacting the last act in Verlaine's prophetic drama? Was he, consciously or otherwise, emulating Verlaine's 'perfect life'? Did he see the bond between them as not only fateful but fatal? Was he doomed to die in a similar squalid fashion? If these thoughts were in Wilde's mind, he must have been aware of the two significant differences between his own life and that of Verlaine.

Following his time in prison, Verlaine had not only written much of his greatest work but had been received into the Catholic Church. Apart from *The Ballad of Reading Gaol* Wilde had written nothing and his efforts to join the Church in the weeks after his release had been singularly ineffectual. Verlaine had fallen greatly and often during the last years of his life but he had clung doggedly to his faith, seeking its sustenance and consolation, and had turned the bitterness of his experience into the beauty of his art. Wilde had little to cling to except self-pity and self-loathing and he had surrendered his bitterness to futility.

As the decadent movement declined, most of its leading adherents were following Verlaine's path, not Wilde's. The seeds sown in decay were springing forth in faith. Aubrey Beardsley, the only figure whose influence rivalled that of Wilde in the English decadence, died of consumption on 16 March 1898. Four days earlier Mabel Beardsley had written to Robert Ross that her brother could not have long to live. 'He is touchingly patient and resigned and longs for eternal rest. He holds always his crucifix and rosary. Thank God for some time past he has become more and more fervent. Pray for him and for us.' On the day he died she again wrote to Ross. 'Our dear one passed away this morning very early. He looks so beautiful. He died as a saint ... He was so full of love and patience and repentance.'[14]

The impact of Beardsley's death was enormous. According to Matthew Sturgis, 'Beardsley's association with decadence had been so complete and so close that his death inevitably broke, if it did not destroy, the movement'.[15] Beardsley was certainly the boy wonder of the English decadence who, still only twenty-five at the time of his death, exerted an influence which belied his youth. 'I belong to the Beardsley Period,' Max Beerbohm had declared and Osbert Burdett entitled his study of the 1890s *The Beardsley Period*. 'The appearance of Aubrey Beardsley in 1893,' wrote Holbrook Jackson, 'was the most extraordinary event in English art since the appearance of William Blake a little more than a century earlier.' Beardsley was 'the unique expression of the most unique mood of the nineties'.[16] In 1894, at the age of twenty-two, his appointment as the art editor of *The Yellow Book* had heralded the so-called 'Beardsley Craze' and, a year later, it had come to an unhappy and abrupt end when Beardsley was dragged down by his perceived association with Wilde. On hearing of

Beardsley's death, Wilde was both shocked and saddened. 'There is something macabre and tragic in the fact that one who added another terror to life should have died at the age of a flower.'[17]

Beardsley's death had a profoundly decisive impact on John Gray who, on hearing the news, was said to have wandered around Piccadilly for hours, murmuring over and over, 'I must change my life.'[18] A few months later he resigned his post in the Foreign Office. On 25 October he took up residence in the Scots College in Rome to train for the priesthood. When Wilde heard news of Gray's decision he must have been reminded of the words of bitterness he had written to Douglas from prison: 'When I compare my friendship with you to my friendship with such still younger men as John Gray and Pierre Louÿs I feel ashamed. My real life, my higher life was with them and such as they.' Possibly the words now twisted in his conscience like a knife. He had forsaken the higher life glimpsed so briefly in prison and was once more an habitué of the world of hard drink and prostitution. Perhaps other words from his past returned to haunt him such as those to Gomez Carillo during a happier stay in Paris in 1891: 'I flee from what is moral as from what is impoverished,' he had told Gomez, 'I have the same sickness as Des Esseintes.'[19]

In fleeing from what was moral Wilde was no different from the other decadents. Their flight was epitomized most memorably by Francis Thompson, described by Osbert Burdett as 'critically considered, the most decadent of writers',[20] who drank the dregs of life, experiencing poverty, prostitution and opium addiction on the streets of London. According to Holbrook Jackson, Thompson's *The Hound of Heaven* serves as 'a symbol of the spiritual unrest of the whole nineteenth century'.[21]

> I fled Him, down the nights and down the days;
> I fled Him, down the arches of the years;
> I fled Him, down the labyrinthine ways
>   Of my own mind; and in the mist of tears
> I hid from Him ...

Wilde was a great admirer of Thompson's poetry and would have known 'The Hound of Heaven', the best known of all his verse. Its image of the sinner being hounded by Heaven until he surrenders to the love of God was one with which Wilde would have empathized. It is an image which resonates in much of his own work, most notably in his most recent, *The Ballad of Reading Gaol*. Unlike Thompson, Beardsley, Baudelaire, Verlaine, Gray, Raffalovich, Ross, Ernest Dowson, Lionel Johnson, Huysmans and a host of others, Wilde was unwilling to surrender. However much he was being hounded, he kept on fleeing.

1 Graham Greene, *A Sort of Life*, London: Bodley Head, 1971; quoted in Ellmann, *Oscar Wilde*, p. 525.
2 Ellmann, *Oscar Wilde*, p. 530.
3 Ibid., pp. 530–1.
4 Ibid., p. 531.
5 Hart-Davis, *Letters of Oscar Wilde*, p. 803.
6 Ibid., p. 828.
7 Ibid., p. 766.
8 Ellmann, *Oscar Wilde*, pp. 531–2.
9 Wilfred Hugh Chesson, 'A Reminiscence of 1898', *The Bookman* (New York), xxxiv, December 1911, pp. 389–94.
10 Ibid.
11 Healy, *Confessions of a Journalist*, pp. 130–8.
12 W.H. Auden, 'An Improbable Life', published in *The New Yorker*, 39:3, 9 March 1963.
13 Ellmann, *Oscar Wilde*, p. 539.
14 Maas, Duncan and Good (eds.), *The Letters of Aubrey Beardsley*, London: Cassell, 1970, pp. 439–40.
15 Sturgis, *Passionate Attitudes*, p. 287.
16 Alexander, *The Catholic Literary Revival*, p. 100.
17 Hart-Davis, *Letters of Oscar Wilde*, p. 719.
18 Sturgis, *Passionate Attitudes*, p. 287.
19 Ellmann, *Oscar Wilde*, p. 325.
20 Osbert Burdett, *The Beardsley Period*, London: The Bodley Head, 1925, p. 174.
21 Holbrook Jackson, *The Eighteen Nineties*, Hassocks, Sussex: Harvester Press edn., 1976, p. 172.

TWENTY SEVEN

Revelations

LORD ILLINGWORTH: ... The Book of Life begins with a man and a woman in a garden.
MRS ALLONBY: It ends with Revelations.

A further nail was hammered into the coffin – or the cross – of the decadents in September 1898 with the death of Stéphane Mallarmé. In the early days, Wilde had sat at the feet of Mallarmé, paying homage to him as mentor and master. As such, his sense of loss would have been considerable. His feelings would no doubt have been akin to those expressed by Huysmans to Paul Valéry: 'D'Aurévilly, Villiers, Verlaine – all those who were precious to me in this age of crassness are dead. And he who was left is gone too. It is not without great sadness that, before withdrawing from the world, one witnesses the disappearance of the only decent artists for years.'[1]

Mallarmé's death added to Wilde's sense of isolation and his feeling of being unwanted and excluded. In both England and France, the decadence was either dead or dying. Wilde was outstaying his welcome, artistically as well as socially. Even those who had not died, such as Huysmans or Gray, were retreating to higher ground – to the cloister or the seminary – where Wilde was unwilling or unable to follow.

At the end of February 1899 Wilde visited Genoa in order to see Constance's grave. He wrote to Robert Ross that it was 'very tragic' to see her name carved on the tomb. It read 'Constance Mary, daughter of Horace Lloyd, Q.C.' with a verse from Revelation. There was no mention of his own name. Wilde placed some flowers on the grave and fought to master his emotions. 'I was deeply affected – with a sense, also, of the uselessness of all regrets. Nothing could have been otherwise, and Life is a very terrible thing.'[2]

Wilde was also haunted by the loss of his children, as an episode in a Parisian restaurant demonstrated evocatively. A young boy clumsily upset a salt-cellar on Wilde's table. When the child's mother scolded him for doing so, Wilde looked at her sadly. 'Be patient with your little boy,' he said. 'One must always be patient with them. If, one day, you should find yourself separated from him ...' At this point the child, emboldened, asked Wilde if he had a little boy of his own. Wilde replied that he had two. 'Why don't you bring them here with you?' the boy asked. The child's mother interjected that he shouldn't ask such questions. 'It doesn't matter, it doesn't matter,' Wilde said, with a sad smile. 'They don't come here with me because they are too far away ...' Then he took the boy's hand and kissed him on both cheeks, muttering in English as he did so, 'Oh, my poor dear boys!' As the child said goodbye he noticed that Wilde was crying.[3] On another occasion Wilde told a friend that he had recently learned of his son Vyvyan's conversion to the Catholic faith. Apparently, Wilde said, Vyvyan had simply declared to his guardian, 'I am a Catholic.' Wilde was also amused to learn that many of his son's mannerisms were similar to his own. He insisted that this proved that his personal gestures, heavily criticized for their artificiality, were never merely affectations.[4]

Shortly after he had visited his wife's grave, Wilde learned of the death of his brother, who had died on 13 March. The brothers had become thoroughly estranged and their relationship poisoned with enmity. Wilde confessed to Robert Ross that wide chasms existed between them. Nonetheless, Willie Wilde's death would have added further to Oscar's isolation. He was now the last surviving member of the family.

Meanwhile, Wilde's life continued as wretchedly as ever. The opera singer Nellie Melba was walking along the streets of Paris one morning when she was approached by a tall shabby man with his collar turned up to his neck. 'Madame Melba,' said a voice, 'you don't know who I am? I'm Oscar Wilde, and I am going to do a terrible thing. I'm going to ask you for money.' The dumbstruck soprano took all that she had in her purse and handed it to him. He muttered his thanks and went. She remembered their first meeting, many years before, when he had said, 'Ah, Madame Melba, I am the Lord of Language and you are the Queen of Song, and so I suppose I shall have to write you a sonnet.'[5]

On 31 January 1900 the Marquess of Queensberry died. His death was to prove as controversial as his life. His will, true to his outspoken agnostic principles, stipulated that 'no Christian mummeries or tomfooleries' were to be performed. He wished to be cremated 'as a Secularist and an Agnostic'. Yet he was nursed in his last days by his brother Archie, a Catholic priest, who claimed that Queensberry had been reconciled to Christianity on his deathbed. He had confessed his sins, was given conditional absolution and was received into the Catholic Church. Doubts have been cast on the honesty of the priest's account of his brother's final days and, without corroborating evidence, Queensberry's eleventh-hour change of heart will remain open to question and shrouded in mystery. The Marquess, like Wilde, had been wedded to controversy and it had followed him all the way to the grave and beyond.

Queensberry's death caused the last bitter feud between Douglas and Wilde. Aside from the meticulous stipulations about 'mummeries and tomfooleries', Queensberry's will had bestowed a personal inheritance of almost £20,000 on Lord Alfred Douglas. Learning of Douglas's changed circumstances, Wilde hoped that he could persuade him to make a small part of his fortune over to Wilde's own use. According to Wilde, this was owed to him. Douglas disagreed and refused resolutely to comply with Wilde's wishes. He owed him nothing. Wilde was devastated. He poured out his feelings to his old friend Frank Harris, tears falling from his cheeks.

Once I thought myself master of my life; lord of my fate, who could do what I pleased and would always succeed. I was as a crowned king and now I am an exile and outcast and despised. I have lost my way in life; the passers-by all scorn me and the man whom I loved whips me with foul insults and contempt. There is no example in history of such a betrayal, no parallel. I am finished. It is all over with me now – all! I hope the end will come quickly.[6]

Barely three weeks after the death of his old enemy came the death of yet another old friend. Ernest Dowson died on 23 February and was buried in the Roman Catholic part of Lewisham cemetery four days later. He was thirty-two. In many respects, Dowson was the English Verlaine, a deeply religious poet who was the slave to strong drink and sexual promiscuity, though Dowson's inclinations were heterosexual. He converted to Catholicism soon after leaving Oxford, without a degree, in the late eighties. As with Verlaine, and indeed Wilde, the depth of Dowson's faith is lost in the weakness of the flesh but discovered in the beauty of the art he produced. The yearning for peace amid the passions of life is a recurring theme in his religious verse. In 'Nuns of the Perpetual Adoration' the peace of the convent is contrasted with the chaos of the world:

> Outside, the world is wild and passionate;
>   Man's weary laughter and his sick despair
> Entreat at their impenetrable gate:
>   They heed no voices in their dream of prayer.

Like Wilde, Dowson longed to see God through stained glass windows but he was as incapable as Wilde of breaching the impenetrable gate.

> Calm, sad, secure; with faces worn and mild:
>   Surely their choice of vigil is the best?
> Yea! for our roses fade, the world is wild;
>   But there, beside the altar, there, is rest.

In similar vein, in 'Benedictio Domini' the Blessed Sacrament is the 'one true solace of man's fallen plight' which is contrasted with 'the world's swift passage to the fire'.

Wilde was 'greatly distressed' at Dowson's death. 'Poor wounded wonderful fellow that he was, a tragic reproduction of all tragic poetry'.[7] 'It is all so sad,' he told a friend, 'Ernest was an *enfant voué au noir.*' A child dedicated to darkness.[8]

Wilde's spirits were lifted in April when a friend, Harold Mellor, financed a trip to Italy. They went to Palermo for eight days, proceeded to Naples and arrived in Rome on Holy Thursday. On Easter Day Wilde managed to obtain a ticket for the Papal audience and received a blessing from Leo XIII. In ensuing days he saw the Pope on several occasions, describing him as a white soul robed in white. His accounts of his sojourn in Rome are curious, a mixture of piety, flippancy and mischievousness, but it is clear from the tone of his letters to friends that he was far happier than he had been for some time. His position, he wrote, was somewhat curious. He was not a Catholic but a 'violent Papist'. He thought Sicily beautiful, Naples 'evil and luxurious' but Rome was 'the one city of the soul'. The waters of the Trevi Fountain were wonderful and soothing.[9]

There was one curious meeting. Wilde was walking through the Roman streets when he came face to face with John Gray who was strolling with a group of fellow seminarians. Their eyes met but they did not speak. Their paths had diverged since the days when Wilde was master and Gray the awestruck disciple. All that remained between them was an awkward silence. It would be the last time they saw each other.

It appears that Wilde's desire for conversion re-emerged during his visit to Rome. He asked Robert Ross to introduce him to a priest with a view to his being received into the Church. Again Ross doubted his friend's seriousness and did not co-operate. Eight months later he reproached himself for not doing so. Shortly before leaving Rome, Wilde repeated to Ross his desire for monastic peace. 'The Cloister or the Café – there is my future. I tried the hearth, but it was a failure.'[10]

In August Wilde met with Anna, Comtesse de Brémont, his mother's old friend, who was in Paris for the Great Exhibition. Wilde was in pensive mood. 'I see so few of my old friends now, and when I do, the meeting is too much for me. I passed a sleepless night – a night of watching – and ...' He paused.

'I, too, watched and prayed through the night,' the Comtesse hastened to say in answer to his unfinished sentence.

'Thank you,' he replied simply.

There was a silence. The Comtesse observed how Wilde had altered since she had last seen him in the days before the debacle: 'there was something indefinable about him that impressed me more than all his former charm and elegance. An atmosphere of spirituality that shone through his changed appearance like the glitter of gold that has been through the refiner's furnace. I felt that he had indeed been refined through suffering.'

The Comtesse asked why Wilde no longer wrote. 'I have not time to write,' he replied. 'My time is short – my work is done – and when I cease to live, that work will begin to live. Ah! my work will live as long as men live to read it; my work will be my great monument!

'Would you know my secret?' he added. 'I will tell you ... I have found my soul. I was happy in prison ... I was happy there because I found my soul.'

The Comtesse struggled to hold back tears which were more of joy than sorrow, but Wilde saw only the tears, not their cause. 'Contessa,' he said. 'Don't sorrow for me, but watch and pray – it will not be long – watch and pray.'[11]

At around this time Wilde discussed his religious feelings with the Paris correspondent of the *Daily Chronicle*. 'Much of my moral obliquity is due to the fact that my father would not allow me to become a Catholic,' he confided in the journalist. 'The artistic side of the Church would have cured my degeneracies. I intend to be received before long.'[12]

Shortly after these comments were made, Wilde's health began to deteriorate rapidly. By the end of September he was bedridden with meningitis. In mid-October he telegraphed Robert Ross to say that he was terribly weak. Ross travelled to Paris and found Wilde in good spirits. He quipped that he was dying above his means but added more seriously that he would not outlive the century. On 3 November the male nurse informed Ross that Wilde's general condition was very serious and that he would not live more than three or four months unless he altered his way of life and stopped drinking. Wilde told Ross that he did not care if he had only a short time to live. He was more concerned with discussing his debts which amounted to more than £400. He was suffering from remorse about some of his creditors and asked Ross to see that at least some of them were paid in the event of his death. Another friend, Reggie Turner, arrived and Wilde told them of a horrible dream the previous night when he had been 'supping with the dead'. 'My dear Oscar,' Turner replied, 'you were probably the life and soul of the party.' This delighted Wilde who instantly became high-spirited.

Wilde spoke lightheartedly about whether Ross had chosen a place for his tomb and he wanted to discuss epitaphs, all of which was disconcerting for Ross who still did not really believe that Wilde's condition was life-threatening. When Ross sought to leave for Nice on 13 November, Wilde became hysterical, seemingly convinced that he would not see his friend again. Ross responded sternly in the belief that Wilde was being unreasonable and departed for Nice as planned.

In Ross's absence Wilde's condition continued to deteriorate. At the consultation on 25 November the doctors gave scant hope of recovery. Wilde knew little of this. His mind was wandering and he was often asleep, partly due to the morphine with which he was being injected. Three days later, Turner wrote to Ross that Wilde had been delirious for two or three days and there was no hope he would recover. Ross rushed back to Paris where he was told by the doctors that Wilde could not live for more than two days. His first sight of the sick man confirmed to him the doctors' opinion. Wilde had deteriorated dreadfully in the fortnight he had been away. He had become very thin, his flesh was livid and his breathing heavy. He was, however, conscious and was trying to speak. Ross asked him whether he understood and Wilde raised his hand in assent.

Ross then went in search of a priest, eventually finding Father Cuthbert Dunne, a Passionist who was, like the dying man, a native of Dublin. When Ross and Father Dunne reached Wilde's room the attendants were asked to leave. Ross knelt by the bedside, assisting as best he could while the priest administered conditional baptism. Afterwards Ross answered the responses while Father Dunne gave extreme unction to Wilde and recited the prayers for the dying. Father Dunne did not endeavour to administer the holy viaticum because of Wilde's extreme condition but he was fully satisfied that Wilde was *compos mentis* and understood that he was being received into the Catholic Church and was receiving the last sacraments. 'From the signs he gave as well as from his attempted words, I was satisfied as to his full consent. And when I repeated close to his ear the Holy Names, the Acts of Contrition, Faith, Hope and Charity, with acts of humble resignation to the Will of God, he tried all through to say the words after me.'[13]

Wilde had reached the moment of death – the one point in every life where fact and truth meet in indisputable unity. Faced with this ultimate reality, this moment of truth, all the illusions and delusions passed away into the realm of insignificance. The *bons mots* had made way for the *bonne mort*. The sublime significance of the last rites administered to Wilde was expressed with beauty and eloquence in the poem 'Extreme Unction' by Wilde's friend and fellow decadent Ernest Dowson, who had reached the same moment of truth a few months earlier.

Upon the eyes, the lips, the feet,
   On all the passages of sense,
The atoning oil is spread with sweet
   Renewal of lost innocence.

The feet, that lately ran so fast
   To meet desire, are soothly sealed;
The eyes, that were so often cast
   On vanity, are touched and healed.

From troublous sights and sounds set free;
   In such a twilight hour of breath,
Shall one retrace his life, or see,
   Through shadows, the true face of death?

Vials of mercy! Sacring oils!
   I know not where or when I come,
Nor through what wanderings and toils,
   To crave of you Viaticum.

Yet, when the walls of flesh grow weak,
   In such an hour, it well may be,
Through mist and darkness, light will break,
   And each anointed sense will see.

Wilde died on the following afternoon, 30 November 1900, in the same garret poverty as Paul Verlaine and Ernest Dowson. Each of them had discovered that every new approach to life led infallibly to the same old truths. The way of decadence was only the way of the Cross.

One of the most descriptive depictions of Wilde's last days was given by Elisabeth Marbury, a leading American play agent:

The last time I ever saw him was in Paris, living in a wretched room in the attic of a squalid little hotel ...

The bed on which his bulky form was stretched was covered with a hideous brown blanket. The furniture was of the ugliest and plainest description. Not a creature comfort of any sort was visible. I recalled the house in Tite Street. The contrast was appalling.

His few remaining friends had given until they could give no more. They at least had kept the roof over his head and had provided him with the necessities of life.

He barely recognized me. The memory of that visit is still painful ...

Yet possibly at no time in his career had this poor soul been so near the recognition of truth which is eternal, as at this bitter moment of his physical disintegration and of his final detachment from that world from which he had been outcast.

I have always maintained that *De Profundis* was his masterpiece and a rich contribution to the treasure house of English literature.

It was conceived and written *in* the depths. It was given to the world as Oscar Wilde's last message to save others *from* the depths.[14]

The last words must belong to Oscar Wilde. It was in his art that he had removed his mask beguilingly to reveal fleeting glimpses of his deeper self. The final words of the final act of *The Duchess of Padua* will serve as the final words of Wilde's life. In his case, more than most, life had followed art.

DUCHESS: ... Oh, do you think that love
Can wipe the bloody stain from off my hands,
Pour balm into my wounds, heal up my hurts,
And wash my scarlet sins as white as snow? –
For I have sinned.
GUIDO: They do not sin at all
Who sin for love.
DUCHESS: No, I have sinned, and yet
Perchance my sin will be forgiven me.
I have loved much.

1 Beaumont, *The Road From Decadence*, p. 176.
2 Hart-Davis, *Letters of Oscar Wilde*, p. 783.
3 Vyvyan Holland, *Time Remembered after Père Lachaise*, London: Gollancz, 1966, pp. 11–12.
4 *La Revue Blanche*, Paris, 15 December 1900.
5 Ellmann, *Oscar Wilde*, p. 538.
6 Frank Harris, *Oscar Wilde*, p. 366.
7 Hart-Davis, *Letters of Oscar Wilde*, p. 816.
8 R.H. Sherard, *The Real Oscar Wilde*, London: T. Werner Laurie, 1915, pp. 417–20.
9 Hart-Davis, *Letters of Oscar Wilde*, pp. 820–8.
10 Ibid., p. 828.
11 Anna, Comtesse de Brémont, *Oscar Wilde and His Mother: A Memoir*, London: Everett, 1911, pp. 176–88.
12 Hyde, *Oscar Wilde*, p. 368.
13 Hart-Davis, *Letters of Oscar Wilde*, p. 857.
14 Elisabeth Marbury, *My Crystal Ball: Reminiscences*, New York: Boni & Liveright, 1923, pp. 99–103.

Index